Accession no.
36176129

WITHDRAWN

THE CULTURE OF EXCEPTION

We live in an ever fragmenting society, in which distinctions between culture and nature, biology and politics, law and transgression, mobility and immobility, reality and representation, seem to be disappearing. This book demonstrates the hidden logic beneath this process; which is also the logic of the camp. Social theory has traditionally interpreted the camp as an anomaly, as an exceptional site situated on the margins of society, aiming to neutralize its 'failed citizens' and 'enemies'. However, in contemporary society 'the camp' has now become the rule and consequently a new interrogation of its logic is necessary.

In this exceptional volume Bülent Diken and Carsten Bagge Laustsen explore the paradox of 'the camp', as representing both an old fear of enclosure and a new dream of belonging. They illustrate their arguments by drawing on contemporary sites of exemption (refugee camps, rape camps, favelas) as well as sites of self-exemption (gated communities, party tourism, celebrity cultures).

Bülent Diken teaches social theory in the Department of Sociology, Lancaster University, UK. His research fields consist of social theory, poststructuralist philosophy, urbanism and migration. His books include *Strangers, Ambivalence and Social Theory*.

Carsten Bagge Laustsen teaches social theory in the Department of Political Science, University of Aarhus. His research fields include political and social theory, psychoanalytical theory and international relations. His publications include *I Terrorens Skygge*.

INTERNATIONAL LIBRARY OF SOCIOLOGY
Founded by Karl Mannheim

Editor: John Urry
Lancaster University

THE CULTURE OF EXCEPTION

Sociology facing the camp

Bülent Diken and
Carsten Bagge Laustsen

LIS LIBRARY

Date	Fund
17/04/13	n-che

Order No
2384607

University of Chester

WITHDRAWN

Routledge
Taylor & Francis Group

LONDON AND NEW YORK

First published 2005
by Routledge,
2 Park Square, Milton Park, Abingdon, Oxon OX14 4RN

Simultaneously published in the USA and Canada
by Routledge
711 Third Avenue, New York, NY 10017

Routledge is an imprint of the Taylor and Francis Group

© 2005 Bülent Diken and Carsten Bagge Laustsen

Typeset in Garamond by Keystroke, Jacaranda Lodge, Wolverhampton

All rights reserved. No part of this book may be reprinted or
reproduced or utilised in any form or by any electronic, mechanical,
or other means, now known or hereafter invented, including
photocopying and recording, or in any information storage or
retrieval system, without permission in writing from the publishers.

British Library Cataloguing in Publication Data
A catalogue record for this book is available from the British Library

Library of Congress Cataloging in Publication Data
Diken, Bülent.
The culture of exception : sociology facing the camp /
Bülent Diken and Carsten B. Laustsen
p. cm.
Includes bibliographical references and index.
1. Social distance. 2. Spatial behavior. 3. Human geography.
4. Camps–Social aspects. 5. Concentration camps. 6. Refugee camps.
7. Gated communities. 8. Sex tourism. I. Laustsen, Carsten B.
(Carsten Bagge), 1970– II. Title.
HM1131.D55 2005
301–dc22
2004026500

ISBN 0–415–35123–5 (hbk)
ISBN 0–415–35122–7 (pbk)

CONTENTS

FOREWORD

Bülent Diken and Carsten Bagge Laustsen have embarked on a bold and risky voyage of discovery – and this book is a record of their findings. Rich record, often startling and occasionally baffling, but continuously, page after page, thought-provoking, and pressing the reader to rethink and revise many common and comfortingly, yet misleadingly familiar (because seldom questioned) images of the world we inhabit. The voyage which Diken and Laustsen undertook led them to uncover the steady and stubborn but undisclosed or covered-up tendency of our times, a tendency powerful enough to frame and shape our shared future if allowed to unravel unhampered.

What Diken and Laustsen suggest in the result of their explorations is the imminent promotion of the 'camp' from the periphery of modern society and the status of a laboratory in which extreme limits of de-humanized life, peeled down to its purely zoological, pre-social or post-social kernel, were bared, experimented with and tested, to the centre of social life; the abnormal, Diken and Laustsen imply, shows all the signs of turning into a norm . . . 'There are emerging', we are warned, 'new social forms characterized by the logic of exemption and self-exemption characteristic of the camp.'

In an astonishing inversion of sociality such as we knew and experienced until recently, the new forms 'promote unbonding as a form of relation'. A century ago Georg Simmel pointed out to the paradox of conflict and strife being major, perhaps even the principal mechanisms of social integration. Diken and Laustsen spot a new, further reaching and potentially much more seminal though no less paradoxical development: it is now 'unbonding' – the dis-connection, dis-engagement un-commitment rather than combat-engagement – that holds society (whatever the current meaning of such a term) together and guides its reproduction. But un-bonding is akin to de-socialization, that trade-mark of camps. Both settings are factories of Giorgio Agamben's 'nuda vita' and both are busy turning out the raw stuff of biopolitics.

Both settings exemplify Carl Schmitt's vision of the rule that exists solely through its exceptions – though Diken and Laustsen suggest that with the present trends in full swing we can assume that it is the exception, the 'outside' of the law and the norm, that is fast becoming the rule. 'We live in a society in which exception is the rule . . . Even normality is today an object of choice, a life-strategy amongst others.' And so they ask themselves, and prompt the reader captivated by the prospects they've sketched to ask. 'What happens when everything residual or exceptional is "normalized", when the society has absorbed every exception, every pathological remainder' and has achieved the degree of fluidity which allows it to take in every remainder as yet unabsorbed and not dissolved into the all-embracing flow?

This book is a diligent and determined attempt to answer that question, which – in as far as the portrait Diken and Laustsen have painted could be taken as a fair representation of contemporary life – would be the most crucial of questions clamouring nowadays for a thorough and credible answer. The authors leave no nook and cranny unexplored. In the search for a convincing answer, they move from refugee detention camps to the gated communities for the rich and settled, and from 'nowherevilles' of the global high and mighty to the urban ghettos for human reject and refuse. They find that 'some camps keep other "out", some "in"', and that 'there are camps for those at the bottom and those at the top', and that there is but a thin line that separates the wild spread of camp living from caringly cultivated dreams of community and belonging.

This book, unashamedly unorthodox and in many ways iconoclastic, radical in its insights and uncompromising in its verdicts, will most probably anger many a reader and baffle many others. But it makes a compulsive reading. Most importantly, it makes you look again at the realities around you, and think again about what makes those realities real and where they are likely to take you as long as they remain real. Not much in the way we now live together/apart will look the same once you have read this book. You would probably note things you had missed before and the things you thought you knew you would and look at in a new and surprising light.

Important questions have been asked, though answering them would probably take the life-time of most readers. Just how credible the answers which the authors tentatively suggest are, remains to be seen. But whatever credibility is in the end proved or discredited will depend also on the seriousness with which we treat the warnings, anticipations and premonitions Diken and Laustsen have distilled from their research and analyses for our use – and our (were we willing to think them through) benefit.

Zygmunt Bauman
December 2004

ACKNOWLEDGMENTS

We are very grateful for the inspiring discussions with Zygmunt Bauman. We are also grateful for comments resulting from meetings with Niels Albertsen, Bob Jessop and John Urry during the writing process of this book. We have greatly benefited from comments on different parts of the book from Jørgen-Ole Bærenholdt, Jennie Edkins, Sümer Gürel, Ulf Hedetoft, Christian Horst, Engin Isin, Lars Thorup Larsen, Enzo Mingione, Per Mouritsen, Mehdi Mozzaffari, Tom Nielsen, Tore Olsen, Eric Pettersson, Rob Shields and Kirsten Simonsen.

We have received very valuable technical support from Helle Bundgaard, Else L. Nielsen, Jonna Kjær, Lone Winther and Mette Ahlers Marino. Many thanks!

Some parts of he book were previously published in *Alternatives* 29(1): 89–113 (2004), *Citizenship Studies* 8(1): 83–106 (2004) and *Space and Culture* 5(3): 290–307 (2004). Thank you for the permission to reprint parts of the articles.

Bülent Diken and Carsten Bagge Laustsen
October 2004

INTRODUCTION

as if at the same time there was nothing more senseless, nothing more hopeless, than this freedom, this waiting, this inviolability.

(Kafka 1976: 105)

The painter of city life is perhaps Eduard Manet, whose city paintings are full of desire for connection and engagement. Hence urban sociology recognizes Manet as an 'artist of displacements' (Sennett 1996: 173). Displacing the familiar frames of reference and, stimulating engagement, his paintings deconstruct one's perception of oneself and the outer world. In this sense displacement is a fundamental experience of city life. In *The Bar at the Folies Bergère*, for instance, it is optically impossible to be facing the barmaid directly and seeing her reflection to the right of her at the same time. In the upper right corner of the painting, reflected in the mirror, we see a man the barmaid is looking at. This man cannot exist optically either; if he did, he would completely block out our direct view of the barmaid – the viewer is standing in front of the barmaid. The drama depicted in the painting is thus: 'I look in the mirror and see someone who is not myself' (ibid.: 177). The city allows you to become yourself by making a stranger of you.

This experience of displacement is increasingly threatened within the horizon of 'camping' today insofar as the camp bypasses the city as a space of exposure and touching. The logic of (self-)exemption tends to turn difference into indifference, while otherness is 'tolerated' but walled-off. The 'tolerance' of the camp neatly places every culture on its own turf in a mosaic bereft of interaction. In its horizon, in other words, tolerance cannot become solidarity and forced contingency cannot turn into a chosen destiny. The city depicted by Manet makes use of the beneficial anarchy of communication between strangers instead of their segmentation in enclaves. The camp, on the other hand, makes it impossible to confront others and to take moral/political choices, because its logic defines the others before they are met.

1

To find, in art, this space of pre-emption, this mutual exclusion, in which reaction comes before action or experience, one looks to the paintings of Edward Hopper. Edward Hopper is the painter of the camp. Decisive in this context is the role of disengagement in his paintings. *Nighthawks* (from 1942), for instance, which evokes the loneliness of New York, depicts a bar occupied by a waiter, a couple and a fourth, unspecific man with his back to the viewer. At first sight, they do not seem to be lonely. But there is a deep sense of loneliness, abandonment and disengagement in the picture, the weight of which cannot be carried by the figures inside the painting alone. Or, loneliness does not come from the picture itself. 'It's from us, the viewer, standing alone in the cold and the dark, looking in at the light through the window. The emotional tug isn't to be found in the picture: it's in our profound reaction to it' (Gill 2004: 41). In the painting, reaction and action, inside and outside, enter into a zone of indiscernibility. The seen and the unseen, the viewer's speculation, coincide. The omitted, off-scene object of the painting, loneliness, becomes obscene precisely at the point at which the viewer's own experience, the fear of loneliness, is directly incorporated in to the picture.

'How strange', writes Januszczak, 'that some artists who are able to capture the most elusive outdoor atmospheres cannot do people' (2004: 7). Hopper, known as 'the very best bad painter ever', is one of them; his kitsch-like paintings are exclusively populated by static, blank people devoid of any interiority whatsoever, 'as if they were furniture' (Gill 2004: 47). They say nothing, they have no dialogue, no touching; they are the monuments of disconnectedness in an interconnected world. Even with Hopper's nudes, depicted as mechanic, empty and silent naked bodies, eroticism and disappearance become indistinct categories. And perhaps herein the difference between Manet and Hopper is at its clearest.

For Manet, displacement is a kind of exception, which is the reserve of the *flâneur*, and as such it is what holds the whole scene, the multiplicity of relations, together. For Hopper, on the other hand, the exception is a rule, depicting a world of incongruities and contradictions in which engagement is impossible. In Manet's bar, displacement as exception leads to an enchanted experience of subjectivity, in Hopper it leads to an experience of *Unsicherheit* and ultimately to a desubjectivation. Thus, as the victims of a voyeuristic/ photographic gaze in a spectacle of suffering, the nighthawks, like the indestructible Sadean object, are subject to a collective enjoyment. In a culture that cultivates the anxiety of boredom, they resemble a sublimated assault on boredom, or, loneliness. Which is why every single one of Hopper's characters suffers from a sensation of inauthenticity, described by Barthes as the 'very subtle moment when, to tell the truth, I am neither subject nor object but a subject who feels he is becoming an object: I then experience a micro version of death: I am truly becoming a specter' (1981: 13–14). Hopper's wooden spectre-like subjects are *homines sacri*, occupying a zone of indistinction between life and death. Boredom? Hopper's loners are suspended somewhere, waiting and waiting, and waiting, unable to escape their fate. In fact, perhaps boredom is the most fundamental human condition. Here is a pertinent example, Hopperesque in *ennui*:

> We are sitting, for example, at the tasteless station of some lonely minor railway. It is four hours until the next train arrives. We do have a book in our rucksack, though – shall we read? No. Or think through a problem, some question? We are unable to. We read the timetables or study the table giving the various distances from this station to other places we are not otherwise acquainted with at all. We look at the clock – only a quarter of an hour has gone by. Then we go out onto the main road. We walk up and down, just to have something to do. But it is no use. Then we count the trees along the main road, look at our watch again – exactly five minutes since we last looked at it . . . and so on.
>
> (Heidegger, quoted in Agamben 2004c: 63–4)

It is here worth noting the lack of a temporal dimension in Hopper's paintings, which all depict an eternal now. In *Nighthawks*, for instance, people do not seem to have a purpose or a plan. This being left empty or abandoned is the essential experience of boredom, in which surroundings become indifferent to us, while at the same time, having no possibility of action, we cannot free ourselves from them (ibid.: 64). Being bored is being held in suspense. As such, boredom reveals an unexpected proximity of human and the animal: 'the man who becomes bored finds himself in the "closest proximity" . . . to animal captivation. Both are, in their most proper gesture, open to closedness; they are totally delivered over to something that obstinately refuses itself' (ibid.: 65). However, boredom paradoxically brings with it a possibility, a potentiality for being (*Dasein*), which has the form of a potential-not-to (ibid.: 67). In other words, the 'proximity' at issue is also a potentiality for the human for distancing itself from the animal. Suspending his animality, man can thus 'open "[a] free and empty" zone in which life is captured and a-ban-doned {*ab-bandonata*} in a zone of exception' (ibid.: 79). Animal is, precisely, defined by the impossibility of such suspension, of breaking down its relation to its environment. Human, in turn, is human because it can non-relate itself. In intense boredom, man can risk himself suspending his relation with the environment; the world becomes 'open' only in non-relating (ibid.: 69–70).

In *Nighthawks*, the bar at first sight appears to be an innocent space. But at a closer inspection it turns into an isolated, Hitchcockian space full of anxiety. Indeed, in stark contrast to Manet's bar, Hopper's is a non-place in the midst of nowhere. The 'city' around the bar is nothing more than a void. 'It's an empty space even though it has been colonised, a wilderness with gas stations, lunch rooms, movie theatres, store fronts' (Jones 2004). It is in this grey, indistinct 'city' lacking any atmosphere that the bar appears as a liminal space of exception, in which the inside and outside become indistinct. Indeed, Hopper himself found it 'difficult . . . to paint inside and outside at the same time' (Kranzfelder 2002: 147). In this respect, the role of the glass, the ultimate transgressor of the public–private divide, is remarkable in *Nighthawks* for it both connects and disconnects the place in relation to the outside.

> Walls almost entirely of glass, framed with thin steel supports, allow the inside and the outside of a building to be dissolved to the least point of differentiation . . . In this design concept, the aesthetics of visibility and social isolation merge.
>
> (Sennett 1986: 13)

Hopper's bar incarnates a kind of isolation-in-visibility, a paradoxical form of inclusionary exclusion, a kind of 'state of exception'. Its darkness is significant in this respect. However, there is light (hope), too, in *Nighthawks*. Indeed, pure light is one of Hopper's returning themes. But light in Hopper never seems to become a line of flight; it always ceases to affect the different fields of colour, each of which constitutes a discontinuous, isolated enclave. Instead, Hopper's 'cold' light often adds a brutalism to the scenes. . . . *Nighthawks* is an early testimony to the fragmentation and brutalization of the city, which is, according to urbanists like Mike Davis, the 'zeitgeist of urban restructuring' (1990: 223).

Hopper himself turned everywhere he travelled into a 'Hopperland', a kind of non-place. When in Paris, for instance, where he made his first picture, he painted the same mood of loneliness. Indeed, as Januszczak remarks, this picture could have been painted in New York with little noticeable difference.

> And my guess is that if you stuck this guy in front of the Taj Mahal on a sunny Indian afternoon, he would still manage to conjure a dingy Manhattan loneliness out of the sights before him, with shadows streaking across it and some alienated American loser at the centre, remembering a hope that got away.
>
> (2004: 6)

A society of exceptions

In this book we argue that ours is a society that increasingly resembles a Hopperland, a society in which exception and normality enter into a zone of indiscernibility. We live in an increasingly fragmented, 'splintering' society in which distinctions between culture and nature, biology and politics, law and transgression, mobility and immobility, reality and representation, immanence and transcendence, inside and outside . . . tend to disappear in a 'zone of indistinction'. The camp, the prototypical zone of indistinction, is the hidden logic beneath this process.

No doubt that the camp was originally an 'exceptional' space, entrenched and surrounded with secrecy. In other words, the camp emerged as the concentration camp, as a space in which the life of the 'citizen' was reduced to 'bare life', life stripped of form and value, where the 'city' turned into a state of nature. However, as the inside/outside distinctions disappear, the production of bare life is today extended beyond the walls of the concentration camp. That is, today, the logic of the camp is generalized; the exception is normalized. Hence it is no longer the city but the camp that is the paradigm of social life (Agamben 1998: 181). But, to stress, our argument is not that contemporary society is characterized by the cruelty of the concentration camps, although camp-like structures such as detention centres are spreading quickly. Primarily, we want to argue that the *logic* of the camp tends to be generalized throughout the entire society (ibid.: 20, 174–5). In this sense the camp signifies a hypermodern differentiation (of 'society'), which can no longer be held together by Durkheim's 'organic solidarity'. Qualitatively, in other words, the logic of the camp marks the whole social field; the camp subsumes the whole society under its paradoxical logic. Indeed, the camp is normalized to that extent that it is necessary to re-construct the sociological 'problematique' on the basis of the paradoxes of the camp. Thus, we investigate the logic of the camp and reflect upon its implications for social theory.

Significantly in this respect, social theory has understood the camp as an anomaly: an exceptional site situated on the margins of the polis to neutralize its 'failed citizens' or 'enemies'. As such, the camp articulates an image of 'society' as if it is dissolved or has disappeared into a state of nature. There are emerging, however, new social forms characterized by the logic of exemption and self-exemption characteristic of the camp. Unlike what sociology conceives of as social relation, these emerging socialities paradoxically promote unbonding as a form of relation. In this, connecting and disconnecting play equally significant and equally legitimate roles (see Bauman 2003: xii, 34, 91). In other words, contemporary social development has transformed the logic of the camp into a form of sociality. The camp is no longer a historical anomaly but the *nomos* of the contemporary social space (Agamben 1998: 166).

It was perhaps Foucault who most persistently approached the society from the point of view of its exceptional, residual zones. Indeed, his 'heterotopias' appear as a shadowy double of the society. As remainders, they constitute 'marvelous empty zones' outside the rhythm of normality. As is well known in this context, for Foucault, the investigation of normality is an investigation of its exception, abnormality (see Foucault 1980: 329). Somewhat similarly, Carl Schmitt understands exception not simply as something linked to the rule in a binary logic, but as something that presents a greater intensity:

> The exception is more interesting than the rule. The rule proves nothing; the exception proves everything: It confirms not only the rule but also its existence, which derives only from the exception. In

the exception the power of real life breaks through the crust of a
mechanism that has become torpid by repetition.

(Schmitt 1985a: 15)

The law is always posited in a negative way. The rule is known through its
transgression, a state through its exception, normal through the pathological,
and so on. To understand the social bond, one thus has to understand what
it excludes. Or, in Schmitt's allusion to Kierkegaard, exception 'explains
the general and itself' (ibid.: 15). Our method is the *via negativa*, which is also
at work in the diverse works of Foucault and Schmitt. But in claiming that
the very distinction between the normal and the exception is dissolving today,
we seek to radicalize their method further. The ontology with which Foucault
and Schmitt operated presupposes the presence of normality as a background
against which the exception can prove itself to be an exception. We argue that
our society is one without such a background. It is, so to speak, a society of
heterotopias. Which is perhaps the true meaning of Foucault's own diagnosis
of the contemporary society as a society in which 'pleasure is the rule' (Foucault
1997: 353). In our terminology, the camp has become the rule.

> Witness the 'Society' column of *Le Monde*, in which paradoxically,
> only immigrants, delinquents, women, etc. appear – everything that
> has not been socialized, 'social' cases analogous to pathological cases.
> Pockets to be absorbed, segments that the 'social' isolates as it grows.
> Designated as 'residual' at the horizon of the social, they enter its
> jurisdiction in this way.
>
> (Baudrillard 1994: 144)

We live in a society in which exception is the rule. Thus progressively more
situations are exceptional, that is, a matter of choice. Even normality is today
an object of choice, a life-strategy amongst others. The question is what
happens when everything residual or exceptional is 'normalized', when the
society has absorbed every exception, every pathological remainder. Namely,
it becomes impossible to decide whether the exception is the residue of the
social or the social itself becomes an exception: 'when nothing remains, the
entire sum turns to the remainder and becomes the remainder' (ibid.). With
the camp, we are witnessing the becoming remainder of 'society'. When the
camp as an exceptional/residual space is generalized, the society itself becomes
a remainder.

Our society sees itself today in the light of the camp. What is crucial here,
however, is not only the fact that the camp is promoted against the 'city' or
'society'; rather, and more significantly, the 'inversion' signals the emergence
of an instability, in which it is impossible to distinguish between the camp as
exception and exception as the rule. That is, the becoming-remainder of the

society signals not only the disappearance of the society but also of the remainder: 'there is "virtually" *no more remainder*' (ibid.: 145). The camp is no longer merely an exception, a remainder. When exception becomes the norm, the norm disappears. But when the norm disappears, exception disappears too. In a sense, therefore, there is no more camp (as exception): all society today is organized according to the logic of camp. 'End of a certain logic of distinctive oppositions, in which the weak term played the role of the residual term. Today, everything is inverted' (ibid.). Following this, we need to imagine a new 'city':

> It is a city made only of exceptions, exclusions, incongruities, contra-dictions. If such a city is the most improbable, by reducing the number of abnormal elements, we increase the probability that the city really exists. So I have only to subtract exceptions from my model, and in whatever direction I proceed, I will arrive at one of the cities which, always as an exception, exist.
>
> (Calvino 1997: 69)

Much has been written on the fragmentation of the contemporary city, e.g. on gated communities, shopping centres, theme parks, holiday resorts, war camps, ghettoes, and other spaces that resemble the camp. But, as if it were mimicking its object of study, this writing itself remains fragmented and is rarely brought together in a broader diagnostic analysis. We aim at such a diagnosis.

Twin camps

The well-known Graeco-Latin myth associates the constitution of the city, Rome, with the twins Romulus and Remus. According to the myth, the king of pre-Roman Alba Longa places his rival's daughter, Rea Silvia, in a sanctuary. However, she is raped by the god Ares and gives birth to Romulus and Remus. The king orders the boys to be drowned. But they were found and suckled by a she-wolf. As adults, the twins lead a revolt in Alba, and restore the government to their grandfather Numitor, who is still alive. At the same time, they decide to found a new city: Rome. But they disagree as to its location: while Romulus chooses a certain site for the new city, his brother Remus choose another one. They consent in settling their quarrel through the flight of vultures, that is, the birds of omen. Romulus sees twelve vultures and Remus only six. Romulus establishes the distinction between the city and the outside by plotting a line. However, Remus knows that Romulus lied about the number of vultures, that is, he transgressed the divine rule, and, being aware of the deceit, ridicules and tries to get in the way of the construction of the city. At some point, he mocks the new lowly walls of Rome and leaps across them, and for his transgression Romulus' men, instructed to let no man cross the new walls, kill him.

There are three dimensions which we find interesting and illuminating in this city myth. First, the city is built on the basis of an inside–outside divide, the walls, which is also a symbol of the law, or, the rule. As such, the origin of the city is posited as a 'distinction' between the law and its outside. Second, the constitution of the city (Romulus) and the transgression of its limits (Remus) are bound together; they are the twin faces of the same relation. In other words, there is no law without transgression, no rule without the exception. Further, the law itself is based on an inherent transgression, Romulus' deceit, just like every rule posits an exception. Power is productive and, by delimiting, it makes possible the proliferation of the transgressive desire. And third, although it relates the city to a distinction between the city and its outside, civilization and the nature, the myth clearly makes reference to a biopolitical zone of indistinction between the city (humans) and nature (wolves). Thus, the twins Romulus and Remus transgress the divide between human and animal, just as they blur the distinction between humans (Rea Silvia) and gods (Ares). In fact, in the myth, the city and the state of nature, man and wolf, coincide in a zone of indiscernibility.

In this book we focus on the same three questions, the rule, the exception and biopolitics, in relation to contemporary society but we do so by imagining a fourth possibility which is left out in this city myth. That is, we also imagine a city in which exception, Remus' transgression, is the rule, in which the camp is the organizing principle. It is significant in this context that the camp comes in twins. The dyadic structure of the camps demonstrates in spite of the absence of immediate physical resemblance a radical ambivalence typical of twinning. The word 'twin' shares the same root with words such as 'twilight' (the zone of indistinction where light and dark become indistinguishable) and expresses a contradictory situation, denoting etymologically both separation and union, a close but troubled alliance. In Middle English to 'twin' meant split or divide; hence 'we two will never twin' meant we will never be separated (Lash 1993: 6). Twins are, however, not necessarily identical twins. Likewise, camps do not necessarily come as conjoined or identical twins but as non-identical twins, which reveal, rather than perfect symmetry, a 'special case of duality in its mode of self-contradiction, the non-resolving duad . . . Twins are parity and disparity, but equality – never' (ibid.). We twin, for instance, detention centres and gated communities as examples of the camp sharing the same logic (of exception) on the basis of disparity and inequality, simultaneously expressing convergence and divergence, similarity and difference:

> A couple of apples is not a set of twin apples . . . Poison one of the two apples and substitute it for the other, and they will become twins. Make the first, unpoisoned apple the cure for the fatal poison of the other, and you have the plot-line for a quest tale based on twin motifs. Likewise, if one apple is reflected in a mirror, it becomes the twin of its counterpart, or if one apple is reflected in two separate mirrors, the

mirror apples are twins of each other as well as twins of the original.
This reveals . . . the odd, astonishing exponential vigour in twinning,
the facile elaboration of 2n, duality carried to the nth power.

(ibid.: 8)

It is here essential to recall the fundamental duality of power: that power is
positive and 'liberating' as well as negative and restrictive. That is, we can
speak of voluntary as well as restraining camps. In some camps the entry is
blocked but the exit is free, in others the entry is free but the exit is blocked.
Some camps keep others 'out', some 'in'. There are camps for those at the
bottom and those at the top. There are camps that are made of bricks and
camps that exist in minds. In each case, however, camps seem to function as
two extreme horizons that attract or repel the consumer-citizens/denizens who
do not know if they will go 'up' (e.g. gated community) or 'down' (e.g. detention centre). Most people seem to be suspended somewhere in the continuum
between the extremes, twin camps, which also materializes the *Unsicherheit*, or
fragility, characteristic of 'liquid modernity' (Bauman 2000).

In certain cases it is thus easy enough to recognize the camp (e.g. refugee
camps, rape camps, favelas, etc.). But nevertheless there are also more 'benevolent' camps (e.g. gated communities, sex tourism, theme parks, etc.) that
repeat the logic of the exception for the 'winners'. They are in a way more
interesting camps precisely because they can appear to be their opposite:
'liberating' alternatives to the 'restrictive' camps. But power catches one
on the flight, at the moment when one thinks one has escaped. The camp is
there where one expects it least. To quote from *The Usual Suspects*, 'the greatest
trick the devil has ever pulled is to convince the world he did not exist'. Thus
we deal not only with compulsory but also voluntary 'camping', which
increasingly signifies a new dream of community or belonging.

Which is why it is essential to examine the camp as a social form focusing
on both similarities and differences between the 'twins'. We do this by tracing
the genealogy of the camp. Even though the camp is that which emerges every
time exception becomes the rule, there is a huge variety to concrete camps.
Hence one must be able to show or prove the existence of an obvious or hidden
but common logic behind seemingly very different camps. In this, we also
show how the logic of the camp allows for a plurality of possible configurations,
depending on contexts.

Overview of the book

Part I delves into social theory and political philosophy for a conceptual
analysis of the camp, relating this analysis to the logic of sovereignty and
territoriality in the context of three *dispositifs* of power: discipline, control and
terror. Addressing different forms of power, politics and social stratification
accompanying different types of societies, we first investigate the camp in its

pre-modern form, that is, before it obtained a permanent spatial demarcation. Then we turn our attention to the camp in its classical *topos*, as a site of spatial enclosure. Following this, we discuss the camp in relation to discipline, control, and terror. By way of this multi-layered genealogy, we can show that sovereignty (abandonment) and disciplinary enclosure are not the only organizing principles of society; social life is also and simultaneously organized according to the principles of control, based on the regulation/coding of flows, and terror, based on naked violence.

Chapter 1 deals with Hobbes's and Schmitt's theories of sovereignty and focuses on the relationship between exception and law. It takes its point of departure in the classical understanding of sovereignty as the practice of abandoning subjects from the polis. Sovereignty is shown to work through an 'untying' rather than bonding. The sovereign is the one who can suspend the law. The symmetrical figure is *homo sacer*, who is banned, excluded and forced to survive outside the *polis*. This uncivilized 'state of nature' does not, however, exist prior to civilization but is established through the ban. Focusing on Schmitt's reading of Hobbes, we understand here the state of nature as a metaphorical description of the political core of law. This logic of the exception and untying is, we demonstrate, also the logic of the camp. The state of exception is the camp in its nascent form, before it can obtain a spatial form. This set-up is then used in outlining a genealogy of sovereignty and naked life, a genealogy that attempts to outline possible configurations of the two terms. We start with *homo sacer* known from the Roman law and end with commenting on the paparazzi hunt on Princess Diana.

Chapter 2 deals with the camp as a spatial reality. It critically combines the literature on camps with major works on biopolitics. As Schmitt argued, the '*nomos* of the earth' is constituted through linking localization and order to each other. However, we cannot but agree with Agamben in insisting on an ambiguity: in the state of exception this link breaks down. The concentration camp emerged when the unlocalizable (the state of exception) was granted a permanent and visible localization, signaling the advent of the political space of modernity itself. Yet, to say that this biopolitical construction is the '*nomos* of modernity' implies that all subjects are reduced to bare life: they become subjects with reference to a fundamental distinction between the sovereign and his subjects. In this sense, the outside of the camp reflects the inside: sovereign power reigns on both sides of the divide as potentiality and as actuality. Modernity creates a zone of indistinction not only between inside and outside (of the nation, the town or the home) but also by cutting through every subject and the political. In this context we undertake a genealogy of the camp in terms of spatial enclosure. We begin with the colonies, move on to the concentration camp via a reflection on the biopolitics of race and then conclude by discussing the camp in terms of deterritorialization or as a denial of settlement.

Chapter 3 focuses on how the production of 'bare life' is extended beyond the walls of the spatial enclosures today as the inside/outside distinctions disappear. The subject produced within the disciplinary *dispositif* was that of the prisoner, whose mobility was constrained through confinement and stigmatization. With control, we have the 'dividual', the subject governed on the move, through multiple systemic inscriptions and codes. The figure of the subject fit for the contemporary risk society is that of the hostage: an anonymous figure occupying a radical state of exception beyond the principle of exchange, alienation and knowledge. The hostage is a truly naked, formless body, which is absolutely convertible. The chapter emphasizes the complex interplay between sovereignty (abandonment), discipline, control and terror. We show how these *dispositifs* co-exist, how their topologies often overlap/ clash, and how they contain within themselves elements of one another, which is why it is difficult to 'distinguish' one form of power from another and why the space of power must be that of a zone of indistinction.

Part II is based on empirical cases. Focusing on the processes in which the citizen's ontological status is transformed into that of *homo sacer*, it elaborates on three pairs of cases selected with regard to the fundamental duality of power as negative/restrictive and positive/liberating. The three chapters here approach the camp from three different points of view: space, the body and ideology. Drawing on symmetrical experiences of the camp both as deprivation and privilege, both as lack and excess, the chapters all start with discussing a subject generally acknowledged as a camp (e.g. refugee camps and rape camps) but then focus on more 'benevolent' camps (e.g. Ibiza as a site of party tourism and gated communities), illuminating how the fundamental logic of the camp remains the same.

Chapter 4 is the first chapter that explicitly addresses empirical situations, looking at the circumstances of the asylum seeker, who, being 'human as such', is an instantiation of the *homo sacer*. Many asylum seekers are literally immobilized in 'non-places', e.g. accommodation centres in which they lead a life of 'frozen transience' and detention centres into which they are forced without trial. The chapter elaborates on the socio-spatial nature of this extreme form of immobilization, relating it to the concept of the camp. It then moves on to discuss some remarkable convergences between refugee spaces and other more respected and more desired contemporary 'camps' such as gated communities that effectively problematize the notions of the city and politics. Gated communities signal the dissolution of the agora and the declining concern for questions of the common good.

Chapter 5 starts with war rape, which historically has been an integral aspect of warfare. The focus is on the practices of rape by the paramilitary Serbian forces on Bosnian soil. As a practice of abandonment, war rape is a bio-political strategy aimed at (ab)using the distinction between the self and the body. The chapter interrogates the complex methods in this regard through a synthesis of the literature on abandonment and abjection. Then the same formal analysis is repeated in a symmetrical case: the 'tourist camps', where, beyond the constraints of daily life, voluntary abandonment is experienced as a hedonistic excess or enjoyment, a process in which the 'naked body' of the tourist borders on *homo sacer*. Due to the emphasis on the deliberate and 'liberating' aspects of this case, the focus of this section is on Ibiza and Faliraki rather than typical cases of 'sex tourism'.

Chapter 6 deals with how the 'network society' produces its own nightmare. Emphasizing the fundamentally political character of September 11, we twin here Bush and Bin Laden, the politics of security and the new terrorism, as two versions of fundamentalism. The fantasy generated within the context of terror is the promise of security, certainty and safety, which calls for the return of discipline as an image of *Sicherheit*, a development that gives rise to new camps and post-political strategies of risk management. This is followed by a discussion of how it becomes increasingly difficult today to distinguish between law and unlaw (the state of nature) and how the question of order, security and certainty re-emerges as a fundamental concern in contemporary society.

Part III opens discussing whether is it possible to re-politicize the social and to re-invent the city as a 'common good'. Is it possible to return from the camps and 'what is to be done' if return is impossible? Here the focus is on what escapes or resists the camp(s). This discussion has two main components articulated in two chapters.

Chapter 7 deals with the sociological consequences of the camp. It asks what happens when the ground concept of sociology, that is, distinction, is replaced with the concept of indistinction. What are the basics of a sociology of indistinction, a sociology fit for the camp? In our discussion we emphasize the paradoxes of (in)distinction, e.g. the question of how distinctions hide indistinctions and vice versa. We focus on the (in)distinction between distinction and indistinction (instead of before/after polarities); between inclusion and exclusion (instead of dichotomous models such as 'space of flows' versus 'space of places'); between normality and perversion (instead of naïve ideals of transgression); between mobility and immobility (instead of the popular dichotomy of immobile nation-states versus global flows); and between the subject as the sovereign and the subject as subjected to the sovereign (instead of the dichotomy of the subject versus power). Against this background, we argue that the existing sociological category of 'relation' is not sufficient to understand the camp. The camp as a sociological object necessitates a new, paradoxical conception of relationality, a sociological sensitivity towards 'nonrelation'. Finally, we ask how sociology can suspend itself, its own relationality, and open a zone of exception in which it can relate to its own limits.

Chapter 8, the final chapter, asks ethical questions about the camp and endeavours to formulate an ethical stance towards the 'human as such'. Modern social theory defined ethics as conformity to the norms but in so far as *homo sacer* is excluded/abandoned from community, the ethics of exception holds that what is shared is that which escapes the social, that is, bare life or nakedness. We interrogate in this respect Arendt's distinction between human rights and national rights that proposes an ethics that takes human 'rights' as rules protecting the subject in its status of being a naked body. This understanding of human rights is close to the original intent of the Declaration but is sadly distanced from contemporary practices; hence it remains a task to think the rights of the stateless, the refugees, or the 'sans papiers' as something more than empty formalisms. Ethics is, we conclude, a gamble. It is a matter of judgment and of running risks; only by becoming minor the other can be truly met. Such culture of hospitality illuminates another, increasingly forgotten face of the camp. The camp is a site of enclosure, abandonment and ethical conformity but it necessarily contains lines of escape, openings, which can turn the camp into something other, a paradoxical habitat of hospitality.

Part I

APPROACHING THE CAMP

1

NAKED LIFE

"camp\'kamp\ *n* 1a: ground on which tents or buildings for
temporary residence are erected b: a group of buildings or tents
erected on such ground c: a temporary shelter (as a cabin or tent)
d: an open-air location where persons camp e: a new lumbering
or mining town 2a: a body of persons encamped b: (1): a group
of persons promoting a theory or doctrine (liberal or conservative
camps) (2): an ideological position 3: military service or life
[Middle French, derived from Latin *campus* "plain, field"].

(*Webster's New Encyclopedic Dictionary* 1993: 140)

The camp is, first of all, a temporary site, a spatially delimited location
that exists only for a limited period. This definition is confirmed by the first
camps set up by the Spaniards in Cuba in the 1890s and by the British during
the Boer War in South Africa. These were followed by the development of
homelands: Bantustans, those large 'camps' within white South Africa, by the
Soviet Gulag, and by the Nazi concentration and death camps. As such, the
story of the camps is part and parcel of European history and cultural identity.
However, the (hi)story has not ended yet. The recent refugee camps, the camp
at Guantanamo Bay and the 'low cost – maximum pain' prisons in the Texan
deserts attest to this unsettling fact. Further, and even more disturbingly, there
seems to be an affinity between the temporary and transitory logic of the camp
and today's modernity. Thus, as we argue later, a decisive amount of contemporary urban structures, e.g. gated communities, shopping malls, theme parks,
campuses, and so on, repeat in their organization and spatial ideology the logic
of the camp.

Second, the camp signifies a position or a doctrine, which is why the
difference between the insiders in a camp is often less important and less
consequential than the difference between its insiders and outsiders. In other
words, the camp is a machine of ordering. Hence Gilroy is justified in claiming
that racism demonstrates a 'camp mentality' because it relentlessly translates
heterogeneity into homogeneity (1999: 188). However, as a machine of

ordering, whose logic is intertwined with that of sovereignty, the camp produces as much disorder as order. Like every order, the camp has to refer to a negativity, a disorder, to be able to constitute itself, and it is crucial to bear in mind that this negativity is a 'product of order's self-constitution: its side-effect, its waste, and yet the condition *sine qua non* of its (reflective) possibility' (Bauman 1991: 7). Consequently, it is always, as a rule, difficult to decide whether the camp produces order or disorder, norm bound regularity or extralegal exceptions.

These two definitions, the camp as a temporary site and as an ordering machine, are of course not unrelated: in order to be identified as a location, the camp must distinguish an inside and an outside, and this takes place through installing a specific principle of order. Which brings us to the third definition, that is, the camp identified with a particular life form. Camps are not only spatio-temporal entities but also social and (bio)political orders producing subjectivities. Different camps posit different life styles, markers, identities and social roles, different ways of acting and thinking.

Interestingly, these three definitions of the camp correspond to the three most central concepts of a theorist who never wrote a word about camps: Carl Schmitt. Let's start with the second definition related to order. For Schmitt the question of order is *the* question of politics, that is, how to install, maintain or question order. Schmitt identifies order with a *nomos*, a principle of ordering, rather than the law. His core concept in this respect is sovereignty. The sovereign is, as he states in *Political Theology*, the one who decides over the exception, that is, who decides when to declare and to end a state of emergency (Schmitt 1985a: 5). The sovereign can, in a perceived state of emergency, suspend the very laws which he is otherwise meant to protect. That is, who incarnates order stands above it. What emerges through this process in which the law no longer applies is the camp as an exceptional space. If, at this point, we link the installment of a *nomos* to the production of subjectivities, we can claim that the camp is a space in which 'bare life' is produced (Agamben 1998). However, the production of naked body also took place before the camp was invented; there was, so to speak, 'camp life' before the camp could be identified in the form of specific locations. Thus, in this chapter, we describe the camp as harbouring mechanisms found long before the camp existed as a location. The focus is, in other words, on the production of naked life.

The sovereign

Schmitt's concept of sovereignty is a 'borderline concept' through which the essence of the political can be uncovered. The concept operates *via negativa*, that is to say, the norm can only be understood through an investigation of the exception. Thus, sovereignty is not to be identified with the presence of a monopoly of violence, the existence of a people, etc., that is, as internal sovereignty. But nor is it to be identified with other states' recognition of a state, as 'external' sovereignty. The 'root' of sovereignty is to be found elsewhere and only to be unmasked in those situations characterized by extreme danger. And the 'root' at issue here is in quotation marks because it cannot be firmly established. Sovereignty manifests itself as an abyssal decision; for Schmitt, all positive systems, be it law, nations or international systems, rest on a decision. And so does the camp. The camp is the exception incarnated. However, as an exception or an anomaly, the camp also allows for an in-depth understanding of 'the political' and 'the social'.

Schmitt's thesis must be read in a non-etatist manner: we do not begin with the sovereign who decides on the state of exception; on the contrary, the one who can declare a state of exception is sovereign. Nuances are important here. The suspension of the law is not illegal but extralegal, hence it cannot be judged according to the distinction between legal and illegal. All legal systems are based on an extralegal and decisionist element, or, in Schmitt's terminology, a 'material kernel'; every legal order 'rests on a decision and not on a norm' (Schmitt 1985a: 10). Following this, because it depends on something external to itself, that is, sovereignty, law cannot be, as most legal positivists think, a self-enclosed and self-referential system. In a sense, therefore, Schmitt posits a paradoxical situation in which the sovereign has the right to suspend the law. It is as if sovereignty is the 'law beyond the law' (Agamben 1998: 59). Likewise, at another level, Schmitt argues that the law depends on the existence of a normality, an everyday frame of life, which provides the interpretative schemes necessary for its functioning and which assures the monopoly of violence that guarantees the implementation of legal decisions (Schmitt 1985a: 13). Every norm or law 'presupposes a normal situation, and no norm can be valid in an entirely abnormal situation' (Schmitt 1996: 46).

Against the background of this normality, the state of exception is limited in space and time: in time, through the declaration of a state of war and by the signing of a peace treaty, and in space, through the indication of its sphere of validity. In *this* period and within *this* space it is as if the statue of liberty has been veiled. Law is, however, not suspended *in toto*, or, the state of exception is not a chaos. Rather, in the state of exception the distinction between a transgression of the law and its execution is blurred (Agamben 1998: 57). The violence exercised 'neither preserves nor simply posits law, but rather conserves it in suspending it and posits it in excepting itself from it' (ibid.: 64). Consequently, there emerges a zone of indistinction between law and nature, outside and inside, violence and law. And yet the sovereign is precisely 'the one who maintains the possibility of deciding on the two to the very degree that he renders them indistinguishable from each other' (ibid.). In the state of exception the distinction between friends and enemies is blurred: the state starts treating its own citizens as potential enemies, as outsiders. The distinction is blurred in that suddenly one's status as a citizen ceases to remain taken for granted and becomes something to be decided upon. In this, what is outside is included not simply by means of an interdiction or an internment, but rather by means of the suspension of the juridical order's validity. The exception does not subtract itself from the rule; rather, the rule, suspending itself, gives rise to the exception. The particular 'force' of law consists in this capacity of law to maintain itself in relation to an exteriority (ibid.: 18).

In Roman law this exceptional act was called 'ban'. Those who were banned from the Empire were treated like an enemy and could be killed without sanctions of any sort. Everybody was entitled to harm, or, in other words, everybody was sovereign in relation to these individuals (ibid.: 104–5). Indeed, the banned individual, or *homo sacer*, seemed to live in a state of exception and as such he was *friedlos*, a 'man without peace' (ibid.: 104). What is crucial here, however, is that such abandonment was not merely a marginal or exotic phenomenon within the Empire. It was, much more significantly, the way biological life was included within the realm of power. Subjects are subjected to the sovereign's will because of his capacity to kill:

> The crimes that, according to the original sources, merit *sacratio* . . . do not, therefore, have the character of a transgression of a rule that is then followed by the appropriate sanction. They constitute instead the originary exception in which human life is included in the political order in being exposed to an unconditional capacity to be killed.
>
> (ibid.: 85)

The term 'sacer' does not, for this reason, refer to the religious domain. To compare and contrast, the sacred in Bataille's sense, for instance, involves the distinction between the sacrificeable and unsacrificeable, a principle according to which *what is useful* is destined to be sacrificed. *Homo sacer*, on the other hand, can be treated violently but not in the form of religious sacrifice; he can be killed but not sacrificed (Agamben 1998: 111–15). *Homo sacer* is excluded from both the *ius humanum* and the *ius divinum*, from both the sphere of the profane and the religious (ibid.: 82). The bare life of *homo sacer* belongs to the domain of (bio)politics, not religion. If the formal structure of sovereignty is untying, or exception, the production of untying is bare life (*zoē*), biological life stripped of (life) forms and political rights and thus located outside the polis (ibid.: 1). Through the act of abandonment, the biological (*zoē*) and the social/political (*bios*) are separated.

Homo sacer and the sovereign are two symmetrical figures: 'the sovereign is the one with respect to whom all men are potentially *homines sacri*, and *homo sacer* is the one with respect to whom all men act as sovereigns' (ibid.: 84). Usually, scholars focus on the first part of the formulation ('the sovereign is the one with respect to whom all men are potentially *homines sacri*'). The obvious reason why is the misguided identification of sovereignty as the state, that is, as a centre, as a certain oneness and indivisibility. This identification is not only wrong; it also blocks the insight expressed in the second part of the formulation ('*homo sacer* is the one with respect to whom all men act as sovereigns'). To clarify this point, Girard's philosophy might be useful. As is well known, his 'scapegoat' is a victim treated as *homo sacer*. As an object of an irrational rage, the scapegoat is not protected by norms and rules, which apply to others, and being considered of no worth, even as an obstacle, he is not worthy of being sacrificed. But, in contrast to Schmitt, Girard understands the archaic form of sovereignty as an exercise of sovereignty by the many over a single individual.

Man is for Girard driven by a desire to imitate his fellow beings, that is, by mimesis. Desire is the other's desire. What is critical here is that the objects of desire are not desired because they are of inherent value but because they belong to the other, or, in other words, one desires what belongs to the neighbour. Thus objects can become a matter of envy, which, further, can develop into outright enmity, that is, 'acquisitive mimesis' can turn into 'conflictual mimesis' (Girard 1977: 1–38). The significance of the scapegoat emerges at this point because, unlike objects, which can only be possessed individually, hatred towards a scapegoat can be shared. Thanks to the scapegoat, people can mimic the other's hatred, which often culminates in violence. Through this projection, the problem of conflict and difference is resolved and unity is reestablished. Therefore Girard sees scapegoating as the foundation of all cultures, as a collective deed fueled by unconscious and unacknowledged desires.

What is significant to us is the Hobbesian aspect of Girard's model. Both Hobbes's state of nature and Girard's origin of culture are characterized by envy, hostility and mimesis. But the way the conflict is overcome is different. Thus, instead of Hobbes's well-ordered state, Leviathan, we have in Girard a lynching mob; the conflict is resolved through the sacrifice of the scapegoat. Or, in our terminology, the scapegoat is abandoned by the community. However, this similarity between sacrifice and abandonment, between the scapegoat and *homo sacer*, must be qualified. Importantly in this context, Girard conflates guilt and innocence in the victim to be able to explain the identity of the sacrifice with the scapegoat. However, since the Bible, the two have been strictly separated:

> The scapegoat, which symbolizes guilt, is not killed but sent out into the wilderness to illustrate that the inability to accept losses for the good of the community signifies the disintegration of the community and its own banishment into the wilderness. Those who refuse to make sacrifices are the scapegoats because they are not willing to make concessions for the good of the community. The proper punishment for such people is the same as for the scapegoat – not death, but banishment. Whereas Girard sees sacrifice as a controlled outlet for violence, the Bible, in differentiating a killing which is not a sacrifice from a killing which is, demonstrates that the significance

21

of the sacrifice is not in release of violence but in the offering of the sacrifice to God according to the laws of the community rather than keeping it for oneself. The man who does not offer the killed animal as a sacrifice becomes guilty of a sin against the community and is cut off from the community, banished like the scapegoat. He is considered guilty of murder because killing must be maintained as a community decision rather than as an individual one . . . The function of the sacrificial goat and of the scapegoat is not to provide a vent for built up aggression but to continually remind individuals of their obligations to the community.

(Pan 1992: 86)

In short, the scapegoat is not merely somebody sacrificed to prevent the community from dissolving. Rather, the scapegoat is really the one who disrupts the mechanism of sacrifice, which is why he or she is banished (abandoned) from the community. In fact, seen in this perspective, Girard's theory shares something in common with Schmitt's: the focus on the negative. In both perspectives, the relation between the exception and the rule is in the forefront. In both, decision (to identify the scapegoat/enemy) is the basis of society. Just as the sovereign exception is the core of law, the scapegoat is what holds culture together (see Palaver 1992).

This is not the whole story, though. Another equally significant parallel exists between the sovereign pardoning and sacrificial forgiveness. Sovereignty can be exercised by granting a pardon. And true sacrifice is sacrificing the sacrifice itself, that is, forgiving the scapegoat. Girard himself finds this motif in Christianity (in the innocence of Christ) and generalizes it to all scapegoats. The scapegoat can be forgiven or pardoned instead of lynching but precisely as such remains under the sway of sovereignty. Sovereignty is both manifested in the decision to wield or rest the executioner's axe (Fiskesjö 2003: 53). This coincidence of pardoning and killing means that sovereign power is per definition arbitrary, that it does not abide rules. If it did, sovereignty would become a form, albeit a perverted form, of justice. But sovereignty is intimately bound to the exception.

Witches and werewolves

Who was *homo sacer*, then? Let us continue with an example from medieval times. In this period witches are one of the recurring groups of people who were treated as *homines sacri*. The witch was seen as a person suffering from an insatiable carnal lust only satisfied through incubus with the devil; we hear about nocturnal gatherings, conspiracies, child sacrifice and other ritual murders, about cannibalism, and more generally about secret plots of malevolence against 'man' (Denike 2003: 18). These women were essentially deemed weak or feeble; however, their weakness was exactly what made them the prime target of devilish seduction. Weak they were but at the same time they were extremely powerful and dangerous: they were seen to be capable of causing death, destroying corps and introducing plagues (ibid.: 14). They were, and that might have been their greatest asset, even capable of transmuting into other shapes and forms, which is why one could never be sure whether one encountered an exemplar of this devilish pack or not (ibid.: 35). Their 'ability' to disguise themselves was, in turn, what made witches a vulnerable target in social and political contexts. Even their normality was thus seen as a proof of their wicked abnormality in the expectation that those who seem most innocent might in fact be the most dangerous witches. The use of torture against these women was thus likened to the activity of peeling an onion, an activity of unmasking or digging to the essential core of identity.

In *Malleus Maleficarum*, perhaps the most important medieval demonology, we are told that 'witchcraft is high Treason against God's majesty' (quoted in ibid.: 25). The person who is accused of high treason is, of course, not an ordinary criminal but somebody who attacks the king in his capacity of being the arbiter of the law. By punishing an ordinary criminal the integrity of law can be sustained, perhaps even strengthened. In the case of high treason, on the other hand, something more is at stake in that the very system of law is under attack. Thus, in such a state of emergency the use of 'illegal' means is accepted. Legal obstacles are removed allowing the inquisitors to unleash their regimes of brutality (ibid.: 29).

The case is, however, more complex than 'just' a suspension of the law. The Inquisition was part of the Church's struggle to enlarge its jurisdiction, which had been diminishing *vis-à-vis* the developing system of public law. Witchcraft in this context was seen as a set of exceptional crimes that allowed for the suspension of ordinary secular judicial procedures (ibid.). The state's growing influence at the cost of the Church could thus be countered. But also the state itself made use of the same trick. Bodin, for instance, one of the most prominent legal theorists of his time, recommended measures that closely resembled those practised by the Inquisition, that is, 'an entirely different exceptional approach' aimed against 'the crimes of Treason against God', a crime which in its wickedness 'outweighs all others' (Bodin, quoted in ibid.: 34–5). The Church and the state thus used the appeal to exception to gain legal monopoly. In both cases, the witch-hunt laid bare the material kernel of law, that is, its extralegal basis.

Among these extralegal means were punitive proceedings, the use of 'judicial' torture, and permission for local courts to function independently of central political and judicial control (Denike 2003: 33). The lower court judges constituted witchcraft as a *crimen exceptum* allowing for a suspension of procedural rules. Women and children were in these unusual circumstances qualified as witnesses; there were no possibility of appealing to higher courts or of having evidence further scrutinized (ibid.). The witches were, so to speak, included and excluded from the law at one and the same time. They were included within the realm of law through the suspension of legal procedures, that is, through exclusion or abandonment.

Another medieval image of *homo sacer* is the werewolf. Edward the Confessor (1030–35) defines the bandit as a *wulfesheud* (a wolf's head) and thus assimilates him to the werewolf (Agamben 1998: 105). The werewolf is neither a beast nor a human being; it dwells within both and belongs to either. Being a hybrid, the werewolf is a threat to the world of culture and order. As is the case with the witch, the werewolf is a master of disguise. And like the witch, the werewolf is an outlaw that can be killed without any legal sanction:

> What had to remain in the collective unconscious as a monstrous hybrid of human and animal, divided between the forest and the city – the werewolf – is, therefore, in its origin the figure of the man who has been banned from the city.
>
> (ibid.)

The space of the werewolf, the forest, stood in medieval times as a metaphor of chaos, that is, an undifferentiated or disintegrated world, a wilderness. The forest or the state of nature, on the one hand and the city, civilization, on the other; this opposition between inclusion and exclusion, between inside and outside, found its best expression in Hobbes's distinction between a state of nature and a commonwealth (Leviathan). Later, Schmitt applied the same distinction to distinguish Europe (the realm of law) and the New World (the realm of nature). Schmitt was of course well aware that Hobbes's state of nature was not to be understood as a chronological period preceding the formation of the legal domain. On the contrary, the uncivilized state of nature is produced from within the legal domain, the forest from within civilization. Just as the gesture of *aban*donment produces *homo sacer* (in the form of the bandit, the witch, the outlaw or the werewolf), the Hobbesian distinction evokes the forest as a retroactively branded counter-image to the city. In other words, civilization does not follow a state of nature; rather, it is the case that through the *ban* we get both civilization and the state of nature (ibid.: 6). A reformulation of the relationship between the forest and the city, between nature and civilization, is thus necessary. The forest and the wolf are nothing but figures that pertain to the state of exception:

> The state of nature is not a real epoch chronologically prior to the foundation of the City but a principle internal to the City, which appears at the moment the City is considered *tanquam dissoluta*, 'as if it were dissolved' (in this sense, therefore, the state of nature is something like a state of exception). Accordingly, when Hobbes founds sovereignty by means of a reference to the state in which 'man is a wolf to men', *homo hominis lupus*, in the word 'wolf' (*lupus*) we

ought to hear an echo of the wargus and the *caput lupinem* of the laws of Edward the Confessor: at issue is not simply *fera bestia* and natural life but rather a zone of indistinction between the human and the animal, a werewolf, a man who is transformed into a wolf and a wolf who is transformed into a man – in other words, a bandit, a *homo sacer*. Far from being a prejuridical condition that is indifferent to the law of the city, the Hobbesian state of nature is the exception and the threshold that constitutes and dwells within it.

(ibid.: 105–6)

In Hobbes, the state of nature survives in the figure of the sovereign. The state of nature is depicted not as a period prior to a civic contract but the moment in which civilization or the city appears to be disintegrated. For the same reason the state of nature becomes the possibility or potentiality of the law, its 'self-presupposition as natural law' (ibid.: 36). Following this, the state of nature comes to resemble the state of exception as a 'complex topological figure in which not only the exception and the rule but also the state of nature and law, outside and inside, pass through one another' (ibid.: 37). Schmitt is thus justified in claiming that Hobbes was a decisionist, and not a liberalist (Schmitt 1996: 55). What matters is not the state as an aggregation of wills, manifested in a contract, but the state's monopoly of violence and, more importantly, its willingness to use it and to suspend the laws in a time of crisis.

Hobbes's metaphors of Leviathan and Behemoth are worth a comment at this point. The two monsters are known from the Book of Job as well as from various texts in the Judean tradition. Leviathan is the gigantic sea monster and Behemoth the earth monster. However, Hobbes understands Leviathan too mechanically, as an accumulation of wills, which leads him to neglect Leviathan's mythic potential. Thus, Leviathan is depicted on the cover of Hobbes's book as a gigantic man composed of lots of miniature individuals, disregarding the image of Leviathan as the strong state capable of suppressing dissent and warding off enemies. Behemoth, on the other hand, serves as an image of a ubiquitous danger of civil war (*Behemoth* is also the title of Hobbes's less well known book on the civil war in England). In short, we have two enormous powers confronting each other. The state of emergency (Behemoth) is countered by a state of exception (Leviathan). These two mythic animals are, according to the Torah, to serve as meat for the feast of the righteous on the final day. Until then, though, they lurk as all-pervading dangers that threaten the commonwealth.

The Hobbesian mythologeme must be understood in terms of the sovereign ban. Indeed, to understand it in terms of a *contract* instead has, as Agamben argues, hitherto condemned Western democracy to impotence every time it confronted the problem of sovereign power (1998: 109). If we understand society in terms of a contract, we necessarily overlook the supreme violence that grounds society and allows for a suspension of its legal order when needed. Power is *potenza*, that is, something which is exercised in exceptional situations and only known as a possibility or a potentiality. In *De Cive* it is 'the body's capacity to be killed that founds both the natural equality of men and the necessity of the "commonwealth"' (ibid.: 125).

The *Muselmann*

One of the most extreme manifestations of the right to kill was the Nazi concentration camps, in which more than four million people were gassed to death in less than four years. These camps manifested the archaic logic of sovereignty in that the camp inmate was a flagrant case of *homo sacer*. A mere 'capacity to be killed' was inherent in the condition of the Jew (Agamben 1998: 134). However, there was something novel in the Nazi camps too. What was previously exercised in singular and marginal cases and punished in spectacular ways was now exercised in the form of a bureaucratized mass murder. Whole groups of people were abandoned. Further, the camp system was designed to blur the distinction between the victim and the executioner. Being the one carrying out 'the dirty work', the *kapo* (those inmates assigned the task of policing fellows prisoners) belonged to both categories. And so did the camp official, who merely 'followed orders', or who, as Eichmann, administered massacres at a distance. And not surprisingly, this blurring had its origin in a legal ambivalence.

The camp was, on the one hand, placed outside the rule of law: the guards could punish the prisoners randomly, without taking any consequences for their acts, just as the murder of the werewolf was not considered homicide (ibid.: 31). On the other hand, however, the camps relied upon the prior legalization, on *Schutzhaft*, and the inhabitants were denaturalized according to legal procedures (ibid.: 167, 132). The exclusion of the Jews, the Gypsies and other enemies of the Aryan race took place from within the realm of law. It was, in other words, a case of inclusive exclusion. During the Weimar years, article 48 of the Weimar Constitution was used several times and for long periods to establish a state of emergency (*Ausnahmenzustand*). On 28 February, when Hitler came to power, he issued a decree for the protection of the people and the state by suspending some basic rights and liberties. The concept of the state of emergency was not mentioned, but the decree remained in force until the end of the Nazi rule, and it thus became permanently impossible to distinguish between the rule and its exception (ibid.: 168). It was a 'Night of St. Bartholomew that lasted twelve years' (Drobisch and Wieland 1993: 26; quoted in ibid.).

Death was the all-pervading reality of the camps, only the method of dying differed. Even those who worked only gained a few extra months compared to those who were gassed immediately. Once, when asked by a group of prisoners about the health of a fellow inmate, the *kapo* simply answered: 'Here there aren't any sick people. There are only the living and the dead' (quoted in Razac 2002: 61). What was killed or what temporarily lived on was something less than a human being; 'extermination happens to human beings who for all practical purposes are already dead' (Arendt 1994: 236). The biological death was in a sense preceded by a moral and symbolic death. The inmates were reduced to the lowest common denominator, that of 'organic life itself', or, in other words, to *homo sacer*.

In this process, all categories used to distinguish the human from the inhuman, e.g. the question of guilt and innocence, became obsolete. The *Muselmann* was, without doubt, the figure who experienced this indistinction at its most extreme. For him, the difference between good and evil, noble and base had no relevance or meaning. His state of being was a consequence of undernutrition, stress and cold. Hence the *Muselmann* had only one aim: survival. Even worse, he did not even register the guardians' physical violence and only occasionally protected himself. Having no sense of a self, the *Muselmann* reminds us of, above all, a walking corpse (Agamben 1999a: 41, 46). The term *Muselmann* originates in Auschwitz and refers to Muslims bending forward in prayer (ibid.: 41). In Majdanek the term in use was 'donkeys', in Dachau 'cretins', in Stutthof 'cripples', in Mauthausen 'swimmers', in Neuengamme 'camels' and in Buchenwald 'tired sheikhs' (ibid.: 44). In addition, Primo Levi's telling term must be included here: the 'drowned'.

In this context Jacob von Uexküll, writing on the animalization of man, is instructive (see Agamben 2004c: 39–62). Uexküll distinguished between *Umgebund* (objective space) and *Umwelt* (the species relative environment), and he saw the *Umwelt* as consisting of a selective sample of marks or 'carriers of significance': some animals cannot distinguish certain colours; some have a better hearing than others, etc. One of Uexküll's experiments was to expose ticks to different membranes filled with liquid. If the temperature was 37 degrees centigrade and the membrane of a certain plasticity, the tick would attach itself to it regardless of what the liquid consisted of. Hence, for the tick the taste of blood is not a carrier of significance, but heat is. Heidegger uses this as a basis to distinguish man and animal: the animal is poor in the world (*weltarm*) while man is rich in his world-forming (*weltbildend*) (ibid.: 51). Only man is capable of shifting between different disinhibitors and thus of posing and exposing himself to different environments. He is not, in contrast to the animal, captivated in his essence. Or, in a nutshell: the animal behaves in an environment; man operates in a world. Another of Uexküll's experiments supports Heidegger's argument further at this point. Uexküll exposed a bee to a cup of honey, and its abdomen is cut away while it sucks the honey. Although all honey is now lost, the bee continues to suck it. It cannot disconnect: it is entrapped in its environment. It cannot close the environment off and thus cannot open itself toward other environments, that is, towards a world. What the *Muselmann* loses is *this* world. Being reduced to animal instinct and impulses, the *Muselmann*'s only concern, or, only carrier of significance, is food.

As such he cannot create a distance between himself and the environment. What is crucial here is, of course, that for the *Muselmann* the camp is an environment, not a world.

The *Muselmann* was a product of absolute power. As is well known from Hegel's master–slave dialectic, death is the limit of power. When the slave dies, the master's power over him disappears too. The Nazis, however, went further and robbed the *Muselmann* even of his own death (Agamben 1999a: 48). In the camp nobody dies in his or her own name (ibid.: 48, 104). The Nazis did not call the inmates by their names but tattooed a number on their skins. Nobody died as an individual but as parts of an industrial production of corpses. They died, in other words, as numbers. Death has always been thought of as a limit, as a figure of nothingness against the background of which the finite, life itself, finds meaning. The Nazis appropriated this limit, reducing the infinite to the finite, or, in other words, turned the exception into the rule. Death was no longer something distant, an external limit, but the condition in which the *Muselmann* lived.

This also explains the rarity of suicides. Suicide is a way of unplugging, a way of creating a minimal distance from the omnipresent reality of the camp (Stark 2001: 100). Furthermore, it was often impossible to identify a suicide. Was it, for instance, a suicide or an attempt at escape, when the inmates ran to the electrical fences (ibid.: 101)? If suicide is a fundamental human act, an expression of freedom and the right to organize one's own life, then the lack of suicide in the camps shows that the inmates were robbed of this possibility (ibid.: 94). On 28 August 1942, five women from Würzburg committed suicide immediately after their deportation. The Gestapo quickly found five replacements for them to thereby punish the Jewish community for the five women's 'initiative'. A survivor from the camps, Filip Müller, a Czech, tells about his suicide attempt by joining other Czechs who were to be gassed. The attempt was prevented by the intervention of the guards. While they beat him, they shouted: 'You bloody ship, get it into your stupid head: we decide how long you stay alive and when you die, and not you' (in ibid.: 97). The minimal form of autonomy characteristic for suicide was unacceptable for the Nazis, even though their project was the elimination of the Jews from the surface of the world (ibid.: 98).

Levi gives three explanations for the low rate of suicide. First, suicide is a human act and therefore unimaginable for one reduced to animal existence. Second, it was, as a form of self-punishment unnecessary; the punishments of the Nazis were abundant: confronted with the mass production of corpses, murder as well as sacrifice becomes meaningless (Arendt 1973: 441). And third, the fight for survival exhausted all the energy of the camp inmates, at any rate of the *Muselmänner* (Stark 2001: 100). Almost regardless of how the *Muselmann* is described, it is not possible for him to attain a reflective distance to himself. To kill *oneself* requires precisely a self, which is what the *Muselmänner* lacked. Conscience, likewise, entails that one can relate to one's self as if it were somebody else, or, to use the previously given distinction, that one can relate to the other as a part of a world and not of an environment.

Starvation was not the only way through which the prisoners were reduced to bare life. The same could be achieved by making an ethically pure position impossible. In the camps, forced complicity as a rule provoked shame and this destroyed the prisoners' moral habitus. Primo Levi's concept of the 'grey zone' is crucial to understand this enforced complicity. In the camps, policing of the inmates was partly conducted by the inmates themselves. In turn, these *kapos* were offered some privileges such as better shelter, a private room or more food, but, at the end of the day, they too were murdered. As such, the *kapos* testify to the fact that in order to survive one was forced to live on others' misery. Perhaps the best description of this is given by Tadeusz Borowski in his *This Way for the Gas, Ladies and Gentlemen* (1976). As he stresses throughout the novel, the prisoners can only remain alive because others keep dying. Hence they start to treat one another instrumentally, without any sign of respect. Some even hit the newly arrived. Consequently, it becomes difficult to distinguish between the victim and the executioner, noble and base, and the human and inhuman. Everybody is dehumanized through the active de-humanization of others. To be sure, the Nazi camps were extreme constellations, but what about their logic? Are extralegal torture, enforced shame, dehumanization of prisoners and other mayhem still with us? Let us now focus on our present predicament.

Prisoners of the United States

Camp Delta (formerly known as Camp X-Ray) is a space perceived to be 'beyond' law. Since the inmates do not touch US soil and since US courts do not consider the Cuban base to be part of the USA, the inmates are denied the rights guaranteed to criminals under the US constitution. Being both inside and outside the USA at the same time, Camp Delta is effectively a zone of indistinction created through the suspension of the law. Thus, the prisoners live at the mercy of presidential decrees and the will of the military personnel. They have now for more than two years been awaiting not their release but simply a decision on their status and a timetable for the future (Fiskesjö 2003: 60).

According to the Geneva Convention, army members automatically qualify for prisoner-of-war status, while others, such as members of guerilla movements, are only accorded this status when the following criteria are met: that one acts as part of a clear structure of command; that one bears a visible sign of participation in a war, e.g. a uniform or carrying a weapon; and that one obeys the laws of war (Sullivan 2002). Referring to these criteria, the Bush administration claimed that neither the Taliban nor al-Qaeda deserve this status: the terrorists do not wear a uniform and in targeting the civilian populations, they break the laws of war (ibid.). It is, however, problematical to treat all the inmates in Camp Delta as 'illegal combatants', regardless of whether they belong to the Taliban or al-Qaeda. There is a significant difference between those who can be directly linked to 9/11 and those who fought to defend Afghanistan against American invasion. Since they were defending a country under attack, the Taliban should automatically be granted status as prisoners-of-war, while the question is less clear regarding al-Qaeda members. Nevertheless, the Convention states that questions of doubt should be decided upon by a court.

Indeed, American courts of appeal have deemed this practice in discord with fundamental principles of American jurisprudence, which is why some prisoners are returned to their country of origin. The only explanation given, after more than two years of imprisonment, is that sufficient evidence cannot be produced. A significant invention meanwhile has been the military tribunals, situated at the base, with the aim of deciding on the status of the prisoners and reviewing the prospect of their release on a yearly basis. The decision might well be a death penalty, which is why the building of a death chamber at the base is to be initiated (Butler 2004: 58). And importantly, these 'courts' are mainly advisory, that is, their decision might be overruled by presidential decree. It is, in other words, administrative bureaucracies and military personnel who decide on the future of the prisoners. And their decisions are bound not by laws but by the concerns for American safety only (ibid.).

The Cuban solution allows for the suspension of cherished principles of Western democracy such as the right to a fair trial before a jury, the right to an attorney, and the idea that one is innocent until proven otherwise. Rules of evidence are relaxed: hearsay and second-hand reports are treated as valid evidence in the military courts.

> If these trials make a mockery of evidence, if they are, effectively, ways of circumventing the usual legal demands for evidence, then these trials nullify the very meaning of the trial, and they nullify the trial most effectively by taking the name of the trial.
>
> (ibid.: 69)

This 'anachronistic' mode of sovereignty manifests itself in all aspects of camp life. For instance, the inmates are locked into small (8 × 8 feet) one-man cages, which are considerably smaller than allowed for in international law. They are protected from the sun only by a roof of metal sheeting; the floor is made of cement and the 'walls' of wire netting; the cells are bathed in electric lighting 24 hours a day, which makes sleep, rest and privacy impossible. When they leave their cells for interrogation and the like, the prisoners are deprived of their senses and isolated from their immediate surroundings (and from each other). Such spatial strategies, which are part of a scheme of continuous torture aimed to retrieve 'actionable intelligence', are thought to 'soften' the prisoners (Danner 2004b). In short, in Camp Delta we are dealing with *homo sacer*.

Since January 2002 the USA has sent more than 700 'illegal combatants' from more than 40 countries to Camp Delta. Many of them are simply people who have been in the wrong spot at the wrong time: there are farmers, cab drivers, a cameraman from al-Jazeera among the detainees, and there are even children between 13 and 16, which the Administration has tried to hide (Butler 2004: 79). Bush designated these people as 'wicked', Rumsfeld as 'well trained terrorists', Heynes as 'exceptional', Hastert as 'unique' and, finally, Cheney as 'really bad people' (ibid.: 90). In the war against terror the enemy no longer represents something, has no reason, etc. The enemy is simply evil, plainly a killing machine, and less than human; hence internment is not seen as punishment but as custody keeping the terrorists away from their targets (ibid.: 74, 79, 83ff.).

The perception of the enemy as inhuman in the war against terror became evident in the scandal that followed the release of torture pictures from Abu Ghraib, the notorious prison which Saddam himself had used for obtaining information from his opponents. The methods of physical and psychological coercion practised in Abu Ghraib varied from hooding (to disorient the inmates and to cause anger and nervousness by making them unaware of how and when they are hit) to handcuffing with flexi-cuffs and beatings with hard objects. The inmates were paraded naked outside their cells, sometimes with women's underwear over their head (Danner 2004a). The inmates were exposed to attacks of dogs and their pictures were taken while posing in humiliating postures. Sexual torture took place often: some prisoners were sodomized with a chemical light or a broom stick, they were forced to perform rape, oral sex and masturbation on each other. What is significant in this respect is that such 'strategy' deliberately blurs the distinction between the animal and the human, the clean and the dirty, the proper and the improper, and strips from the prisoners the status of citizen or of legitimate enemy, reducing their life to *homo sacer*'s bare life.

Among the known photographs are: a man covered in a dirty carpet and with a sand bag on his head posing like Christ. There are wires attached to his fingers and genitals, threatening with a deadly electric shock if he fell down from the box on which he stands. Another picture shows seven men forming a sort of human pyramid. They are all naked and hooded with sand bags. And perhaps the most distressing depiction is the one in which Private Lynndie England holds a prisoner on a dog leash. She is grinning at the camera, pointing at the prisoner's genitals with her right hand and flashing a thumbs-up with her left. It has not been proven that they were instructed to use sexual torture but the official discourse certainly encouraged such acts by portraying these people as subhuman. It is also plausible that there have been some coordinated reflections on how most effectively to break the prisoner's resistance. A pamphlet, along with a one-week course on Iraq's customs and history, was given to the American Marine Corps before going to war. Here are some admonitions from the pamphlet:

Do not shame or humiliate a man in public. Shaming a man will cause him and his family to be anti-Coalition. The most important qualifier for all shame is for a third party to witness the act. If you must do something likely to cause shame, remove the person from view of others. Shame is given by placing hoods over a detainee's head. Avoid this practice. Placing a detainee on the ground or putting a foot on him implies you are God. This is one of the worst things we can do. Arabs consider the following things unclean: Feet or soles of feet; using the bathroom around others. Unlike Marines, who are used to open-air toilets, Arab men will not shower/use the bathroom together.

(quoted in Danner 2004b)

Indeed, it is telling to compare this 'cautious' material with the practice of torture which reversed all the advice in an attempt to maximize the amount of shame. The following is part of a sworn statement of an as-yet-anonymous prisoner given to the military's Criminal Investigation:

Some of the things they did was make me sit down like a dog, and they would hold the string from the bag and they made me bark like a dog and they were laughing at me . . . One of the police was telling me to crawl in Arabic, so I crawled on my stomach and the police were spitting on me when I was crawling and hitting me . . . They took me to the room and they signalled me to get on to the floor. And one of the police he put a part of his stick that he always carries inside my ass and I felt it going inside me about 2 centimetres, approximately. And I started screaming, and he pulled it out and he washed it with water inside the room. And then two American girls that were there then they were beating me, they were hitting me with a ball made of sponge on my dick. And when I was tied up in my room, one of the girls, with blonde hair, she is white, she was playing with my dick . . . And they were taking pictures of me during all these instances.

(testimony quoted in ibid.)

Here is another testimony:

Ahmad said he was forced to insert a finger into his anus and lick it. He was also forced to lick and chew a shoe. . . . Sattar too said he was forced to insert a finger into his anus and lick it. He was then told to insert this finger in his nose during questioning, still kneeling with his feet off the ground and his other arm in the air. The Arab interpreter told him he looked like an elephant.

(ibid.)

In a kind of reversed Orientalism, the American soldiers understood themselves as sexually liberated and the prisoners as constrained by custom and religion. 'Sexuality and especially homophobia were their vulnerable aspects. They decided to use these weak points in interrogations. And concentrated on humiliating scenes with a sexual character' (Evren 2004). Nakedness is thus emphasized as an instrument of humiliation and the inmates were often treated like Sadean victims. We also have the forced contamination by licking dirty objects (shoes . . .) and contact with filthy fluids (excrement on a finger that is licked). And finally, we have the practice of making inmates behave like animals (like dogs, elephants . . .).

Trophy shots are a manifestation of sovereignty. People pose with a foot on the killed animal to show that in the battle of man against animal, man is superior. The same kind of superiority is depicted in the pictures from Abu Ghraib. What is striking is that these pictures do not show any sign of hatred. Hatred would at least display some kind of stained respect (like the respect offered an enemy). Instead, what we have here is victims reduced to just bodies, to objects (Sante 2004). As such, the pictures can be compared to those from the beginning of the twentieth century in which black people are shown being lynched while the perpetrators do not feel any guilt or shame in their giddy postures and grins (ibid.).

Notably, the American authorities were more concerned about the fact that the pictures were published than with the content of the pictures (Sontag 2004). The pictures were claimed to misrepresent what America stands for: democracy, freedom, equal worth, etc. Yet, it is possible to say that the pictures represent the underlying truth of the downside of these values. Which is perhaps why the striking familiarity of the pictures is more terrifying than what they depict. As such, the pictures are a testimony to the extent of voyeurism and brutalization present in today's society. 'Considered in this light, the photographs are us' (ibid.). The pictures signify a normalization of what has hitherto been an exception: the extreme exercise of a sado-masochistic ritual (e.g. a young woman leading a naked man around on a leash).

> It is hard to measure the increasing acceptance of brutality in American life, but its evidence is everywhere, starting with the games of killing that are the principal entertainments of young males to the violence that has become endemic in the group rites of youth on an exuberant kick. From the harsh torments inflicted on incoming students in many American suburban high schools . . . to rituals of physical brutality and sexual humiliation to be found in working-class bar culture, and institutionalised in our colleges and universities as hazing – America has become a country in which the fantasies and the practice of violence are, increasingly, seen as good entertainment, fun. What formerly was segregated as pornography, as the exercise of extreme sado-masochistic longings – such as Pasolini's last,

near-unwatchable film, *Salò* (1975), depicting orgies of torture in the fascist redoubt in northern Italy at the end of the Mussolini era – is now being normalised, by the apostles of the new, bellicose, imperial America, as high-spirited prankishness or venting.

(ibid.)

So, insofar as torture has a ritual aspect, and insofar as they were subjected to insult and torture, the Iraqi prisoners also tasted a dose of the downside of 'American culture', which constitutes the necessary supplement to the proclaimed values such as democracy, freedom, personal worth, etc. (Žižek 2004). 'Remember: Just because torturing prisoners is something we did, doesn't mean it's something we would do' (the comedian Rob Corddry quoted in Danner 2004b). It is telling that Rumsfeld's first response to the public disclosure of what happened in Abu Ghraib was to ban the possession of digital cameras (ibid.).

'All photographs are *memento mori*. To take a photograph is to participate in another person's (or thing's) mortality, vulnerability, mutability' (Sontag 1977: 15). In Abu Ghraib the camera functions as an inventory of torture and death. Indeed, in the remarkable private England scene, the camera coincides with the gun. In this moment, when the camera fixates/mortifies the inmate, shooting pictures and shooting people overlap.

Princess Diana

'Strictly speaking', writes Metz, 'the person who has been photographed . . . is dead . . . The snapshot, like death, is an instantaneous abduction of the object out of the world into another world, into another kind of time' (1990: 158). Hence the frequent comparison between the camera and the gun, on the one hand, and photographing and murdering on the other (Sontag 1977: 14–15). One example that comes to mind here is Princess Diana, perhaps the most photographed person on earth (Caputi 1999: 104). 'Press coverage of her death received more column inches per week [in the two months following her death] in the British papers than did World War II' (Chancey 1999: 163). No wonder that, as a multi-billion dollar industry, Diana has been an 'object of global fascination and obsessional documentation in the mass media' (ibid.) since she started dating Prince Charles in 1980 until her death in a car crash which was caused by the celebrity-chasing paparazzi in 1997.

Photojournalistic sleaziness and the intrusiveness of the media made a substantial contribution to the image of Diana. Wherever she went, she was literally chased by the 'stalkerazzi', which induced both fear and irritation in her. Thus, already in 1981, the Queen called a meeting with the media to be able to protect the privacy of the then-pregnant Diana. However, this only intensified the intrusion of the paparazzi. In 1993, Diana announced her desire to retire from public life and, once more, asked for more privacy, which only made stronger the media's urge for 'hunting'. Hence no wonder that two photojournalists specialized in pursuing Diana describe in their book *Dicing with Di* (Saunders and Glenn 1996) their activity of shooting Diana's pictures with violent and sexualized metaphors (e.g. 'doing Di', 'to bang', 'to rip', 'to whack'), and, characterizing Diana as 'unstable' and her attempts to protect her privacy 'bizarre', they claim: 'our job is to take pictures . . . We do not accept an accusation of harassment, intrusion, or invasion of privacy' (ibid.: xi, 2; quoted in Chancey 1999: 167–8; Hubert 1999: 132; Caputi 1999: 116).

The 'joy of shooting with impunity' corresponds to the act of abandoning *homo sacer*. In this respect, the images of the photojournalist as somebody 'doing his duty' (which brings to mind Eichmann's infamously cynical self-defence regarding his activity in the camps) and of the impunity attached to the paparazzi's practice (again, reminiscent of the camps) mean more than a mere 'objectification' of Diana's life. Being victimized by the paparazzi in a 'spectacle of suffering', Diana bore the burden of a collective enjoyment as an indestructible Sadean object. In a culture that eroticizes the celebrity, speed and crash, her death came to resemble, as Rushdie put it, a 'pornographic' death in a 'sublimated sexual assault' (quoted in Caputi 1999: 9). 'The camera as phallus' (Sontag 1977: 7). What is crucial in this respect is the nature of the objectification brought out by the camera:

> It is the Princess's indestructible beauty . . . that discloses the truly Sadean nature of the press's relationship with Diana. Like Sade's heroine Justine . . . the sufferings of the Princess never diminish her beauty in the fictions written and reproduced by the media, never leads to the point where she is dismembered and destroyed . . . In a Sadean manner, the grace and beauty of Diana function to support, that is maintain, sustain and even provoke, the spectacle of suffering.
>
> (Wilson 1997: 2–3)

It is not difficult to recognize *homo sacer* in this zone of indistinction between subject and object. Indeed, with the disappearance of rites in contemporary society, photography may correspond to the interference of 'a symbolic Death, outside of religion, outside of ritual, a kind of abrupt dive into literal Death. *Life/Death*: the paradigm is reduced to a simple click' (Barthes 1981: 92). A 'simple click', which brings with it a non-symbolic, sacred death: the 'flat death' (ibid.) of *homo sacer*. As a media star longing for privacy, as a bad girl/whore and a fairytale princess, as an enemy of the dynasty who remained an aristocrat, etc., Diana incarnated some contradictions which blurred the borders between her private and public life and turned her body into a 'war zone' (Braidotti 1997: 10). In this regard she 'embodied a series of female archetypes equally potent but at odds with one another. For instance, she was both Hollywood star and charitable and compassionate missionary. Mother of future kings and lonely and abandoned woman' (ibid.: 8). From the perspective of *homo sacer*, it can be claimed that the 'most photographed woman's' extreme inclusion (in everybody's habitus) turned into its opposite, total exclusion. Hence her complaints of loneliness in the aftermath of the media scandals resulting from her love affairs (ibid.: 7). What is the explanation for Diana's 'contradictory' oscillation between exclusion and inclusion, between victimization and power, then? Which brings us back to the relationship between *homo sacer* and the sovereign. Remarkably in this respect, the 'contradictions' mentioned above disappeared immediately after Diana's death:

> At the same time as her death crystallized the iconic image of Diana, another image was withdrawn from media circulation: the image of the Princess dying in the crumpled Mercedes taken by the 'paparazzi.' A taboo was placed on those images that recorded her dying moments, unconscious or in pain. They were subject to universal moral censure, deemed to constitute the very limit of intrusive prurience, the accursed part of the photo-archive, the dazzling, unbearable core of the story that must be covered over.
>
> (Wilson 1997: 1)

Why this moralism by the very media that destroyed Diana by turning her into an image? Why did the photographs censor Diana's 'contradictory' character, eliminating the sex scandals, depressed and thin-looking series of photos, bad cellulite days, street brawls, or, in short, 'the ugly, inappropriate, or transgressive in favour of emphasizing the traditionally feminine aspects' (Chancey 1999: 6)? Such unanimous reaction ought to provoke more reflection than has been the case. Let us, to reflect on this question, go back to Kantorowicz's thesis on the king's two bodies (1957). Here, mentioning the apotheosis of Roman emperors in which a wax effigy of the sovereign was treated as his living person, Kantorowicz suggests that the effigy is set in relation to the perpetual nature of sovereignty ('the king never dies'). Agamben corrects this thesis by relating the role of the effigy to the absolute nature of sovereignty, a relationship through which 'the political body of the king seemed to approximate – and even to become indistinguishable from – the body of *homo sacer*' (1998: 94).

In the age of Antonius, for instance, the consecrated emperor was burned on the funeral pyre twice, *in corpore* and *in effigie*. Hence, contrary to usual practice, public mourning and the state funeral only began after the emperor's corpse was buried and his remains deposited in the mausoleum. This state funeral, the 'image funeral', concerned the wax effigy made after the image of the sovereign and treated as the emperor himself (e.g. a slave kept flies away from the face of the doll):

> the wax effigy, which is 'in all things similar' to the dead man, and which lies on the official bed wearing the dead man's clothes, is the

emperor himself, whose life has been transferred to the wax doll by means of . . . magical rites.

(ibid. on the basis of Bickermann 1929)

What is significant here is the function of the effigy or the image as being beside the corpse, 'doubling' rather than substituting the dead (Agamben 1998: 95). The image represents the part of the person that is consecrated in death and that, insofar as it occupies the threshold between the two worlds, must be separated from the normal context of living. The separation usually happens at the time of death, through the funeral rites that re-establish the proper relation between the living and the dead (ibid.: 98).

Thus, only until the rite of image (following her death) Diana remained a paradoxical being (neither alive nor dead, neither human nor image . . .). The paparazzi pictures of Diana represent, in a sense, her consecrated life that should be separated from her after her death. She had, as the sovereign (the fetish object, the princess of the 'people'), a supplement of sacred life, which was freed by death and then neutralized by means of her image as the 'fairy princess' cleansed from the accusation of 'bad girl/whore'. Diana had two bodies, one natural and one sacred: the latter survives the first, and dies first after the image rite.

> It is as if, by means of a striking symmetry, supreme power . . . required that the very person of the sovereign authority assume within itself the life held in its power. And if . . . for the sovereign death reveals the excess that seems to be as such inherent in supreme power, as if supreme power were, in the last analysis, nothing other than the capacity to constitute oneself and others as life that may be killed but not sacrified.
>
> (ibid.: 101)

Homo sacer and the Friedlos, the werewolf and the witch, the *Muselmann*, the prisoners at Guantanamo and Abu Ghraib and finally Diana. These limit figures are, one could say, homological; they are different in their similarity and similar in their differences. The point is that 'every society – even the most modern – decides who its "sacred men" will be' (ibid.: 139). Their similarity is based on their reduction to bare life, to *hominis sacri*. To conclude, we have so far sketched four constellations of sovereignty, bare life and exception. First, there is the archaic form of sovereignty: the sovereign, who suspends his own laws and abandons *homo sacer*. Second, we have the relation between the one and the many sovereigns, between the lynching mob and the scape-goat, or, between the paparazzi and their shooting targets. Third, there must be distinguished between the singular and spectacular act of abandoning a subject, and the biopolitical stripping of prisoners of their humanity, culminating in a bureaucratized mass murder. Fourth, there are those who are

37

abandoned through extreme deprivation and neglect, or those who suffer from too much exposure and excessive richness. And finally, we argued that the camp, at least its logic based on the twinning of sovereignty and bare life, has existed since the ancients. Now it is time to show that at a certain stage in history, the camp evolved into a semi-permanent spatial constellation.

2

ENTRENCHED SPACES

In the beginning was the fence.
                    (Jost Trier, quoted in Schmitt 2003: 74)

Landnahme, the taking possession of land, is, Schmitt claimed, what gives society its order and orientation (ibid.: 80). The origin of culture and law is not the word, which links strangers together, but the fence, which separates them. However, despite its importance, Schmitt was mistaken in seeing territorialization as *the* beginning. Which is why he ignored the nomadic tribes by reducing them to pre-social and pre-historic phenomena, thereby turning land appropriation into an unproblematic act. Therefore, on Schmitt's account, the Greek, Italian, Germanic, Slavonic and Magyar clans, tribes and retinues affected land-appropriations only after settling down and thus gave Europe its birth as a political and legal entity (ibid.: 81). Before this sedentary turn took place, Europe did not exist. In Locke's formulation, also appropriated by Schmitt, 'in the beginning, all the world was America' (quoted in Agamben 1998: 36). 'America', for Schmitt, signifies not a true beginning but merely an undifferentiated wilderness populated by rootless, barbaric inhabitants, a virgin land waiting to be formed and fertilized. History and civilization began with the arrival of the conquistadors. For this 'new world' the fence was the true beginning. It is no accident that fence and defence share common origins, relating to the Latin *defendere* – *de* (off) and *fendere* (strike) – to strike off.

Hence the significant link between the Nazi concept of *Lebensraum* and Schmitt's insistence on *Landnahme*. Both relate social forms to the possession and ordering of space. But unlike the Nazi concept, which was one of *Blut und Boden*, Schmitt's account of land appropriation was shaped by an interest in space only. In other words, Schmitt's racism was not a biological but a spatial racism. Therefore, when he attacked Jewish scholars, for example, the legal positivists, he accentuated their lack of roots and their neglect of the significance of land. In this, he subscribed to the age-old hatred against the mobile – the primitives in the New World, the Jews and the Gypsies during the

Reich, and the refugees and stateless people of today – which invites the zealous attempt to encamp and control them through spatial means. Indeed, one is tempted to say that the fence is not just a possible beginning but also a dramatic end. Spatial ordering frames some social forms, destroys some others.

For Schmitt, the '*nomos* of the earth' was spatial ordering, that is, the linking together of localization (*Ortung*) and order (*Ordnung*): order is conceptualized on the basis of an inside–outside divide, that is, in spatial terms, as homes, towns and nations; on the outside, disorder reigns. But there is an ambiguity in this: in the 'state of exception', the link between localization and order breaks down. What is significant regarding the camp is the permanency of the state of exception. That is, the concentration camp first emerged when the unlocalizable (the state of exception) was granted a permanent and visible localization. This coincidence of order without territory (the state of exception) and territory without order (the camp as a permanent space of exception) signals, in turn, the advent of 'the political space of modernity itself' (Schmitt 2003: 20, 174–5). In other words, the location of unlaw within the law is not merely an historical anomaly but is characteristic of modernity. The camp transforms the whole society into an unbounded and dislocated biopolitical space. To discuss this, we start with focusing on a direct genealogical link between the discovery of the 'new world' and the origin of the camp.

The colonies

Schmitt claims that land was 'the mother of law'. He specifies in this respect three ways in which land serves to measure and nominate law and justice. The fecundity of the fertile soil is a measure of human toil and trouble: the earth rewards justly through growth and harvest. Second, the soil engraves 'firm lines' through which human divisions become visible. And finally, the earth is 'delineated by fences, enclosures, boundaries, walls, houses, and other constructs' in which 'the orders and orientations of human social life become apparent' (Schmitt 2003: 42). The Greek word for land appropriation, that is, for the primordial division, is *nomos* (ibid.: 67). Significantly, *nomos* does not refer to law but to what lies behind the law and gives it its order and orientation. As such, *nomos* is the precondition of the legal order, a constitutive event, which renders the legality of the law meaningful and illustrates the meaninglessness of the perception of law as a self-enclosed, self-referential system (ibid.: 42, 48, 69).

By the '*nomos* of the earth' Schmitt means those common rules for the partition of the world. Until World War I, the *jus publicum Europaeum* governed the ways in which land could be taken into possession. Through customs and contracts, a system, characterized by equality of members, that is, of states, was established. However, this system required a free and 'juridically empty space' unbounded by common law: an extra-European combat zone which limited war among European powers by exporting it overseas (ibid.: 66). This space was the new world, America, distinguished spatially from the old world through concepts such as 'amity lines' beyond which the law of the strong applied. That is, beyond the amity lines, the quest for land appropriation knew no bounds (ibid.: 94).

Or, to put it differently: Hobbes's 'state of nature' is not a non-place or utopia. It is to be sure a no man's land but this, however, does not imply that it exists nowhere. Hobbes locates it in the 'new world', which was in legal terms an open and empty space (ibid.: 95–6). In this no man's land, man was no longer *homo homini homo*, that is, 'a man to man', but *homo homini lupus*: a man who is a wolf to other men (ibid.: 95). The 'new world' was a 'wolfland', a land 'beyond the line', a friction-free and empty space. The amity lines, in other words, created a distinction between the realm of law and the realm of nature (ibid.: 97–8). All of which, of course, served to legitimize the territorialization of the conquered lands:

> Colonial occupation itself was a matter of seizing, delimiting, and asserting control over a physical geographical area – of writing on the ground a new set of social and spatial relations. The writing of new spatial relations (territorialization) was, ultimately, tantamount to the production of boundaries and hierarchies, zones and enclaves; the subversion of existing property arrangements; the classification of people according to different categories; resource extraction; and finally, the manufacturing of a large reservoir of cultural imaginaries.
> (Nbembe 2003: 25–6)

The introduction of barbed wire in the USA, in 1874, is a telling example of such 'writing'. It was a cheap multifunctional product easy to handle. Thus the farmers started to use it to fence in their land. However, what made barbed wire really significant was the colonization of the 'great plain'. Hence the 1862 Homestead Act gave all landless farmers 160 acres of public, that is, Indian, land on the condition that it was cultivated (Razac 2002: 7–8). Barbed wire served here a dual purpose: it both protected the land from wolves and from the 'wolfish Indians' (ibid.: 90). Soon afterwards the period of the legendary cowboys driving the cattle around and nomadic Indian tribes was over. The appropriation of land and the mass-killings of bisons pushed Indians towards the west. As the USA grew, the tribes were relocated in settlements in less fertile land according to the 1887 Dawes Act, which offered each Indian family 200 acres of reservation land (ibid.: 17). The barbed wire, which was initially used to fence in the white farmers' cattle, was now used to entrench the reservations. This Act not only reduced Indian land but also destroyed Indian life form by pulverizing their tribal 'mass' in the hope of producing sedentary citizens. This assault on their nomadism was the reason why many Indians sold their newly 'acquired' land and, refusing to disappear as nomads, drove off to remote and undesirable parts of the country (ibid.: 20–1).

The Indian genocide was only one among many. In South Africa, for instance, the Hottentot tribe was massacred and the size of the Congo population was dramatically reduced (Arendt 1973: 185). The Europeans did not consider these massacres as mass murder. Because the tribes lived in accordance with nature and treated it as their undisputed master, that is, because they lacked a purely human world distinguished from a natural one, they appeared to their colonizers as ghostlike phantoms (ibid.: 192). However, the black slaves quickly became the only working people. It was, as Arendt stresses, the contempt for labour that gave the concept of race its distinct meaning (ibid.: 193). The Boers lived on their slaves in exactly the same way as the natives had lived on nature (ibid.: 194). And, as a consequence, the Boers' world was not a common world; in it, there was no space for the colonized 'other'. Not surprisingly, the British colonies were characterized by a similar hubris. Just like the Boers, the British colonizers treated the colonial population as mere things. Thus, one word that continuously pops up in Arendt's description of the Britons and Boers is 'aloofness':

> Aloofness became the new attitude of all members of the British services; it was a more dangerous form of governing than despotism and arbitrariness because it did not even tolerate that last link between the despot and his subjects, which is formed by bribery and gifts. The very integrity of the British administration made despotic government more inhuman and inaccessible to its subjects than Asiatic rulers or reckless conquers had ever been. Integrity and aloofness were symbols for an absolute division of interests to the point where they are not even permitted to conflict. In comparison, exploitation, oppression, or corruption look like safeguards of human dignity, because exploiter and exploited, oppressor and oppressed, corruptor and corrupted still live in the same world, still share the same goals, fight each other for the possession of the same things; and it is this *tertium comparationis* which aloofness destroyed.
>
> (ibid.: 212)

And it was the same aloofness that paved the way for the introduction of the camps on European soil. With the camps, the distinction between Europe and the 'new world' was reintroduced within Europe (Rasch 2003: 130). During World War II, therefore, it became possible to employ in Europe methods previously reserved for the 'savages'. Indeed, the prohibition of mixed marriages, forced sterilization, and the extermination of vanquished peoples were all techniques that had hitherto been tested in the colonial world (Arendt 1973: 185–221):

> It should never be forgotten that while colonization, with its techniques and its political and juridical weapons, obviously transported

European models to other continents, it also had a considerable boomerang effect on the mechanisms of power in the West, and on the apparatuses, institutions, and techniques of power. A whole series of colonial models was brought back to the West, and the result was that the West could practise something resembling colonization, or an internal colonialism, on itself.

(Foucault 2003a: 103)

Above all, it was the logic of biopolitical engineering that was acquired in the distant camps. Then the camp was re-introduced in Europe as a means of repression, to eliminate the danger posed by its own 'barbarians': the abnormal, the criminal, and so on. However, Foucault's point is significantly more inclusive: the biopolitical skills inherited from the colonies address not only those 'othered' on the margins of the society but the whole society, every single subject, or, to be more precise, the whole population. A marginal phenomenon, a practice aimed at just certain segments, is generalized to include the whole society. The crucial tool here is the concept of race.

Biopolitics of race

Biopolitics addresses not the singular body of *homo sacer* but a 'multiple body', a body with countless heads (see Foucault 2003a: 245). This multiplicity is constituted in the form of aggregates such as the labour force, the old, the young, the sick, etc., and, as is the case with other objects of political steering, a whole range of technologies and scientific knowledge is produced to contain and transform this multiplicity. In this endeavour, power captures every domain of life and even a biological problem, age, mortality, general state of health, workability, and so on, become power's problems (ibid.: 245; 2002: 216–17):

So after a first seizure of power over the body in an individualizing mode, we have a second seizure of power that is not individual-izing but, if you like, massifying, that is, directed not at man-as body but man-as species.

(ibid.: 242–3)

Significantly in this respect, with the introduction of biopolitical strategies, a new understanding of death emerges. The crucial problem here is no longer that of momentary epidemics but 'endemics', that is, the threats to the population's general health. Instead of short periods of mass death, the concern is now for permanent factors, such as working hours, housing, public hygiene and the hydrographic environment, or, in short, all factors that influence the population's health. Death, in this, becomes something permanent, which

43

slips into life and diminishes it (ibid.: 244). The singular death is confronted individually and it is unpredictable, but, taken together, individual deaths form a pattern that can be assessed though statistical forecasts and estimates (ibid.: 246). The character of political intervention acting on these figures differs from that of the sovereign right to take life or let live. The new power, in contrast, is one of 'making live and letting die' (ibid.: 247). And finally one further difference relates to the significance of the norm *vis-à-vis* the law:

> Law cannot help but be armed, and its arm, par excellence, is death; to those who transgress it, it replies, at least as a last resort, with that absolute menace. The law always refers to the sword. But a power whose task is to take charge of life needs continuous regulatory and corrective mechanisms. It is no longer a matter of bringing death into play in the field of sovereignty, but of disturbing the living in the domain of value and utility.
>
> (Foucault 1978: 144)

Thus, at first sight, Foucault's and Agamben's takes on biopolitics appear to be essentially different. For Foucault, biopolitics is a novel invention, while, for Agamben, it has been with us since ancient times, which is why the production of a biopolitical body is the most originary and most authentic activity of sovereign power (Agamben 1998: 6). Further, while Agamben deliberately conflates sovereignty and biopolitics, in Foucault's work, the terms mark distinct periods. For Foucault, sovereignty is just one *dispositif* of power among others, as a form that has become increasingly more inflexible and obsolete. Although the old *dispositifs* are still partly in use and may intertwine with novel forms of power, one is still justified in describing the historiology of power as one in which sovereignty lead to discipline and discipline to biopolitics. With the advent of biopolitics, sovereignty is replaced by a concern for life and more specifically for the citizens' well-being. Biopolitics is the politization of life. Thus, the 'life' relevant to 'biopolitics' is not, by any means, the singular life of *homo sacer* but the life of aggregates such as populations, not of man as an individual being but of man as a species. And finally, while Agamben focuses on the suspension of law and thus on the production of exception, Foucault's focus is on the production of normality.

However, if we take Foucault's less-known seminars into account, some significant parallels proliferate. In his seminar on racism, for instance, Foucault (2003a) describes the death of one race as the precondition of the life of another. In racism, sovereignty and biopolitics coincide, life and death overlap. Or, to put it somewhat differently, racism is at one and the same time both ancient and modern. Here, Foucault asks:

> If it is true that the power of sovereignty is increasingly on the retreat and that disciplinary or regulatory power is on the advance,

> how will the power to kill and the function of murder operate in this technology of power, which takes life as both its object and its objective?
>
> (ibid.: 254)

How can killing contribute to life? It can when one form of life is perceived as a threat to another, that is, in racism (ibid.: 256). Racism, or the differentiation and categorization of people, has of course been known for a long time, but, when inscribed in the mechanisms of state power, its form changes; racism goes biopolitical. With the advent of biopolitics, racism necessarily turns into state racism (ibid.: 254; 1980: 55). It is no longer a matter of defending oneself against society, but to defend society, the social body, against biological threats (2003a: 62). 'Society Must be Defended!' By whom? The state now starts to act as if it were in a state of war, not against other states but against all that which threats the population's biological well-being. The state exists to protect the race: it is a shepherd looking after its flock. And here we encounter the concept of *nomos* once more but this time with a new accent: 'The word nomos (the law) is connected with the word nomeus (shepherd): the shepherd shares out, the law apportions. Then Zeus is called Nomios and Nemeios because he gives his sheep food' (Foucault 2002: 304). It is, however, not just a matter of feeding the sheep. To protect them, one also needs to kill the wolves, an aspect which was underdeveloped in Foucault's writings on pastoral power from which the metaphor of the shepherd originates. 'If you want to live, the other must die' (2003a: 255). Other less dramatic methods might be segregation of the sick, monitoring of contagions, and exclusion of delinquents. Thus killing is no longer related to war because the enemy is no longer a political adversary but a biopolitical threat. Killing ceases to be murder and becomes merely the elimination of a danger. Concomitantly, instead of heroic battles, we now get struggles for existence, the instruments of which are 'exposing someone to death, increasing the risk of death for some people, or, quite simply, political death, expulsion, rejection, and so on' (ibid.: 256). Instead of singular deaths, we now meet a statistical death, and instead of the former ritualized murder, the spectacular death in the guillotine, by hanging, etc., death becomes something to be hidden away. Thus, while natural death is privatized and tabooed, political death is secreted in death camps (ibid.: 247):

> In the right of sovereignty, death was the moment of the most obvious and most spectacular manifestation of the absolute power of the sovereign; death now becomes, in contrast, the moment when the individual escapes all power, falls back on himself and retreats, so to speak, into his own privacy. Power no longer recognizes death. Power literally ignores death.
>
> (ibid.: 248)

LIBRARY, UNIVERSITY OF CHESTER

Decisively in this context, racism is a way of 'introducing a break into the domain of life', a break which leads to the fragmentation of the biopolitical field, a break between those who are to die and those who are to live (ibid.: 254–5). A binary rift within the society, between a super-race and a sub-race, or, between 'us' and 'them', just and unjust, rich and poor, masters and those who must obey (ibid.: 61, 74). It is telling in this context that after the imprisonment of political opponents by the Nazis, the next wave consisted of people who were 'work-shy' or 'asocial'. Then came the beggars, vagrants, people with venereal diseases, prostitutes, homosexuals, alcoholics, Gypsies, and so on, that is, 'anyone and everyone who had fallen out of favor with some authority or with an informer in the neighbourhood' (Sofsky 1997: 33). In short, the biopolitical rift which racism introduces is that of between the 'normal' and the 'abnormal'. It is an 'internal racism' against the abnormal (see Foucault 2003b: 316–17).

Indeed, it is no coincidence that German psychiatry and the Nazi ideology worked well together (ibid.: 317). Indeed, in the Third Reich the politician directly took over the psychiatrist's role, that is, screening the society and diagnosing its abnormal elements. The first 'Operation Against Asocial Elements' (*Asocialen-Aktion*) took place in April 1938. Some 1,500 were captured and sent to labour camps. In February 1940, a secret meeting took place in Berlin, a meeting in which three doctors, Hevelemann, Bahnen and Brack, discussed the measures to authorize the 'elimination of life unworthy of being lived'. The aim was no longer just to keep the 'asocial' elements in custody and force them to work; all dangerous elements were now to be eliminated. This was the birth of the euthanasia programme planned for the *Gnadentod*, 'the mercy killing' of, for instance, the mentally ill (Agamben 1998: 140). And then again, the more the programme developed, the longer grew the row of *Untermensch* in need of elimination. Another project, though never realized, was the idea of a national X-ray examination. Those with lung diseases should then be sterilized or eliminated on the orders of the Führer (Arendt 1973: 416). Which is also to say that Hitler planned to eliminate large sections of the German people (Arendt 1994: 235). In the final days of the war, he even promised 'an easy death for the German people by gassing them in case of defeat' (1973: 348).

The concentration camp

This biopolitical stance manifested itself most directly in the Nazi politics towards the East. Without access to soil, to a *Lebensraum*, the Aryan race would vanish. The Germans were perceived to be a nation of settlers, *Siedlers*. They were not fighting other nations merely for economic gain. What mattered was to settle down, to resettle in the old home, *Heimat* (Plet 1994: 84–5). Himmler was the architect of the programme to resettle ethnic Germans in occupied territories, which were seen to be originally German due to the fact that they contained some historic buildings, such as German castles. Such heritage was, in Himmler's words, memorials of 'the right to life and the will to persist of the whole German nation in the East' (quoted in ibid.: 85). The resettlement programme demanded the elimination of non-Germanic races to reintroduce Germanic culture and life forms. Everything should be rebuilt and reformed (ibid.: 86–7). The symbiosis with Germanic soil should be re-established to allow Aryan culture once again to blossom.

The concentration and death camps in the East, just like the labour camps, constituted an important part of this programme in serving a dual purpose: encamping hostile sub-races and exploiting them for work. Camps such as Sachsenhausen (in Oranienburg, north of Berlin), Buchenwald (outside Weimar) and Mauthausen (near Linz) were established near major towns and with access to natural resources such as forests, sand, granite, clay and other materials needed to produce bricks and the like. Most camps were placed along major transportation lines, usually railways, making the transportation of bricks to the building projects in Berlin as easy and cheap as possible.

Auschwitz, for instance, to take the best-known camp, was built near a sand factory. However, this was not the sole reason for the choice of location. Nearby there was a Polish town housing a large group of ethnic Germans. The town was planned to become a centre of massive industrial activity and was estimated to grow to accommodate a population of 47,000 (ibid.: 81). What is crucial in the plan is that the infrastructure was to be financed by the revenue from the camp Auschwitz. In other words, the *Übermensch* and the *Untermensch* had to be close neighbours. Thus, in the first map of the camp/town, planning utopia borders on terror:

> Not only does it show the concentration camp itself (usually designated as Auschwitz 1), located to the left – with its barracks, roll-call place, hospital, prison, work shops, and auxiliary structures such as the Kommandantur, the offices of the Gestapo, the barracks for the SS men, and so on – but it also shows, to the right, a pleasant village for married SS men and their families, including a hotel, shops, sport facilities and, on the edge of the barbed-wire fence close to the prisoners' hospital, a primary school. The plan symbolizes but does not exhaust the juxtaposition of nightmare and dream.
>
> (ibid.: 82)

The larger of the two sections of Auschwitz-Birkenau was planned to contain 97,000 inmates while the other, smaller, section was to be used to quarantine 17,000 inmates. However, the final plan was projected to contain 125,000 inmates, due to budget cuts and the growth in the number of prisoners. Overcrowding escalated the mortality rate dramatically, necessitating a constant influx of new prisoners to keep the facilities running. Himmler responded to the lack of labour force by deeming still more groups dangerous. First, he ran short of political prisoners. Then came the 'asocial elements', and then the POWs from Russia and finally a vast numbers of Jews. A lethal circle was established: to make room for new, fit labour power, the SS started to kill or starve the non-able-bodied prisoners to death (Sofsky 1997: 38).

The initial rationale for the camps was economic, which, however, proved to be at odds with the ideology of *Über*- and *Untermensch*. A precondition for the continuous extraction of labour power from the prisoners was reasonable living conditions, proper food and hygienic facilities. The Nazi elite was not prepared to meet such expenses and, more importantly, the shortage of space and food was a means to produce the *Untermensch*. The decisive shift in priority occurred following the decision on the 'final solution'. Following this decision, in December 1941, mobile extermination vehicles were put into use at Chelmno, and later came the 'showers'. That is, the development of the camps was an unpredictable and complex affair in which the original plan (labour camps) and implementation (death camps) came to differ considerably.

Auschwitz-Birkenau was one among many camps. Fifty-nine early concentration camps existed and during the war twenty-three new ones were established. Other camp-like structures included those for foreign forced labourers (*Arbeitserziehungslager*), camps for criminal prisoners and POWs, 'transit camps' (*Durchgangslager*), 'collection camps' (*Sammellager*) and of course the Jewish ghettoes (ibid.: 12–13). And then there is the difference between the death camps such as Chelmno, Belzec, Sobibór and Treblinka and the concentration and labour camps. Auschwitz and Majdanek were exceptions belonging to both categories. These camps differed in several ways: in size, regarding the kind of prisoners they contained, the standard of living that could be obtained, and the guards' behaviour towards the prisoners. Buchenwald, mentioned before, was the classic model for the camps: a space entrenched by electrified barbed wire and overviewed by the watchtowers. Its inside consisted of rows of barracks in front of which there was a place for roll calls and the entrance gate. Everything was built according to a design philosophy aiming at enhancing visibility and filtering undesired spontaneous behaviour. There were no curves, arches, or blind spots (ibid.: 52).

Within the camps, spatial differentiation, e.g. between the women's and the men's areas or between different groups of prisoners, was created through the use of barbed wire (Arendt 1973: 288). The camp administration and housing for the SS were located just outside the camp. Differences were further accentuated though stigmatic patches on inmates' clothes, a system which also regulated the distribution of misery. The *kapos*, for instance, were given temporary privileges. Together with them, the political prisoners, especially the Germans, formed the upper strata of the camp population. The Jews, the Poles and the Russians made up the bottom.

One common and perhaps the most significant characteristic shared by all camps was total isolation: there was no way to escape from the camps. In other words, the most important distinction related to the camps was that between the inside and outside: the fence. 'Anyone entering the camp had to forget what he knew before. . . . Here, another sort of money was in circulation' (Razac 2002: 61).

Forgetting one's former self for the sake of survival in this autarkic space involved learning how to cheat on others, how to avoid the guards, show humility and be as invisible as possible, etc. In short, one should adjust oneself to a 'Hobbesian universe of theft and bribery, mistrust and animosity, the struggle of all against all' (Sofsky 1997: 24).

A further defining aspect of camp life was the lack of space, which served to deprive the prisoners of their dignity, privacy and the basic conditions necessary for the maintenance of personal hygiene. Usually four inmates shared a bed-section, giving them no more space than that of a large coffin. It was so tight that it was extremely difficult during the night to remove the corpses of those who died during the night. Thus, often, the inmates were forced to sleep with the dead (Plet 1994: 100). When one wanted to turn in bed, all had to turn at the same time (Sofsky 1997: 71). Such conditions stirred up rivalry. Hence there was a constant struggle for everything, for space in the bed, access to the latrines, time at the washbasin, and so on. In Birkenau there was one washbasin per 7,800 inmates and one latrine per 7,000 inmates. Prisoners often suffered from diarrhoea or dysentery but were only allowed to use the latrines for certain periods and for maximum of ten minutes. This 'excremental assault' aimed to destroy the inmates' sense of dignity (Plet 1994: 106). All were covered with mud and faeces, stank and were full of lice. The pressure on the facilities was so great that the prisoners could not avoid soiling each other. In short, characteristic for the camps is a biopolitical engineering which systematically reduced the inmates to the *Untermensch*. The concentration camp is the place in which people are metamorphosed into scraps, vermin, or parasites:

> You see, they are animals, and the worst species, as well. You've been told this. They are ugly, they stink, they are weak, they are cowards and they fight each other to eat. No Aryan would do such a thing.
> (Hitler, quoted in Razac 2002: 93–4)

Interestingly in this context, there existed two kinds of labour in the camp: slave labour and terror labour. In extracting slave labour from the inmates, a minimum of respect was shown. Which is what explains, for instance, why Ivan Denisovich Shukhov, the protagonist of Solzhenitsyn's *One Day in the Life of Ivan Denisovich*, keeps working in a Soviet gulag to be able to keep his dignity, even when he does not have to. In this novel, we meet no prisoner living on others' misfortune or death. The prisoners share food, help each other against the guards, and so on. It is precisely this sense of dignity the German camps aimed to destroy. In this, labour became merely a way of progressing towards death. Thus, there is a crucial difference between the forced labour in the Russian camps and the death labour in the German ones:

Forced labour as a punishment is limited as to time and intensity. The convict retains his rights over his body; he is not absolutely tortured and he is not absolutely dominated. Banishment banishes only from one part of the world to another part of the world, also inhabited by human beings; it does not exclude from the human world altogether. Throughout history slavery has been an institution within a social order; slaves were not, like concentration-camp inmates, withdrawn from the sight and hence the protection of their fellow-men; as instruments of labour they had a definite price and as property a definite value. The concentration-camp inmate has no price, because he can always be replaced; nobody knows to whom he belongs, because he is never seen.

(Arendt 1973: 444)

Especially after the decision on the 'final solution', the concentration camps functioned in a purely anti-utilitarian way, only serving to illustrate two things: the absolute power and the superiority of the master race, and the worthlessness of the imprisoned scum (Arendt 1994: 233). The gas chambers radicalized this even further. They were costly and drained the resources, military and otherwise, which could have been used in the war; they demoralized the military forces and interfered disastrously with some parts of the populations in the East (ibid.: 236).

If power is to be total, it must defy regularity and rationality. It has to become arbitrary and thus unpredictable. It must, in other words, turn to terror. And inversely, terror would no longer be terror if it were predictable. In the camp nothing was predictable and the prisoners lived in 'an eternal yet irregularly pulsating present, an endless duration that was constantly interrupted by sudden attacks and incursions. In this world of terror, a single day was longer than a week' (Sofsky 1997: 24). Absolute power aims at nothing, except proving this 'power of power', a decisive will and an unconstrained ability.

The Trojan ass

When the concentration camp was introduced on European soil, the 'Jew' became the stereotypical figure of the camp inmate for the reason of not being settled and thus defying the identification of birth and earth (nation). The 'Jew' is the symbol of being 'off space' in the sense of being not assimilated and of not fitting in with respect to the link between citizenship and nationality/ birth (Sofsky 1997: 179). What first appeared in the form of the 'new world' later re-appeared in the concentration camps and, in our present predicament, re-presents itself in newer forms of unbelonging. Thus, one of the contemporary incarnations of *homo sacer* is the illegal migrant, who is often reduced to a naked body outside the reach of the social and cultural systems of the receiving country. To give an example, this situation is perhaps most dramatic for international female sex workers and temporary workers. The case of 'Natashas', for instance, illustrates both. It is well known that the demise of Soviet Union resulted in considerable out-migration and many illegal 'sex workers' started to travel to diverse destinations ranging from Turkey to South Europe to Norway. In Turkey, for example, which has become a major destination for the sex industry, sex migration is based on a 'circular' or 'oscillating' mobility of sex workers who commute between Turkey and the former Soviet Union and Eastern Europe:

> Arriving in Turkey with an initial sum of approximately US$ 1000–2000, these individuals buy goods (such as clothes, small household commodities) from local merchants and then return to their countries of origin to sell these products at a profit. Continuing the cycle, they then return to Turkey with small commodities, selling these and buying more goods to take back to their own countries. The term 'suitcase industry' stems from the fact that these goods are often transported in suitcases or plastic bags. This type of trade activity has been documented for individuals from many countries of the Former Soviet Union and Eastern Europe, including Poland, Romania, Russia, Ukraine and the CIS . . . In contrast to their male counterparts, large proportions of women from these countries also supplement their incomes in Turkey with sex work.
>
> (Gülçür and Ilkkaracan 2002: 413)

What is significant here is that this migration takes place in a juridical no man's land because sex work is not considered illegal in Turkey. Politically and culturally, 'Natashas' are completely on the 'margin' of society because of a *laissez-faire* type of regulation. Excluded from all existing social systems, the sex workers constitute 'a mass of . . . bodies which have to survive somehow on their own' (Luhmann 1994: 4). Such migration can, however, take place in more 'organized' ways. For instance, in the case of temporary migration between Russia and Norway, migration is legally regulated and this presents an even more interesting case in relation to the camp (in the sense that the suspension of the law is legalized through the law).

As Aure (2004) documents in an interesting study, the dismantling of the Iron Curtain created new interactions across the Russian and Norwegian border. Being also Schengen and thus the European Union border, this location marks the 'end of Europe'. Here there is a considerable amount of highly regulated migration from one of the most poverty-stricken regions of Russia to rich fish plants in Norway, e.g. from Teriberka to Båtsfjord, which constitute Aure's case study. Most migrants are female. Geographical closeness makes oscillation between the two contexts easy. The Russian migrants, expectedly, do unskilled jobs. Hence both conservative and social democratic politicians have been actively engaged in lobbying for liberalization of working permits for Russian temporary workers. Consequently, Teriberkan workers can come to northern Norway to work for a well-defined period of time, which is followed by a period of 'quarantine' back home. Even though the Russian workers have the ordinary rights related to employment in Norway, this situation of 'regulated' in-between-ness makes it impossible for them to accumulate rights based on duration. In their case, temporariness becomes a permanent situation:

> They arrive when there is a need, and disappear when there are lay-offs . . . The unemployment benefits [the temporary] migrants are entitled to require just a few weeks' work, but the *level* of the benefits is based on average income over the last three years. The short permits make it impossible for the migrants to reach a decent level unemployment benefit. When there are lay-offs, most Russian workers will therefore leave for Russia because without work there is no reason to stay in Norway. The low level of benefits makes it difficult to manage the high costs in Norway, while the living expenses in Russia are much lower.
>
> (ibid.: 12)

Their flexible lives and 'dislocated localization' mean that although they have rights at a formal level, these rights do not materialize and accumulate, e.g. in the form of seniority or increments. They are even entitled to sick leaves, but in practice they cannot afford becoming sick because they will be the first to lose their jobs in case of sickness. What is significant in our context is that this migration characterized by temporary localization or dislocated temporality is made possible and sustained by Norwegian law, which would have been impossible without the logic of the camp, the exception, which generates a zone in-between Norway and Russia. The Russian migrants are, in a sense, 'legal serfs', or, the 'Trojan ass' of the Fortress Europe. As John Berger wrote of migrants in similar situations:

> They are not born: they are not brought up: they do not age: they do not get tired: they do not die. They have a single function – to work. All other functions of their lives are the responsibility of the country they come from.
>
> (Berger and Mohr 1975: 64)

'Natashas' are, again, a significant part of this picture, states Aure. In contrast to Turkey, their presence in Norway is regulated and legal. But in both cases the worker, legal or illegal, is reduced to a naked body, to Berger's migrant who does not age, get tired, or die. The Sadean victim as an indestructible body. Small wonder that everywhere, in North Europe as well as in South,

'Natasha' is constructed as promiscuous, while the male illegal worker is 'criminal'. The reduction to a naked body never comes without a loss of dignity.

Women on waves

It was perhaps Foucault who most tenaciously approached the city or society from the point of view of residual zones, or off-spaces mentioned above. Indeed, his 'heterotopias', exemplified by fairs, boarding schools, spaces of deviance, military spaces, brothels, and so on, appear as a shadowy double of the city. As such, they constitute 'marvelous empty zones' outside the rhythm of normality. And they have a dyadic structure: one enters heterotopias either by force or by submitting to some rites of purification (Foucault 1997: 356). At both extremes, however, heterotopias 'presuppose a system of opening and closing that isolates them and makes them penetrable' (ibid.: 355–6). The heterotopia *par excellence* is the ship:

> Think of the ship: it is a floating part of space, a placeless place, that lives by itself, closed in on itself and at the same time poised in the infinite ocean . . . Then you will understand why it has been . . . the greatest reserve of imagination for our civilization from the sixteenth century to the present day. The ship is the heterotopia *par excellence*. In civilizations where it is lacking, dreams dry up, adventure is replaced by espionage, and privateers by the police.
>
> (ibid.: 356)

'Have you ever been on a cruise?', asks Nikki Katz. 'If so, you've probably noticed that you can gamble once you cross into international waters.' The activist group 'Women on Waves' has taken this 'heterotopic' knowledge to a new level by launching the first-ever floating medical clinic to give abortions in countries where it is illegal. Its mission consists in: preventing unwanted pregnancies; ensuring safe and legal abortion; reducing unnecessary suffering and deaths from illegal abortions; empowering women so that they can make well-informed choices; and re-energizing pro-choice activism (see Katz 2000).

From the outside, the *Aurora*, Women on Waves' ship, also called the 'abortion ship' in the media, seemed to be ordinary, a 40-metre Dutch fishing vessel, except that it was accompanied by police everywhere it was illegal to have abortions. Since the ship is only subject to Dutch law, it can offer legal abortions 12 miles offshore in international waters. The *modus operandi* of the team is, in other words, exception. But the team is not authorized to perform surgical abortions. Obviously, they tried and failed to get the necessary paper-work from the Dutch government. Therefore, they are content to distribute the RU486 abortion pill instead (Osborn 2003).

One of the countries in which Women on Waves produced much controversy was Poland where abortion had been legal until 1993. Then a law sponsored by the Church stipulated that abortion could only be allowed to protect the mother's life. Doctors performing abortions face imprisonment of up to three years and, consequently, safe and legal abortion is only accessible to women who can afford to travel abroad or have an illegal abortion in a private clinic at astronomic costs. It is, however, estimated that from 80,000 to 200,000 illegal abortions are performed each year.

There are three significant characteristics of Women on Waves' *modus operandi*: first, it operates in a zone of indistinction between law and unlaw. 'Abortion with impunity', so to speak, parallels a sovereign decision. In this the team seeks, especially in its struggle against the Church, to take women's bodies out of the domain of religion. The body thus enters the domain of (bio)politics. Second, Women on Waves politicizes the body, or, 'life itself'. And third, the team justifies itself with reference to human rights as a suprapolitical instance. 'We are here in support of Irish women who have been denied their human rights and we are calling on women all over the world to support us' (Dr Gomperts, quoted in Cowan 2001).

As such, it seems to us that Women on Waves is a post-political (biopolitical) organization insisting that their actions are only humanitarian and not political. Yet this stance 'above' politics is attainable only paradoxically and when the women become a referent for biopolitics, that is, *homines sacri*. In a sense, therefore, there is a clandestine unity between the humanitarianism of Women on Waves and the biopower it fights against. Women on Waves addresses the same bare life which power is parasitic on. The naked body is the privileged site of its 'humanitarian intervention'.

Shortly after Women on Waves was launched, Philip Nitshke, an Australian doctor, was planning to establish a floating euthanasia clinic off the UK to administer lethal injections and drug dosages. His was an unrealized attempt to 'raise the political profile of the mercy killing debate' (Batty 2001). Obviously, his plan, travelling to the Netherlands to buy a Dutch-registered ship so he could legally end the lives of the terminally ill, was clearly influenced by Women on Waves. And not surprisingly, Rebecca Gomberts, the senior doctor behind Women on Waves, backed Dr Nitschke's plans. However, the Dutch health ministry found the project impossible under their legislation because the patients must have a long-standing relationship with their doctors and need to get a second opinion from another physician in such cases (ibid.). What makes this case interesting from our point of view is again the status of death in biopolitics:

> Euthanasia signals the point at which biopolitics necessarily turns into thanatopolitics . . . If it is the sovereign who, insofar as he decides on the state of exception, has the power to decide which life may be killed without the commission of homicide, in the age of biopolitics this

power becomes emancipated from the state of exception and transformed into the power to decide the point at which life ceases to be
politically relevant.

(Agamben 1998: 142–3)

This is nowhere as visible as in the case of new biotech economies focused on
distinguishing between human embryos to be wasted or spared. As Roberts
and Throsby argue, these economies depend on the donation of embryos from
assisted reproduction and thus it is essential to 'consider the broader context
of embryo donation and to understand precisely how some embryos are framed
as "spare" and therefore as suitable for donation' (2003: 18). Indeed, this logic
of 'selection' between spare and waste seems to be functioning as a new version
of the sovereign decision as to life and death. Which implies that 'the sovereign
decision on bare life comes to be displaced from strictly political motivations
and areas to a more ambiguous terrain in which the physician and the sovereign
seem to exchange roles' (Agamben 1998: 143).

Interestingly, the *Aurora*'s voyages attracted immense international media
interest. The reaction to the *Aurora*'s visit, described in the following by the
crew themselves, is telling in this respect:

> During three weeks everybody talked about abortion, in the media,
> in the parliament, on the street, in bars . . . Most of the international
> media also covered the story. BBC news broadcast several news reports
> and there have been articles in all main American and European
> newspapers. The project has been filmed by a crew of the BBC pro-
> gramme *Correspondent* and the 45-minute documentary will be shown
> sometime this fall.
>
> (Women on Waves 2003)

Women on Waves became so spectacular that in the process it became a
concept, or rather a conceptual project. Even before the team visited Portugal,
for instance, its concept was exhibited as an artwork in Porto where Rebecca
Gomperts participated in an art event as an 'artist/gynaelogist' with the
'project' Women on Waves (Veloso 2004: 143). The project was introduced in
the following way:

> The base for the activities of the Women on Waves project is a mobile,
> portable gynaecological unit designed by the Dutch group Atelier van
> Lieshout . . . This unit can easily be loaded on a ship, which enables
> it to travel worldwide to wherever it is needed. The first operation
> of this unit was in the summer 2001 when it went on a chartered
> Dutch ship to Ireland, which created a big debate in the media and
> caused some conflict between Ireland and the Netherlands. The legal
> situation is that although abortion is illegal in Ireland, as soon as the

ship leaves the coastline and reaches international waters, Dutch law applies and Women on Waves can deliver an abortion pill until the ninth week of pregnancy.

(Bauer, quoted in ibid.)

Turning into a concept, Women on Waves became 'a media event' (ibid.: 144). It no longer consisted of a material 'clinic' but of the idea of it. As such the project 'capitalized on the already existing media attention and, in return, media attention is what made the project "successful" as an artwork' (ibid.). Art became, in short, a kind of 'international waters' for Women on Waves (ibid.: 146). 'International waters' is here a zone of indistinction in which art meets the world, in which the body without word (bare life) meets the word without the body (the concept). In the heterotopia, biopolitics meets the society of spectacle.

Women on Waves went to Portugal virtually, before going there physically. In a sense, one could say that the ability to suspend its physical materiality was its power. Sovereignty, after all, is a play of presence and disappearance; it can suspend itself (in virtuality) without becoming less real at that.

Biopolitics is, above all, a way of suspending a person's legal status. Biopolitics bypasses the legal subject and operates directly on the body. And as with all forms of power, biopolitical power is not only negative and restrictive but also positive and constructive. Further, it operates not in spite of but because of this ambivalence. Thus, it not only represses but also promises liberation. It not only entrenches but also permits flow. In short, power can let sail in the heterotopia as well as it can fix in the panopticon. In this respect, there is a direct genealogical link between the discovery of the 'new world' and the origin of the camp; and between the concentration camp and contemporary political spaces.

3

THE CAMP AS DISCIPLINE, CONTROL AND TERROR

In the contemporary equivalent of solid modern Utopias, happiness is linked to mobility, not to a place . . . The liquid modern equivalents of the Utopias of yore are neither about time nor about space – but about *speed* and *acceleration*.

(Bauman 2002: 241)

A man enters a public toilet cubicle and sits down on the toilet. From the cubicle next door he hears 'Hello'. He ignores it, embarrassed, a little apprehensive at the invasion of his privacy, he looks down to the floor to observe the other man's shoes, the only visible part of him. Another 'hello' comes, to which this time the man feels obliged to return an awkward hello. 'How are you? How was your day?' etc. follows to which the man politely returns answers and a return 'How was your day?' At which point the camera withdraws to the exterior of the cubicle and the man who we first heard say hello says: 'Just a minute. There is a guy who keeps answering all my questions.' It is only then that we realize he has been talking to someone else on a mobile phone.

This is how a Mexican TV ad proceeds to make its point: the promise of the mobile phone is a paradoxical exterritoriality that consists in both making obsolete the inside–outside divide by creating a neutral space, almost an insignificant 'wilderness', around itself and, at the same time, constituting an invisible shield against the intrusion of the environment. That is, the mobile phone is an instrument of self-exemption from and abandoning an immediate place simultaneously. Reaching far behind the physical limits of a concrete locality, it makes the inside–outside distinction specific to a concrete place irrelevant. And at the same time, it minimizes and sterilizes the contact with the immediate surroundings. Hence mobility becomes an assault on one's immediate surroundings.

Significantly in this context, the mobile phone reduces the contact with others to a visual contact, which brings with it more indifference than a desire to relate. 'Connecting' elsewhere means local dislocation. To re-paraphrase

Simmel: someone who sees and hears without connecting is much more uneasy than someone who sees without hearing (who is, admittedly, more uneasy than someone who hears without seeing). In this there is something characteristic of the sociology of the camp. Never before have people been so included in each other's private life and never before have they been so excluded from each other's public life. Demonstrating the paradoxes of the experience of (self-) exemption, instruments like the mobile phone make the distinction between the private and the public obsolete. Sociality fit for the camp is as much about disconnecting as connecting, unbonding as bonding.

And indeed, the state of (self-)exemption created by technologies of mobility has a family resemblance with the 'state of exception'. The mobile phone, for instance, is more than anything else an instrument of self-exemption (abandoning immediate sociality) and exemption (abandoning others from one's domain of significance). Just as the sovereign exception does not leave in peace what it 'abandons', the mobile phone user does not merely 'ignore' or 'exclude' people around but paradoxically 'includes' them by excluding, e.g. in a noisy, overheard conversation. One's freedom (of mobility) becomes another's unfreedom (being fixed to the place of another's non-place).

In other words, the new technologies of mobility also function as technologies of 'camping'. Thus they increasingly reshape the relationship between subjective experience and power. To discuss this, we focus on three *dispositifs* of power: discipline, control and terror. Our main argument is that disciplinary confinement, and thus exclusion and normalization, constitutes only one of the three spatial principles embodied in the camp. The camp is also a space of control, which does not demand the delimitation of movement but rather abstraction and speed. In contrast to discipline and control, which operate, respectively, in terms of enclosure and flow, terror functions against the background of fear related to uncertainty, insecurity and unsafety. Terror immobilizes through fear; that is, it is disciplinary without the spatial confinement of discipline and the functional regularity of flows. To end with, we focus on how attempts at escaping from one form of power sediment other, more advanced forms of power, and on how what appears as freedom in one context might turn into repression in another. In this, we emphasize the inter-relations between discipline, control and terror and their internal ambiguities, which is central to the understanding of the contemporary camps.

Discipline

In *The Panopticon Writings* (1995), Bentham describes the production of bare life, but he does so with a spatial emphasis. Thus panopticism has often been understood as a technique of immobilization. There are, however, at least two ways to read Bentham's text. Foucault's reading of panopticism in *Discipline and Punish* (1977) is the first, according to which sovereignty and discipline, conceptualized by Bentham, are to be clearly distinguished. Yet, second, it is possible to understand discipline as a new technique of abandonment, that is, as a technique through which sovereignty is still present. In fact, even though Foucault had examined the prison as the paradigmatic political space of modernity, leaving the camp out of consideration (Agamben 1998: 20), it is possible to see the prison as a manifestation of the logic of the camp. Curiously, this possibility is ommitted in Agamben's considerations of the camp.

Let us start with focusing on Foucault's position. The distinction between sovereignty and discipline is perhaps clearest when Foucault juxtaposes the treatment of the leper and the plague. The first case manifests the way of sovereign abandonment; the latter the use of disciplinary techniques, which Foucault claims is a 'non-sovereign' power (Foucault 2003a: 36):

> If it is true that the leper gave rise to rituals of exclusion, which to a certain extent provided the model for and general form of the great confinement, then the plague gave rise to disciplinary projects. Rather than the massive, binary division between one set of people and another, it called for multiple separations, individualizing distributions, an organization in depth of surveillance and control, an intensification and a ramification of power. The leper was caught up in a practice of rejection, of exile-enclosure; he was left to his doom in a mass among which it was useless to differentiate; those sick from the plague were caught up in a meticulous tactical partitioning in which individual differentiations were the constricting effects of a power that multiplied, articulated and subdivided itself; the great confinement on the one hand; the correct training on the other. The leper and his separation; the plague and its segmentations. The first is marked; the second analysed and distributed. The exile of the leper and the arrest of the plague do not bring with them the same political dream. The first is that of a pure community, the second that of a disciplined society.
>
> (Foucault 1991: 198)

This disciplinary *dispositif* is alien to law and sovereign will. It is not a code of law affecting only those who transgress them but a mechanism of normalization (Foucault 2003a: 38). Hence, Foucault's aim is to free the analysis of power from the three assumptions related to the subject, unity and law (ibid.: 44–5). Or, to put it metaphorically, the goal is to 'cut off the king's head' (ibid.: 59). And then we get a series of differences between sovereignty and discipline, all recurring Foucauldian themes: whereas sovereignty puts death into play, discipline aims to correct the living; whereas sovereignty focuses on the body, discipline emphasizes the individual as a conscious being that can be corrected; whereas sovereign power is exercised over the few, discipline is employed against all; whereas sovereignty plays at the potentiality (of the ban), discipline acts on the actuality. And finally, sovereignty is about exception, discipline on the maintenance of order.

It is significant that the panopticon was invented as a universally applicable diagram of surveillance to be used in all institutions, e.g. schools, hospitals and workhouses as well as in prisons (Bentham 1995: 31–4). In each case the institution was to be organized around the gaze of a central authority 'seeing without being seen'; the inmates could not, and should not, know when they were under the scrutiny of the central authority (ibid.: 34, 43). This threat of being seen by an omnipresent gaze was to make the inmates survey themselves (ibid.: 43).

Bentham was a utilitarian obsessed with maximizing utility and minimizing costs. Punishment was to be accepted only when it served a higher goal, that is, more utility (Miller 1987: 10; Bozovic 1995: 3). The function of punishment was not revenge or an act aimed at inflicting the same amount of pain on the doer as suffered by the victim. The feeling of pain could not be compensated for (Miller 1987: 10). If, however, punishment prevented others from acting out similar wrongs, then the overall utility would increase (Bozovic 1995: 3). In this sense, the panopticon was built to remind the outsiders of how much their utility would decrease if imprisoned (ibid.: 4). The building should be visible from all over the town, preferably built on a small mountain. It should be non-transparent and dark. Bentham insists that people in the surrounding town should be convinced that the prison was a real institution. Likewise, the prisoners should be certain that the person in the central tower was not a wooden replica; the best way to sustain the fiction of the omnipresent gaze was, in other words, to have a real panopticon signaling the potentiality of a ban (ibid.: 7).

As the prisoners internalized the gaze of authority, the citizens would internalize the risk of imprisonment. The ban could strike all; again, sovereignty reigns *in potentia*, omnipresent yet not necessarily real or actual. 'It is the apparent punishment, therefore, that does all the service, I mean by the way of example, which is the principal object. It is the real punishment that does all the mischief' (Bentham 1988: 170, quoted in Bozovic 1995: 4). The sovereign shows himself only through his acts of abandonment, which is also why the 'outsiders', the citizens, can be disciplined without confinement. Sovereignty is about, to use a Chinese proverb, 'killing the chicken to scare the monkeys' (Fiskesjö 2003: 49).

When the prison was opened to the public, the prisoners should wear masks corresponding to their crimes. The mask was, Bentham thought, more real than what it concealed. It ensured that the criminal looked repelling so that the visitors did not feel (irrational) pity for him. Also, the mask ensured that the punishment achieved the right (rational) goal, and only this goal. If the prisoners could be recognized after their release, a further irrational punishment would be enforced: the public might avoid the ex-prisoner, inflicting pain on him and thus reducing his utility:

Guilt will thus be pilloried in the abstract, without the exposure of the guilty. With regard to the sufferer, the string of shame will be sheathed, and with regard to the spectators, the salutary impression, instead of being weakened, will be heightened, by this imagery. The scene of devotion will be decorated by – why mince the word? – by a masquerade: a masquerade, indeed, but of what kind? Not a gay and dangerous, but a serious, affecting, and instructive one.

(Bentham 1995: 100)

The panopticon sought to manipulate the visual image to maximize utility; fictions built into a spatial design could have real effects. Reading Bentham this way, one's attention is turned to non-spatial forms of power. The panopticon is a technology constructed to make people internalize the sovereign gaze. Sovereignty becomes omnipresent through invisibility; its mystery lies in the paradox of absence and presence. The primary goal of the panopticon was, therefore, not confinement but the manipulation of self-consciousness. Bentham was interested in creating a God-like effect in the minds of both prisoners and citizens (Miller 1987: 5; Bozovic 1995: 14–15). Above the inspector's lodge a chapel was to be placed and through a vicar, visible through the windows above the cell door, God should make his presence felt in the prison (Bentham 1995: 41).

The panopticon was above all an apparatus, a machine (ibid.: 31); and in many ways it was a forerunner to other self-sustaining systems. It is a 'complex system of cogs and gears' that does not rely on single individuals for their running (Foucault 1980: 158). As the guard surveyed the prisoners, the public surveyed the contractor; the contractor surveyed the other contractor through competition, etc. (Miller 1987: 8–9); 'all by a simple idea in Architecture!' (Bentham 1995: 95). Through this simple idea, power over the minds of fellow men could be obtained without 'unpopular severity, not to say torture – the use of *irons*' (ibid.: 49). The guiding idea is self-governance. Inside the panopticon, the walls need to be thick preventing escape, in the penitentiary house they may be thinner and in the hospital just a cloth will do (ibid.: 77). Outside the panopticon, one does not need walls; they can be invisible as the moral law. Outer walls exist to generate inner walls. When the guard becomes the super-ego, people may very well be given their 'freedom' for they will discipline themselves. The prisoners inside the panoption, and the citizens living outside scared about the risk of imprisonment, are both reduced to bare life. The prison signals, as the forest previously did, the potentiality of abandonment and hence the omnipotence of the sovereign power.

Bentham never saw his ideas realized, but they were, for instance in totalitarian states, which replaced the prison guard with 'the party' with secret agents, informers, etc. Bentham's philosophy was totalitarian: *everything* could be reduced to and measured according to its utility (Miller 1987: 5). What Bentham wanted was total control and transparency:

A fear haunted the latter half of the eighteenth century: the fear of darkened spaces, of the pall of gloom which prevents the full visibility of things, men and truths. It sought to break up the patches of darkness that blocked the light, eliminate the shadowy areas of society, demolish the unlit chambers where arbitrary political acts, monarchical caprice, religious superstitions, tyrannical and priestly plots, epidemics and the illusions of ignorance were fomented.

(Foucault 1980: 153)

One could go further, as Agamben does, and claim that the central authority could be 'the People', that biopolitics does not necessitate a totalitarian party. What looks like a welfare-machine turns up as an apparatus reducing people to bare life. This ambivalence was utterly visible in the panopticon regarding the function of the 'speaking-tubes'. A system of tubes had to be installed, linking the inspector's lodge and the cells so that the authority could hear the slightest whisper and command every single prisoner through his speaking trumpet (Bentham 1995: 36, 112). The omnipresent gaze thus finds its parallel in 'walls with ears'. Yet the same technology could be employed in hospitals, replacing the guard with another authority, the doctor. In the hospital:

> the use of the tin *speaking-tubes* would be seen again, in the means they would afford to the patient, though he were equal to no more than a whisper, of conveying to the lodge the most immediate notice of his wants, and receiving answers in a tone equally unproductive of disturbance.

(ibid.: 84)

In Kafka's short story, 'Der Bau', the nameless animal that narrates the story is obsessively engaged in building an inexpugnable burrow. The burrow, however, turns into a trap with no way out. Agamben asks:

> Isn't this precisely what has happened in the political space of Western nation-states? The homes – the *Fatherlands* – that these states endeavored to build revealed themselves in the end to be only lethal traps for the very 'peoples' that were supposed to inhabit them.

(2000: 140)

The rights won by individuals in their struggle against state authority pave the way for the inscription of lives within state power, hence laying the foundation of the power from which they wanted to liberate themselves (Agamben 1998: 121). The struggle for rights enables a biopolitical paradigm to reduce subjects to bare life:

Everything happens as if, along with the disciplinary process by which State power makes man as a living being into its own specific object, another process is set in motion that in large measure corresponds to the birth of modern democracy, in which man as a living being presents himself no longer as an *object* but as the *subject* of political power. These processes – which in many ways oppose and (at least apparently) bitterly conflict with each other – nevertheless converge insofar as both concern the bare life of the citizen, the new biopolitical body of humanity.

(ibid.: 9)

As confinement becomes a trap, masters and slaves become interchangeable. The prisoners of the panopticon are slaves restricted in all aspects of their being in a gigantic calculation of utility. Inversely, the patients are masters whose slightest whisper works as a command. Or is it the other way around? Who is surveying whom? Who is the sovereign? The more one tries to understand the panopticon, the harder it becomes to distinguish between master and slave, subject and object, inside and outside, and reality and fiction: the terms merge into each other and enter into a zone of indistinction.

Modernity creates a zone of indistinction not so much between inside and outside (of the nation, the town or the home) but by cutting through every subject and the political. 'The borderline between political existence and bare life' moved inside every human life and every citizen. Bare life is no longer confined to a particular place or a definite category of people. It now dwells in the biological body of every living being (ibid.: 140). Instead of the excluded 'abnormal' elements, we now have the camp as a condition lived by all, as a condition of hypermodernity in which the processes of differentiation are taken to their logical (and paradoxical) consequences. It is, however, essential that this condition is not just one characterized by the quantitative increase in the number of people abandoned. Rather, as we discuss in the following, the method or the *dispositif* of abandonment itself continually changes.

Control

On the same day *The Independent* published the front-page picture of the naked Abu Ghraib prisoner cowering before US guards and their dogs, it also brought news about a new scanner that will soon be coming to UK airports (see Woolf 2004). The body scanner, which can see straight through clothing by using a special light frequency, is designed to detect guns and other offensive metal weapons concealed on the body and is expected to be employed within a year in British airports as part of the war against terror. It captures the 'naked image' of a traveller but, to protect people's modesty, it comes replete with 'fig-leaf technology' that can detect the body parts that need screening out. It can focus, that is, on the parts of the body rather than the unity of the body, which means that the body without word (naked, biological body) and the word without a body (image, password) finally coincide. And the fig-leaf technology can show on the screen an a-sexed, or 'castrated' body without sexual organs. The ultimate, naked image of *homo sacer* as a non-erotic 'body' that only consists of dismembered 'organs'. Which is also the ultimate image of the subject in what Deleuze (1995) called 'control society':

> While . . . the disciplinary establishments increase, their mechanisms have a certain tendency to become 'de-institutionalized', to emerge from the closed fortresses in which they once functioned and to circulate in a 'free' state; the massive, compact disciplines are broken down into flexible methods of control . . . Sometimes the closed apparatuses add to their internal and specific function a role of external surveillance, developing around themselves a whole margin of lateral controls.
>
> (Foucault 1977: 211)

Foucault operates with two images of discipline: first, the enclosed institution 'on the edges of society, turned inwards towards negative functions', and, second, a *dispositif* that improves the exercise of power 'by making it lighter, more rapid, more effective' (ibid.: 209). It is the latter image that Deleuze draws on to discuss the emergence of post-disciplinary 'societies of control', insisting that contemporary technologies of mobility constitute a new social topology, in which the geographical/institutional delimitation of discipline, that is, the inside–outside distinction, has become obsolete. As against the persistent image of discipline as an 'anti-nomadic technique' that endeavours to 'fix' mobilities (ibid.: 215, 218), today, power itself goes nomadic.

In control societies, one no longer moves from one closed site to another (family, school, barracks, prison, etc.) but is increasingly subjected to free-floating, nomadic forms of control (Deleuze 1995: 178). Inclusion and exclusion thus take place through continuous, mobile forms of surveillance as is the case with electronic tagging, risk management in relation to 'networks', or cross-border regulation with respect to divergent sets of flows of subjects and objects. Whereas discipline worked as an 'instrument of immobilization', post-panoptic forms of power target the conduct of mobile subjects (Bauman 1998b: 51–2). Neither demanding nor promising normalization, they engage in pre-emptive risk management (Rose 1999: 234).

Control is digital, it translates everything into the logic of codes and passwords, and thus transgresses the duality of mass and individual. 'Individuals become "dividuals," and masses become samples, data, markets, or "banks"' (Deleuze 1995: 180). Focusing on biosurveillance methods through access to tissues, fluids and images available from the body itself, control transforms 'the body into a password' (Lyon 2001: 75). Post-panoptic power can interpellate the subject *in absentia* through electronic lists (see Poster 1996). Such lists can be used by businesses to differentiate and filter customers and to regulate access to the net (Lyon 2003: 107). Regulating a fluid and endlessly divisible, fractal, 'multitude' rather than 'peoples', control produces a hybrid, metastable subjectivity that no longer corresponds to stable identities of the disciplinary society (Hardt and Negri 2000: 331–2).

Indeed, in control societies, sociality seems to follow the pattern of the airport. Which is, above all, a site in which the agora is transformed into Benjamin's 'phantasmagoria', because all belonging in the airport consists in representation (Wong 2004). Through the passport and other signs, which recognize the subject only as a sign, as a number, the airport works as a machine of representation that produces and reproduces the subject as a representation, as a 'word without body'. Small wonder that one cannot exist in the airport without a passport. On the other hand, though, the airport transforms the agora into a kind of 'zoopolis', in which 'citizens' are reduced to naked bodies, because the biometric technologies of surveillance can only 'scan' and recognize the subject as a body or body parts. In short, the airport is a 'transitional' space in between the two extremes of spectrality and biopolitics:

> To the media devices which control and handle the public word thus corresponds the technological devices which register and identify the naked life: between these two extremes of a word without body and a body without word, the space of what we formerly called politics is increasingly more reduced and more exiguous.
>
> (Agamben 2004b; our translation)

Significantly in this respect, control brings with it an infinite intensification of discipline in a smooth space devoid of enclosures; control is discipline without walls, a mobile form of discipline that regulates humans and non-humans on the move. Nomadism was once a critical tool against discipline, a 'line of flight' out of the panopticon, but control society captures nomadic 'war machines', accommodating them for its own purposes (see Deleuze and Guattari 1987: 387). Moving from 'exceptional discipline' to 'generalized surveillance' (Foucault 1977: 209), control extends the logic of the camp. With intensified and direct biopolitical access to bare life, control 'knows no outside' (Hardt and Negri 2000: 413). Its logic transgresses the binary logic of the inside–outside distinction for it is a 'decentered and deterritorializing apparatus of rule' (ibid.: xii). Modern discipline had played upon the distinction between inside and outside; post-modern control, in contrast, constitutes an *ou-topia*, a non-place (ibid.: 190). When there is no outside left, the zone of indistinction opened up by the camp becomes the smooth space of control, a generalized space of indistinction. Which turns discipline itself into a simulacrum: hence in control society 'prisons are there to hide that it is the social in its entirety, in its banal omnipresence, that is carceral' (Baudrillard 1994: 12).

The city as a complex technological artifact illuminates the logic of control. Systems of control are urban phenomena; cities constitute nodal points in mobile societies of surveillance, and even cyberspaces are congested 'around conventional urban areas' (Lyon 2001: 53–4). Yet this is misleading because the 'conventional city' no longer exists. The contemporary city is no longer founded on the divide between its 'intramural' population and the outside; 'it no longer has anything to do with the classical oppositions of city/country nor centre/periphery' (Virilio 1997: 382, 390). The city of control is an immanent space, a reticular *ou-topia*, sharing with all other networks a 'fibrous, thread-like, wiry, stringy, ropy, capillary character that is never captured by the notions of levels, layers, territories, spheres, categories, structure, systems' (Latour 1996: 370). It is Rem Koolhaas' fractal 'generic city', which 'cannot be measured in dimensions' (Koolhaas *et al*. 1995: 1251). With Derrida, the city of control cannot be *Whole*; with Baudrillard, it cannot be *Real*; and with Virilio, it cannot be *There* (see ibid.: 967).

The new urbanism refuses 'meticulous definition', 'the imposition of limits' and a 'definitive form' (ibid.: 969). Tom Nielsen (2000) has coined the concept of 'surplus landscapes' to conceptualize this 'formless' city. What was hitherto formless, the indistinct zones in-between centres and peripheries, now tends to extend to the whole landscape, including the city itself. Transgressing its limits and its inside–outside divide, the city is becoming an indistinct space: a 'camp'. Bataille had contrasted the solid forms of 'architecture', that is, homogeneity or the law, with 'fluidity', that is, heterogeneity or transgression (Bataille 1997: 121). The generalization of the 'formless', of the camp, is the normalization of Bataille's utopia. Hence the main attraction of the generic city 'is its anomie' (Koolhaas *et al*. 1995: 1251). The generic city is, in a sense, the 'ecstasy' of the city: 'If, in fact, the era of transgression has ended, it is that things themselves have transgressed their own limits' (Baudrillard 1988b: 82).

Does the generic city, then, consist of an undifferentiated fluidity? No. There are three imperatives of control. First, control is all-inclusive on the basis of an undiscriminating universal notion of right fit for the generic, smooth space. But, second, it involves a moment of re-differentiatiation, e.g. in terms of informational or cultural identities, which functions as an apolitical impetus for identification. This differential moment is followed by the management of differences through 'circuits of movement and mixture' that replace the disciplinary enclosures (Hardt and Negri 2000: 198–9). Flows of 'dividuals' are channelled or blocked in prescribed ways (e.g. one is not expected to sleep in a shopping mall), 'submitted to a system of interior/exterior traffic control' (Virilio 1997: 381). In 'Traffic in Democracy', Sorkin writes:

> Flow seeks to increase speed (and save time) by prioritizing the faster means of movement. Safety is often foregrounded as the reason for this system of preferences; the potential for danger, confusion and slow-down resulting from the undisciplined mix gives rise to elaborated

structures for vetting what traffic engineers call 'conflict' between modes. Typically, this means slower vehicles yield to faster ones and pedestrians to all, walkers deferring to cars, cars to trains, trains to planes, and so on. Modern city planning is structured around an armature of such conflict avoidance.

(1999: 1–2)

Conflict and danger arise when flows intersect in unexpected, unwanted ways; flows are 'purposeful, repetitive, programmemable sequences of exchange and interaction between physically disjointed positions' (Castells 1996: 412). If functional flows cannot connect with or bypass one another, the traffic control is broken down, of which Baudrillard allegorically writes:

All over the US, they have adapted the sidewalks to afford access to motorized handicapped persons. But the blind who used to be guided by the curbs are disoriented, and often are run over. So they came up with the idea of a handrail for the blind along the street, but then the handicapped get caught on these rails in the wheelchairs.

(Baudrillard 1990: 30)

Further, a paradoxical consequence of mobility is immobility, and this paradox marks the city of control, in which sedentariness/inertia is more a post-mobility situation than one that precedes mobility. 'Sedentariness in the instant of absolute speed. It's no longer a sedentariness of non-movement, it's the opposite' (Lotringer and Virilio 1997: 68). Thus, 'the generic city is *sedated*, usually perceived from a sedentary position' (Koolhaas *et al*. 1995: 1250). In Virilio's account, the life of Howard Hughes, one of the most mobile people in the twentieth century and a famous producer of transportation (cars) and transmission (movies), epitomizes life with speed. Hughes was a person obsessed with speed but he ended up a technological monk in Las Vegas, without getting out of bed at all, avoiding all external stimuli. He spent his last fifteen years shut up in a single room, watching films, always the same ones, trying to create a private world of inertia. Hughes was a mobile person who 'lost the world' (Lotringer and Virilio 1997: 76–7). Along similar lines, Sorkin mentions Walther Hudson, the world's fattest man, who was forever confined to his bed:

Hudson's 'luxurious' occupation of physical space bore a striking resemblance to the delimiting privileges of the global elite, who circle the globe with effortless efficiency immobilized in their business-class seats, strapped and wired in . . . This global movement system trades access for privacy: constant surveillance is the price of 'freedom' of movement. Ironically, this surveillance is at its most Draconian for those with the greatest 'rights'. World travelers, for example, are subject to microscopic attention, their activities recorded, correlated, and made available to an enormous invisible government of customs authorities, shadowy credit agencies, back-office computer banks, market research firms, private security companies, advertisers, database gatherers an endlessness of media connections. Pull out your Amex card and we know exactly where you are. Turn on your home security system and we know you've left. Order a special meal and we know there's a non-smoking Muslim in seat 3K.

(Sorkin 1999: 8–9)

Kafka's 'Der Bau' again, but this time in the form of permanent movement that pacifies and leads to inertia. Control is a line of flight that escapes disciplinary entrenchment, but it has its own discontents, bringing with it nomadic forms of repression, and turning the freedom of movement into a new form of sedentariness. What kind of a line of flight, then, can emerge in societies of control? What happens, when the codes of the flows break down?

Terror

The great transparency of the world, whether through satellites or simply tourists, brought about an overexposure . . . [which] led to the need to surpass enclosure and imprisonment. This required the promotion of another kind of repression, which is disappearance. (Gangsters had already invented it by making bodies disappear in cement.)

(Lotringer and Virilio 1997: 87)

Within the disciplinary diagram of exception, a single central authority watches individuals immobilized on the 'edge' of society; with the diagram of control (e.g. the global market), multiple, deterritorialized authorities watch the mobile 'dividuals', the multitude, through generalized biopolitics. Yet control is prone to immanent problems. As flows traverse the surface of control society, their complex global interdependencies bring forth an inherent danger, that any problem at any singular point may potentially have direct effects on all other points. In other words, the virtual centre of control society can be accessed from any point, because every point is potentially its centre, and thus any crisis in control society may lead to an *omni-crisis* (Hardt and Negri 2000: 58, 340). The nightmares of the disciplinary society were entropy (lack of centralized co-ordination) and sabotage (opposition); in control society, 'the passive danger is noise and the active, piracy and viral contamination' (Deleuze 1995: 180). 'Noise' emerges as a problem of miscommunication between the codes and the programmes of the horizontally differentiated function systems (see Luhmann 1989). The 'viral', on the other hand, emanates in the form of metastasis and remains indifferent to control, bringing with it transparency (disappearance).

Transparency is a flattening process characterized by the exacerbation of indifference and the indefinite mutation of social domains (Baudrillard 1990: 7, 50). When everything becomes political, politics disappear; when everything becomes sexual, sex disappears; when everything is social, the social disappears, and so on. With the obscenity of the transparent, 'there is nothing but the dilation of the visibility of the things to the point of ecstasy' (ibid.: 55). As is the case with pornography, extreme visibility leads to the loss of the invisible (seduction). Control society is in this sense not a scene but obscene, off-scene: social change tends to lose its historical dimension, information ceases to be an event, physical geography is cancelled by networks, the political is foreclosed in transpolitics, and the real implodes into simulation. In short, transparency is the answer to the question: 'Why does the World Trade Center have *two* towers' (Baudrillard 1988a: 143)? The twin towers of the WTC were perfect parallelepipeds whose smooth surfaces merely mirrored each other, confirming the irrelevance of distinction and opposition in a postmodern world. Cancelling out difference, upon which politics is based, the WTC was a symbol of transpolitics: an obscene system in which dialectical polarity no longer exists, a simulacrum, where acts disappear without consequences in indifferent 'zero-sum signs' (Baudrillard 1994: 16, 32).

Yet, for all that, transpolitics is not a peaceful order: the foreclosure of the political and the implosion of the social provoke new, obscene forms of violence: terror, which is not a product of 'a clash between antagonistic passions, but the product of listless and indifferent forces' (Baudrillard 1993: 76). No wonder that it is terrorism, naked violence, that demolished the WTC. Transpolitics and terror mirror each other in a smooth space of indistinction; they are the twin faces of control society.

Because control society is a virtual order, a simulacrum, its 'hysteria' is the production of the real (Baudrillard 1994: 23). This hysteria is, for instance, exemplified by the reality-TV show *Big Brother* with its tragicomic reversal of panopticism: 'today, anxiety seems to arise from the prospect of not being exposed to the Other's gaze all the time' (Žižek 2001a: 249–51). Transparency is the very source of anxiety of control society. When the social disappears, the extreme disenchantment with life becomes an object of perverse desire, invested in the hope that the real will return when the veil of simulacrum is lifted from everyday existence . And terror is a traumatic intervention of the 'real' into the virtual, symbolic 'reality' (see ibid.). Terror takes place in the 'desert of the real itself' (Baudrillard 1994: 1):

> If there is any symbolism in the collapse of the WTC towers, it is not so much the old-fashioned notion of the 'center of financial capital-ism,' but, rather, the notion that the two WTC towers stood for the center of the virtual capitalism, of financial speculations disconnected from the sphere of material production. The shattering impact of the bombings can only be accounted for only against the background

of the borderline which today separates the digitalized First World from the Third World 'desert of the Real.' It is the awareness that we live in an insulated artificial universe which generates the notion that some ominous agent is threatening us all the time with total destruction.

(Žižek 2001a: 4)

Terror confronts the *Matrix* of control society, the truth of which is 'the de-materialization of "real life" itself' (ibid.). In this 'desert', terror confronts us with a real catastrophe: 'terrorism is always that of the real' (Baudrillard 1994: 47).

The subject produced within the disciplinary *dispositif* was that of the prisoner, whose mobility was constrained through confinement, stigmatization, and so on. With control, we have the 'dividual', the subject controlled on the move, through multiple systemic inscriptions and codes. The figure of the subject regarding terrorism is that of the hostage: an anonymous figure who occupies a radical state of exception beyond the principle of exchange and alienation (1990: 34–5). Beyond the principle exchange, the hostage is a truly naked, formless body, which is absolutely convertible: anybody and everybody can be a hostage. Killing a hostage sends no messages; it does not have any political efficacy or meaning. Terror is 'an event without consequences (and always leads to a dead end)' (ibid.: 40).

The situation of the hostage can no longer be related to the idea of freedom based on individual responsibility (discipline) or to the instances of security based on risk management through 'objective systems' (control). In stark contrast to both situations, terror does not place responsibility in a definite actor or system; it can hit any individual, without any systemic instance being objectively responsible for it. The absolute convertibility of the hostage brings with it a new constellation of responsibility. Replacing individual and systemic violence with spectacular anonymity, terror generalizes responsibility through the logic of the hostage. Anybody can be hit; thus everybody is blackmailed by (and responsible for) terrorism, which

> insinuates a wholly different type of relation to power than that based on the violence of interdiction. The latter had a specific referent and an object, and therefore transgression of it was a possibility. Blackmail, however, is allusive, and is no longer based either on an imperative or on the utterance of a law . . . but plays on the enigmatic form of terror.

(ibid.: 42)

Every war is 'original' in that it redefines the enemy and the borders of the battlefield, but with terrorism, the enemy remains unclear and the battlefield ceases to have demarcations; terror is a 'formless war' (Lotringer and Virilio 1997: 173). It creates a zone of indistinction, a camp, which we all inhabit. However, not only terror but also the contemporary (trans)politics of security has much in common with the camp:

> Today we face extreme and most dangerous developments in the thought of security. In the course of a gradual neutralization of politics and the progressive surrender of traditional tasks of the state, security becomes the basic principle of state activity. What used to be one among several definitive measures of public administration until the first half of the twentieth century, now becomes the sole criterion of political legitimization.
>
> (Agamben 2001)

As security is becoming the dominant discourse, it is today redefining what it means to be a subject subjected to power. Yet there is a paradox in this: the instruments of security and control are fluidity, liquidity and speed, but politics requires time for reflection and dialogue. Speed and politics form a self-destructive relation: speed is *beyond* politics; 'exceeding politics, speed blinds it' (Lotringer and Virilio 1997: 86–7). Power based on the speed of flows escapes political territories, disengaging itself from the agora (Bauman 1999: 87).

Forms of life and forms of security are interrelated; security creates society as much as society creates security (see Dillon and Reid 2001). Security is a formative, productive and dynamic aspect of social life (Dillon 1996). Yet, in contemporary society, this relationship is overlooked while it is firmly held that it is a 'moral duty' to wage war against terror, whose definition, however, remains obscenely indistinct (e.g. Bin Laden: created by the CIA and wanted by the FBI). The threat against civic culture is, therefore, Janus-faced: terrorism and the (trans)politics of security must be thought of together. Both operate in a smooth space, both speak the language of deterrence ('if you do not . . . '), and both are inherently opposed to the law. Security can easily turn into a perversion: terror: 'The thought of security bears within it an essential risk. A state which has security as its sole task and source of legitimacy is a fragile organism; it can always be provoked by terrorism to become itself terroristic' (Agamben 2001).

When the police and politics merge, and when the difference between terror and the state disappears in obscenity, they start to justify each other, terrorizing the political itself by transforming it into a hostage: the state of emergency. Significantly in this context, the discourse of security conceptualizes the 'networks of terror' in timeless frames devoid of casual explanations, and seeks an 'infinite justice' fit for the smooth network space. Post-political governance attempts to control disorder through risk management. In other words, it does not seek political solutions to political problems, and in the absence of an original political strategy . . . the state becomes desocialized. It no longer works on the basis of political will, but instead on the basis of intimidation, dissuasion, simulation, provocation or spectacular solicitation. This is the *transpolitical reality* behind all official policies: a cynical bias towards the elimination of the social.

(Baudrillard 1993: 79)

When blackmail, intended as a pre-emptive form of action (where is the next war going to take place to prevent war?), becomes the law, 'society' implodes into the state, both ordinary and political violence turns into terror. The camp is symptomatic of both security and terror.

No wonder that, with control and terror, urban politics too is depoliticized, and the disciplinary interest in 'social justice' (Harvey 1973) and 'collective consumption' (Castells 1977) tends to disappear. Yet, ironically, as the production of security is fast becoming the key factor that is transforming the city, the city itself seems to be assuming the status of an object 'beyond control'; thus, in the 'chaos' of the generic city, control is an illusion (see Koolhaas *et al.* 1995: 969, 971).

There is in this image an aggressive assertion of something beyond human control: a restless, if impersonal hostility, an antagonism whose source cannot be located entirely in the human, in the common antagonisms of social life. It is as if we were suddenly placed on the side of *Das Ding* and viewing human life . . . with respect to the Real. But where lies the inhuman *Das Ding*, there is always its human agent. Lacan called it 'Sade'.

(MacCannell 2000: 678)

Transpoliticization leads to the image of a Sadist city, against which the 'citizen' only can assume the passive role of the Sadean victim. With its gated communities and ghettoes (disciplinary enclosure), closed-circuit cameras (the obscene), communication and information technologies (control), terrorists and psychopaths (naked violence), and anthrax in the mail (the viral), the contemporary city prescribes security as a lifestyle (see Davis 1990: 226–336). As exception becomes the rule, the 'urban' (law) turns into a 'jungle' (perversion), assuming a capacity beyond human control. The 'urban jungle' is a zone of indistinction, in which the figure of the citizen meets *homo sacer* in a struggle for survival:

Cutting oneself off. Locking oneself in, hiding – these are today's most common ways of reacting to the fear of the things happening 'out there' which seems to threaten us in a variety of masks. Deadbolts on the door, entrance locks, multiple security systems, alarms and surveillance cameras have spread from upper-class villas to middle-class areas. Living behind a wall of mechanical locks and electronic walls, whistles, pepper-sprays, tear-gas guns or tazer guns is part of individual urban survival orientation

(Hinzler quoted in Bauman 1999: 50)

However, as security is seen as an absolute achievement, the price to pay is high: the return of discipline, the burrow becomes a trap. In the disciplinary era, exception was enclosed inside the panopticon, and the 'ghetto' of those defined as 'other' constituted a 'camp' in the form of an island of disorder a midst order. In control society, there emerges a smooth space of discipline beyond the ghetto walls. Yet, at the same time, due to the problems of noise and the viral, anarchy spreads, too. As 'disorder' is generalized across the smooth space, the disciplinary situation is reversed; what has hitherto been exceptional becomes normality. Consequently, there emerge islands of order amidst disorder. These 'gated communities' refer to particularistic orders (e.g. cultural, ethnic or class-based), where risks are sought to be minimized in secured zones of discipline, while outside, in the 'urban jungle', horror lies in wait. In short, we are witnessing a cyclic process of creating spaces of indistinction: discipline followed by control, followed by terror, and then the return of discipline as the reversed panopticon.

Escape

On the one hand, modern life is more and more characterized by connectionism, facilitated by the technologies of mobility. But on the other, we have a growing social distance between mobile individuals and groups 'camping' without the 'social' bond in the form of organic or mechanic solidarity in classical sociological sense. To end with, we want to reflect upon this paradoxical relationship between increasing mobility and the subsumption under the logic of the camp, or, between quantitative and qualitative generalization of the camp. What is decisive in this respect is the fact that the camp no longer needs walls and borders, that it has, so to speak, become liquid.

Historically, civilization or the 'city' has been imagined as a disciplinary space entrenched by 'walls', originating in an act of inclusion/exclusion. Entrenchment establishes a clean-cut distinction between insiders and outsiders, between the subjects and the outlaws. The 'outside' is distinct from the city, but it becomes so primarily through a sovereign act dividing the urban from the non-urban. The question is whether this idea is still adequate to describe the contemporary city characterized by cross-border flows in multiple directions. As we argued, today, disciplinary enclosure seems to be only one among three organizing principles of modernity. Contemporary life is also organized according to the principles of 'control', based on the regulation/coding of flows, and naked violence, 'terror'.

Discipline establishes sovereignty by creating zones of exception through confinement, a logic in which it proves difficult to sustain the difference between the master and the slave, between the free subject and the inmate, for they are all subjects of a bare life. Control reverses this, realizing the fantasy generated by the disciplinary society, that of breaking through the wall. Free movement becomes a necessity. However, this gesture brings with it an even more sinister, mobile power. Then, again, master turns into slave. 'Freedom' of movement (along strictly regulated flows) coexists with confinement and fixation; sheer movement leads to inertia. Thus the utopia generated by control society is that of an unregulated, anarchic flow.

Terror emerges in this sense as a utopia specific to control society, as its line of escape. It invests in insecurity, uncertainty and unsafety, turning citizens into hostages, to *homines sacri*. In the transpolitical war against terror, the state extends exception as a permanent state along a totalitarian line (of flight from terror). The fantasy generated by terror is, in other words, based on the promise of security, certainty and safety. Which brings us back to disciplinary entrenchment as protection against terror. Discipline opens the space for control, control for terror and terror for discipline.

Then, discipline, control and terror do not merely create zones of indistinction in a chronological order. What is interesting is how escape from discipline enables control, how from within control society terror emerges, and how the territorial logic of discipline resurfaces in the aftermath of terror. Discipline, control and terror co-exist, they contain within themselves elements of one another, and their topologies often overlap/clash, which is why it is difficult to 'distinguish' one form of power from another and why the space of power must be that of a zone of indistinction.

Clearly though, as one moves from one 'camp' to another, power becomes increasingly more difficult to escape. Thus, '[c]ompared with the approaching forms of control in open sites, we may come to see the harshest confinement as part of a wonderful happy past' (Deleuze 1995: 175). It is relatively easy to escape discipline, finding a line of flight; with the transpolitics of control, escape becomes difficult. 'There Is No Alternative' is the order-word of the control society, in which politics is foreclosed, and this provokes transpolitical violence, terror, as a suicidal line of flight. And when the logic of terror and state power merge, when power becomes obscene, there is nowhere to escape. It's over, that was it, curtains. But, then, is this not precisely the conclusion demanded by the transpolitics of security? Is there really no genuine possibility of escape?

All *dispositifs* of power 'are defined much more by what escapes them or by their impotence', insist Deleuze and Guattari (1987: 217). There is always a line of flight, but all lines of flight have their own dangers. *This* is, we think, extremely relevant to recall in the control society, which makes escape infinitely easy, and infinitely dangerous. A line of flight can always become re-stratified; a line of flight deterritorializes, but only in order to invent new territories, longing for safety: discipline. Or, it can turn into a line of death, into total de-stratification: terror. Terror is the result of an intense line of flight wanting self-destruction (see ibid.: 230).

Only if a line of flight can preserve its immanence, its creative potentials, can it remain truly 'nomadic' in the Deleuzian sense. In this respect the definition of nomadism and its relation to mobility are crucial. Nomadism is related to *deviation*, however slowly, from fixation or the linear movement of flows (ibid.: 371). It is by deviation and not necessarily by physical movement that the 'nomad' creates an*other* space. It is no surprise, therefore, that Deleuze, who is often criticized for 'romanticizing' mobility, is not so keen on travelling. 'You shouldn't move around too much, or you'll stifle becomings', he writes, adding with reference to Toynbee: 'the nomads are those who don't move on, they become nomads because they refuse to disappear' (Deleuze 1995: 138).

Acknowledgments

Parts of this chapter were previously published in *Space and Culture* 5(3): 290–307 (2004). Used with permission.

Part II

A TALE OF TWO CAMPS

4

FROM REFUGEE CAMPS TO GATED COMMUNITIES

We should not forget that the first camps were built in Europe as spaces controlling refugees, and that the succession of internment camps – concentration camps – extermination camps represents a perfectly real filiation.

(Agamben 2000: 22)

What the European Christian bourgeoisie could not truly forgive regarding Hitler was 'not the crime of genocide, but the crime of having applied to Europe the colonialist actions' (Bauman 2002: 109). The Nazis' real crime was to bring the *homo sacer* to Europe. It is in this respect significant that the first camps built in Europe were spaces to contain and control refugees (Agamben 2000: 22). Being 'human as such', the asylum seeker is an instantiation of the *homo sacer*. In this respect the confrontation with the refugee remains an acid test for politics, recurrently bringing into play the 'scandal of the human as such' (Dillon 1999: 114). Indeed, as Arendt pointed out long ago, the notion of human rights, which presupposes the existence of a 'human being as such', is drawn into a crisis whenever it is confronted with real people without qualities except, that is, that of being human: the refugees (Arendt 1973: 299).

As is well documented in cultural studies, the refugee conveys a grey zone of ambivalence as to his internality/externality *vis-à-vis* the society, and this provokes a fundamental undecidability. Indeed, our society seems unable to decide whether the asylum seeker is the true subject of human rights, which it invites everybody to accept as the most sacred of the sacred, or simply a criminal, a thief, who threatens 'us' with abusing 'our' welfare system. Further, like Simmel's stranger, the refugee is 'both inside and outside', close to and remote from the context in which he 'comes today and stays tomorrow' (Simmel 1971: 143). As such, the refugee is a constant threat to the image of order, signalling the horrifying impossibility of occupying one pure and distinct position. 'Building and keeping order means making friends and enemies, first and foremost, however, it means purging ambivalence' (Bauman 1992: 120). And in this process of ordering, the refugee is excluded from politics: whereas the refugee wants to 'participate without identification', he is nevertheless forced to 'identify without participation', a process that pushes the refugee further and further away from the political to the anthropological domain along the lines of today's dominant essentialist politics of difference (Sennett 1996: 193).

For all the merits of this image of thought, though, a crucial point needs to be clarified: sovereignty does not work merely according to the logic of a one-way exclusion. The refugee is excluded from the domain of the law but remains subject to it. Thus, the life of the refugee is strictly regulated and restricted by the law, which applies even to his or her private life (e.g. marriage), even in countries that champion democracy and human rights. The refugee is, in other words, radically internal to the processes of ordering; order not only seeks to 'purge' the ambivalence of the refugee but emerges and expands in relation to this ambivalence. The refugee is included while being excluded and excluded while being included; this zone of indistinction between inclusion and exclusion, in which the life of the refugee borders on the life of the *homo sacer*, is the very place of sovereignty.

The refugee as exception

The Netherlands, end of August 2002: a politician from the List of Pim Fortyn, Hilbrand Nawÿn, the former head of the Dutch Immigration Office and now the Minister for Asylum Affairs, put forward a proposal that, in spite of its populist triviality, reveals the core of contemporary migration debate. According to Nawÿn, those foreigners who already have acquired Dutch citizenship should, if they commit crimes, be denaturalized and denationalized so that as a sanction they could be sent back to their 'home' countries. Putting aside the question of what will happen to the Dutch citizens who commit crimes, moreover, this is an idea that is not new. Certainly, since World War I many European states have passed laws allowing denaturalization of their own citizens, and in this respect one should not forget that '[o]ne of the few rules the Nazis constantly obeyed throughout the course of the "final solution" was that Jews and Gypsies could be sent to extermination camps only having been fully denaturalized' (Agamben 1998: 18, 22). What is equally notable in Nawÿn's gesture is its endeavour to establish a sovereign exception through suspending the law and abandoning the citizen.

Foucault, and later Deleuze and Guattari, observed that the foundation of sovereignty is normalizing or capturing the outside. 'The law of the State is . . . that of interior and exterior. The State is sovereignty. But sovereignty only reigns over what is capable of internalizing' (Deleuze and Guattari 1987: 360). Sovereign power internalizes excess through interdiction and constructs a social space, an interiority, which only 'lines of flight' can 'break through'. That is, in this perspective, the refugee represents the nomadic excess that the state seeks to capture and normalize through panoptic confinement, e.g. in refugee camps. However, Agamben gives a significant twist to such an analysis, complementing it with the concept of 'indistinction'. The launching of the 'state of exception' plays a crucial role in this respect.

As we mentioned in Chapter 1, the origin of sovereignty is the state of exception, the ban: the *aban*donment of subjects to a condition of bare life, stripping them of their political rights. Nawÿn wants to abandon the 'criminal' citizens with foreign origins to: what? It is the answer to this question that is tricky in our context because the ban involves not a simple exclusion but an inclusion by exclusion in the sense that what is excluded or abandoned at the margins of politics, of the *polis*, maintains its relation to the law as its suspension. Nawÿn's secret appeal is thus to a sovereignty that recognizes the refugee as its genuine subject. The refugee is abandoned only to be included in the domain of power.

Thus, one must not be deceived here by the fact that Nawÿn wants to send the refugee 'home'. The ban is a kind of relation with no positive content, 'the simple form of relation with the nonrelational' (Agamben 1998: 29). In this sense the refugee is a 'limit concept'; 'the law applies to him in no longer applying, and holds him in its ban in abandoning him outside itself' (ibid.: 23, 50). According to the diagram of sovereign exception, power emerges not as an expression of the social bond but as an un-bonding; 'the sovereign tie is in truth only an untying' (ibid.: 90). The social bond itself has the form of exception, or un-bonding, in which an exclusionary inclusion politicizes the subject, in our case the refugee. Thus, every time the refugee is 'excluded', we should be looking for the inclusive gesture that follows it, which is part and parcel of the social bond between 'us' and 'them'. Because untying is not merely exclusion and because it at once excludes the bare life of the refugee as its outside and captures it within the realm of the law, the sovereign decision is a kind of localization that does not distinguish between inside and outside 'but instead traces a threshold (the state of exception) between the two' (ibid.: 19). The refugee inhabits this zone of indistinction.

Enter the camp Woomera, the infamous and now closed detention centre in Australia. A detainee said: 'When we came first to Woomera, we didn't believe we were in Australia . . . Because the things that happened – they wouldn't happen in Australia. It must be another country' (quoted in Campbell 2002: 26). 'Woomera *is* another country', Campbell wrote, commenting on his interviewee's utterance. However, the point is rather that Woomera, established and run by Australian authorities alone, was effectively a frustrating zone of indistinction between inside (law) and outside (unlaw), a space in which the link between localization and order breaks down, a space that can materialize only when exception becomes the rule. It is the location of the unlaw within law in the form of an exception that turned Woomera into an unbounded space. Hence the confusion whether it was inside or outside Australia. Needless to say, the paradox here consists of sovereign power being both inside and outside the juridical order at the same time.

When the frustrating experience of indistinction abounds in open-ended incarceration, the asylum seekers became desperate in Woomera, which the staff called a 'war zone', and collapsed in hopeless acts of protest (e.g. hunger strikes, slashing themselves, hanging themselves from the razor wire, swallowing shampoo and sleeping pill cocktails, or digging their own graves . . .). Fifty of them broke out of the camp in 2002; most were captured: 'but they are unlikely to be prosecuted or jailed – if they were, they would have visiting rights and a definite length of imprisonment, luxuries denied them as asylum seekers inside Woomera' (ibid.: 27). The detainees were legally abandoned outside the legal system through exceptional practices that held them under their ban. The detention centre, *per se*, is a 'hybrid' in which the distinction between the legality and illegality of what happens in it does not make sense. Its essence is the materialization of the state of exception, constituting a space topologically different from that of mere enclosure, e.g. a prison, for it at once belongs to the inside and the outside of the normal order (Agamben 1998: 169). It is the reason why the inmates of Woomera could find the panopticon luxurious compared to their camp. After all, panopticon was 'a model of mutual involvement and confrontation' that required the constant mutual engagement of power holders and those subject to power (Bauman 2000: 10). The power based on abandonment refers, in contrast, to a model of disengagement; it is, to use Bigo's concept, a 'ban-opticon' in the sense that it seeks proactive control and risk management rather than normalizing (Bigo 2002: 82).

Denmark, Hanstholm Refugee Center, July 2002. In the centre, the asylum seekers have some rather simple daily responsibilities, e.g. cleaning their own rooms and the immediate environs, cooking, etc., and legally they are not required to participate in other activities. However, the Municipality of Hanstholm illegally stopped paying the support payments, which the refugees are legally entitled to, as a sanction when some refugees refused to participate in Danish language classes. Consequently, the asylum seekers lodged a complaint, and when the media became involved, the Danish Parliament asked Bertel Haarder, the Minister of Refugees, Immigrants and Integration, to explain the juridical practice in the field. Haarder's answer was not insignificant. He writes that after the incident in Hanstholm, the Danish Home Office (Udlændingestyrelsen) 'clarified' for the Municipality of Hanstholm that the responsibilities of the refugees do not include participation in language classes, and thus municipalities cannot legally take action in such cases. Haarder goes on to point out that after this clarification the Municipality of Hanstholm has paid back the support payments to the refugees in question. Thus, ignorance of the law is turned to serve as an excuse for the illegal actions of the municipality! There is more to it, however, for at this point Haarder gives to the unfolding of the event an interesting twist:

> I can add that the government has established a working group with
> the aim of strengthening the initiatives of activation and education in

asylum centers. Among other things the working group aims at evaluating the valid rules in this field . . . In my opinion the system of support payment and its refusal should from now on work smoothly. I have therefore asked the working group to consider more closely whether in future the operators [of the asylum centers] should be able to take decisions on refusing to make support payments to refugees without any involvement of the Home Office.

(Haarder 2002)

Instead of taking action against the illegal practice, the minister finds it more appropriate to change the law. This move pushes the asylum centres into the territory of vigilantism; a paradoxical territory that can be defined neither as a situation of fact nor as a situation of right. This is 'the ultimate meaning of the paradox that Schmitt formulates when he writes that the sovereign decision "proves itself not to need law to create the law"' (Agamben 1998: 19). Power is beyond the law.

The idea of exception permeates every aspect of refugee life. For instance, recently, it was revealed that the French company, Sodexho, running a new detention centre near Heathrow airport in the UK, is supported by the British government in paying refugees 34p an hour for cleaning and cooking, less than one-tenth of the British minimum wage. This procedure was made possible by the logic of exception: that 'the legal obligation to pay the minimum wage has been waived for UK Detention Services' (Bright 2001). This suggestion is reminiscent of forced labour camps and their economy of exception, i.e. 'slave labour' schemes and undoubtedly would contribute to the creation of an underclass of denizens.

And last but not least, the exception lasts for a very long time. Even when the asylum seeker is successful in crossing the indiscriminating barrier of 'refuse and return' policies and attains the status of refugee, starting to lead a 'normal life', his life remains subject to exceptions. Here is another example, from Danish psychiatry. Facts: a middle-aged man from the Middle East comes to Denmark with his two eldest children of 5 and 7 years of age, and gets asylum. His wife and the youngest child are left in the home country. He manages life in Denmark relatively well, finds a job, and can take care of his children. He gets his wife to Denmark after a long waiting time, meanwhile repressing, according to the psychologist we interviewed, the fact that his marriage had been problematical in the past. At this stage he starts showing symptoms of depression, anxiety and apathy, although it was unclear to the psychologist whether these were signs of post-traumatic stress disorder following war, violence and seeking refuge; he became increasingly paranoid, which is a usual symptom of traumatic experiences. When the wife arrives, the marriage shatters. All his hopes had been invested in re-establishing the marriage, and when this is not realized, he cannot bear the frustration, becomes aggressive, threatening and sometimes violent. He is taken to the court for violence. They get a divorce. The wife moves out with the three children and he is forbidden to contact his ex-wife and children. Consequently, for some years he totally loses contact with his children, gets more and more lonely, and increasingly psychotic, with hallucinations he experiences as demons which will punish him for his wrongs – he blames himself for losing contact with his children.

'Normally', that is, if this were a Danish family with 'problems', the psychologist notes, 'the authorities would try to make sure that there are arrangements so that the father and the children can keep in touch.' In this case, however, the authorities did literally nothing to this end. The man was threatened with compulsory internment each time he attempted to contact his children. In other words, normal rules, procedures and ethical considerations were suspended. Instead, the authorities have treated the man as automatically being at fault. Indeed, our interviewee suggests that the man came to function as an easy target for the latent aggression and anxiety, which the public employees involved in this case and the authorities as such bear in relation to the 'evil, inhuman, and violent, other': the immigrants in Denmark. As basic norms are thrown into relief (e.g. as a psychiatrist one is supposed to believe in what the patient says as long as the opposite has not been proven) and in this case an opposite procedure emerged. The patient was hit twice: as mentally ill and as 'ethnically different'. It is significant that the psychiatrists did not try to establish the necessary documents which may contribute to the diagnosis (e.g. the documents from the refugee centre could have counted in the direction of post-traumatic pain). Such is life as an 'exceptional' figure even when you come out of the asylum centre. The interval between diagnosis and the juridical consequences delimits an extratemporal and extraterritorial threshold in which the refugee is separated from normal scientific/juridical process and abandoned to an extreme misfortune, that of the *homo sacer*.

The refugee as *homo sacer*

Having left behind his origin and been stripped of his former identities, the refugee is socially a 'zombie' whose spectral past survives in a world in which his symbolic capital does not count, and whose present takes place in a condition of 'social nakedness' characterized by the lack of social definition, rights and responsibilities (Bauman 2002: 116). Or, a werewolf: neither a beast nor a man, an outlaw that can be exposed to violence without facing legal sanctions (Agamben 1998: 104–5). 'They are dealing with us as animals, not as human beings', said the detainee in Woomera (quoted in Campbell 2002: 26). In the detention centre the human and the inhuman enter into a biopolitical zone of indistinction, and the detainees can be subjected to all sorts of physical and symbolic violence without legal consequences. Banned and excluded from the city, the werewolf is forced to survive in the forest. Banned and excluded from society, the detainee is forced to survive in an open-ended period of

incarceration, sealed off by barbed wire and surveillance cameras. It is important, however, to bear in mind that this 'ban-opticon' does not exist outside
society but is radically internal to it, just as the 'state of nature' does not exist
prior to 'civilization' but is established through the ban.

Clinging to trains, attempting to cross the Channel in boats, hiding among
the refrigerated vegetables in long-distance lorries, and all that to become the
'bandit' against whom 'citizens' unite without feeling any political or moral
obligation. One of the globally relevant features of the contemporary discourse
is, indeed, the criminalization of the asylum seeker. The contemporary discourse of immigration, which creates the asylum seeker as an 'outsider inside',
is based on the sovereign myth and its body politic that conceives of the state
as a container, as a 'body endangered by migrants' who 'penetrate' its borders
(Bigo 2002: 68–9). It is the very equation of the bandit and the refugee that
makes it possible to locate the refugee in a zone of indistinction, in which
the refugee is excluded from the domain of ethical responsibility and exposed
to violence both from civil society and the state without legal consequences.
The bandit/refugee steals our wealth and enjoys it in excessive ways, all at the
expense of our own enjoyment, our own wealth. Thus, the then Home Secretary,
David Blunkett, could time after time describe asylum seekers as 'swamping'
British medical services and schools (quoted in White and Travis 2002). In a
similar spirit, the Danish Prime Minister Anders Fogh Rasmussen proposed
that the 'newcomers' must wait seven years before they can access the Danish
welfare system: 'That will be a way to protect our welfare' (quoted in Osborn
2001). That is, the refugee is the 'other' who threatens 'our' wealth, promising
no more than uncertainty, insecurity and danger. A clever ascription, it is
through this figure – the 'theft of enjoyment' – that the other is othered. 'This
would be the most general formula of the modern racism we are witnessing
today: a hatred of the particular way the Other enjoys . . . the Other as he who
essentially steals my own enjoyment' (Jacques-Alain Miller, quoted in Žižek
1993: 203). As a bandit, the refugee is not simply excluded from the law in
an indifferent manner but rather abandoned by it, that is, rendered vulnerable
on a threshold in which life and law, outside and inside, become indistinct.
It is in this sense difficult to decide whether the refugee is inside or outside;
he is at once at the mercy of the juridical context in which he seeks asylum and
is exposed to any kind of (cultural, social, religious, political, economic) threat
and violence.

As *homo sacer*, the asylum seeker is the political figure *par excellence*, for 'from
the point of view of sovereignty only bare life is authentically political'
(Agamben 1998: 106). Breaking the continuity between man and citizen, as
homo sacer, the refugee brings to light the real condition of sovereignty and the
contradictory character of the attempts by committees and organizations dealing with the refugee's 'human rights', which insist that their actions are only
humanitarian and not political. Yet this post-political stance that represents
itself outside and above politics is attainable only when, and paradoxically, the

refugee is considered as *homo sacer*, as a referent of biopolitics. This separation between politics and humanitarianism, or between the rights of the citizen and the rights of man, thus signals 'a secret solidarity' between humanitarianism and the powers it should fight (ibid.: 133). Humanitarian organizations need the same bare life which power feeds upon.

The concept of 'post-politics' is interesting regarding the point of interference and the inherent complementarity between humanitarianism and power. The dominant form of politics in the field of asylum is post-political in the sense that it disavows politics as such, which, however, takes place not by 'repressing' politics but by 'foreclosing' it (see Žižek 1999a: 198). What is precluded in the post-politics of asylum is the gesture of politicization proper. The metaphoric universalization of particular demands, which is 'not simply a part of the negotiation of interests but aims at something more': at the restructuring of the social space (ibid.: 204–8). Thus the aim of the politics of asylum is pre-emptive risk management, to make sure that nothing disturbing really happens, that 'politics' does not take place. Of course, there exists a cacophony of discourses in the context of asylum in contemporary societies, and of course this multiplicity of the discourses constitutes a struggle for hegemony. However, it seems that the discourse of securitization has articulated its rivals within its own horizon and has thus become a meta-discourse in the field of asylum (see Bigo 2002). It is small wonder that the politics of asylum is increasingly drawn into the orbit of the global post-politics of security (and fear). And significantly in this context, even the critical discourses that do not perceive the asylum seeker as an existential threat to national identity too often argue this 'by accepting the framing of a different domain of security beyond the political – one linked with emergency and exception. In doing so, they agree with the idea of an "exceptionalization," or a "beyond the law" politics' (ibid.: 73).

The refugee camp as a non-place

Most refugee spaces, both more 'open' ones (e.g. interchangeably called refugee camps, accommodation centres, or, reception centres) and 'closed', prison-like structures (e.g. detention centres) are instantiations of what Augé called 'non-places': they do not integrate other places, meanings, traditions and sacrificial, ritual moments but remain, due to a lack of characterization, non-symbolized and abstract spaces (Augé 1995: 82). As non-places, most refugee spaces are spaces of indistinction: 'a person entering the space of non-place is relieved of his usual determinants' (ibid.: 103):

> A world where people are born in the clinic and die in hospital, where transit points and temporary abodes are proliferating under luxurious and inhuman conditions (hotel chains and squats, holiday clubs and refugee camps, shantytowns threatened with demolition and doomed

to festering longevity); where a dense network of means of transport which are also inhabited spaces is developing; where the habitué of supermarkets, slot machines and credit card communicates wordlessly, through gestures, with an abstract, unmediated commerce; a world thus surrendered to solitary individuality, to the fleeting, the temporary and ephemeral, offers the anthropologist (and others) a new object.

(ibid.: 78)

This new global object Augé announces is the 'non-place', or, as we would rather call it, the camp. What they share in common are exterritoriality (they are 'in' but not 'of' the contexts in which they are located exceptionally), disposability of meanings, fluidity of identities and the permanency of transience, that is, the constitutive tendencies of 'liquid modernity' (see Bauman 2002: 113). What is the mechanism, then, behind the formation of such spaces?

Refugee camps are often located outside cities, in suburbia or in rural areas, as a rule, in demonstratively peripheral sites, the contemporary strategy behind which is the dispersal of the asylum seekers. As a Home Office (2002) press release tells, for instance, the new British asylum accommodation centres are all planned on former military sites in rural areas isolated from the amenities and cultural facilities concentrated in cities. Needless to say, because it will be difficult for asylum seekers to afford transport on their small support payments, it is most likely that they will spend most of their time confined to the centres, and, coupled with the size of each centre (750 places each), this may become a 'recipe for frustration and tension within the centres and between asylum seekers and the existing local communities' (Cambridgeshire Against Refugee Detention 2002: 2). Basic to the strategy of dispersal are economic considerations (e.g. cheaper land) and social concerns against the formation of 'refugee ghettos' in metropolitan and urban centres. However, the practice of dispersal itself leads to ghetto formations in isolated locations. In such locations they come to look like islands, or, like 'neutral cities' (Sennett 1990: 170), characterized by a sterilized, mono-functional enclosure: contact with the outer world is physically minimized behind the fences, which yield no permission to touch the outer world, resulting in the complete isolation of the refugee from public life. In contemporary politics of asylum, the refugee invokes this fear and the related feeling of uncertainty, and the refugee camps are perfect materializations of a 'fear of touching' made obvious by their very architectural design, their anti-urban ideal and their idealization of the sterile as an image of order. Indeed, the refugee camp can be considered as, to use Sennett's apt metaphor, an 'urban condom' (Sennett 1994: 228).

Not surprisingly, therefore, the strategies of dispersion directly aim at *not* integrating asylum seekers, neither in the local context, labour market, nor in schools, keeping them in limbo in sites of confinement until they acquire the status of refugee, which clarifies whether they are going to be sent 'home' or not. Indeed, from the systemic point of view, refugees embody those people who are excluded from several function systems at once and thus whose lives are reduced to bare life; in Luhmann's words: 'bodies which have to survive somehow on their own, and not so much as a kind of parts, or kind of persons used for whatever purpose in function systems' (1994: 4). Thus, the most basic four characteristics of camp life consists of: living on small amounts of support payments or even food vouchers with no cash allowance, which pushes the asylum seeker out of the normal functioning of the economic system; to be prevented from finding paid work; living according to the government's choice of residency; and minimum geographical mobility.

In short, the life of the asylum seeker is marked by an extreme isolation; not only physically but also socio-economically and culturally. His social contacts often depend on the good will of (especially the voluntary) staff in the camps. An important factor in this context is of course the barrier of language, reducing the asylum seeker's capacity to participate in civic activities. Further, there is the economic barrier: transportation to the closest cities, for instance, as all other civic activities, costs more than the asylum seeker can afford, which reduces their mobility to short-distance movements. For those who do not have their own means, there is no possibility of work except in the 'black' economy, which, apart from the inequalities related to it and difficulties of finding it in isolated or 'dispersed' sites, can result in the involved asylum seeker being sent from the refugee centre to the detention centre. The only possibility for the asylum seeker to avoid forced residency in a refugee centre, a possibility that emerges only in some countries once the reception period is over, is to apply for permission to reside outside the centres. In Sweden, the UK, France and the Netherlands, for instance, asylum seekers are entitled to keep a minimum amount of their support payments if they can find a residence outside the camps themselves, and they can use 'activation' and educational offers. In countries such as Denmark and Austria they lose their rights to receive support payments, to participate in activation schemes and to use the health system, if they choose not to live in the camps. Germany is even more restrictive: here, refugees have to live in the refugee camps chosen for them by the authorities, and have to ask for written permission when they wish to travel more than a few kilometres away from the centres (ECRE 2002: 33). One step further is Australia, where all asylum seekers are detained.

As mobility today is increasingly becoming a determining factor of social change and social stratification, and as the distinction between *Gesellschaft* and *Gemeinschaft* consequently tends to be displaced onto a new distinction between the mobile and the sedentary (see Bauman 2000), the asylum seeker is held in a condition of immobility. Distances disappear and the globe shrinks for the mobile, but, as Bhabha says, 'for the displaced or the dispossessed, the migrant or the refugee, no distance is more awesome then the few feet across borders' (quoted in Graham and Marvin 2001: 219). Across the borders, immobility persists, not only in the geographical sense but also in terms of sociality and the objects that hold sociality together. The regulation of the support payments and residencies, for instance, fix refugees geographically in a world of flows, the paradox being that, whereas network mobility is reshaping the relationship between physical and social proximity today, the refugees' lives remain indexed to an image of sociality that demands both physical and social proximity.

It is significant in this context that the refugee camps are an integral part, a product and manifestation of processes of contemporary globalization as are Augé's non-places. In terms of global mobility, refugee non-places have in common several significant characteristics. First, they are places in which exception becomes the rule. Thus, the German *Durchgangslager* or *Aufgangslager*, for instance, can grant admittance or rejection to refugees without the intervention of the ordinary citizenship rights. Second, and akin to the mobile character of the refugee identity itself, such spaces are in general close to central transportation nodes and borders and thus directly involve mobility in their regulatory matrix (Verstrate 2001). Thus, the police can immediately send refugees back, transportation companies are obliged to check if people have visas, and so on. It is therefore not a coincidence that refugee camps mirror the contemporary technologies of *speed* (that make it possible to get rid of the refugee as soon as possible), *escape* (from political publicity) and *passivity* (neutralizing the refugee as stranger), all of which are concepts Sennett (1994) used in characterizing modern urban design. And third, such places are organized around a 'pre-emptive' logic of risk management, with the police seeking to operate *before* potential problems occur, e.g. before the refugees enter the country. The aim is, in a sense, to control 'eventualities' before the 'event' takes place (Lyon 2001: 54), turning the 'exclusion' of the refugee into a pre-emptive action.

However, although the refugee is seen as a sign of displacement, and although his routes are densely controlled by infrastructures of mobility, his own life in the camp can only be described as immobility. The camp is officially a transitory, so to say, an 'exceptional' space, in which the refugee is supposed to spend only a limited amount of time. Yet, everywhere the refugee camp has today become a 'permanent' location and the transient condition of the refugee extends indefinitely, becoming an irrevocable and permanent situation, freezing into non-negotiable, rigid structures:

> Refugee camps boast a new quality: a 'frozen transience', an on-going, lasting state of temporariness, a duration patched together of moments, none of which is lived through as an element of, and a contribution to, perpetuity. For the inmates of a refugee camp, the prospect of long-term sequels and consequences is not part of the experience. The inmates of refugee camps live, literally, from day to day — and the contents of life are unaffected by the knowledge that days combine into months and years. As in the prisons and

'hyper-ghettos' scrutinized by Loïc Wacquant [2001], camped refugees 'learn to live, or rather survive [(sur)vivre] from day to day in the immediacy of the moment, bathing in . . . the despair brewing inside the walls'.

(Bauman 2002: 114–15)

Among the different camps dealing with asylum seekers, the detention centres are the most rigid. Asylum seekers are sent to detention centres in three different situations. First, for clarification of their identities and travel routes but especially when asylum applications are refused. In French international airports, for example, this is the case 'during the four days foreigners may be kept in the zone d'attente before the intervention of French judicial authorities' (Agamben 2000: 42). Second, Australia, for instance, has a policy of mandatory detention and, assuming that asylum seekers are all 'bogus' until proven genuine, that is, until they 'deserve' the status refugee, detains every asylum seeker, a system also called the 'Pacific Solution'. And third, the refugees who have committed crimes (e.g. by working in the 'black' economy, or by being violent or by threatening the camp staff) can be 'imprisoned' until their applications are processed. It is significant that in most Western countries theft of around £50 by an asylum seeker can result in detention. And the interpretation of what counts as 'threatening' behaviour often depends on the personal and arbitrary tolerance threshold of the staff. Many refugee centres operate with 'zero-tolerance' policies so that asylum seekers can be sent to detention centres even for relatively small crimes.

In general, the atmosphere of the detention centre is characterized by latent threats of violence, which at times are actualized in concrete violence and even cause deaths, while the constant presence of the police strengthens the image of it as a prison. As a consequence, the violations of human rights abound. By way of example, 'the detainee was handcuffed, shackled, placed in a windowless room for six days, denied medical treatment and held in detention for more than twelve months in 1996 and 1997' (Human Rights and Equal Opportunity Commission 2002). Indefinite imprisonment, not being told of one's rights, delays in responses to requests for legal assistance, being held in isolation from other parts of the detention centre, the use of force, and poor general conditions regarding food, medical services, privacy, sleeping arrangements, the level of personal security, and education and recreation facilities: these are the most common characteristics of life in most detention centres all over the world.

What is most significant in this respect is the increased use of forced detention. When Blair's government came to power in 1997, around 700 people were imprisoned in detention centres at any one time in the UK; the figure is today around 1,800; and the government promises to increase the numbers to 4,000 with the new detention centres called 'removals centres'. The government claims that these numbers cover:

'failed' asylum seekers who will be held for a few days prior to deportation. On past experience this seems unlikely – according to recent government statistics only 4% of detainees were awaiting imminent removal action, with some 60% not even having received an initial decision on their asylum applications, and most of the rest awaiting the results of appeals – and many detainees have been held for months or even years.

> (Cambridgeshire Against Refugee Detention 2002: 5)

Denmark: *Sandholmlejren*, or, the camp Sandholm. In number 17 two women reside: N. Jamshidi and H. Elmess, respectively from Iran and Lebanon. They are there not because they have committed crimes but because their asylum applications are rejected and they are waiting to be sent home. Jamshidi says she is 'going crazy from sitting here' – she is afraid of going back and eventually risking her life in a country, from which she has escaped. And the same frustration again:

> I feel nothing any more. No hope. No hunger. I just want some peace. Formerly I cried all the time, I missed my freedom, I missed my children, now I am just unconcerned . . . Eating time, shout the personnel at 12. Eating time, they shout again at 17. At 22 we go to bed. It is the same every single day. I can just as well go back to Lebanon and get killed. Inside I am already dead. . . . I am nothing.
>
> (our interview)

Is it, one wonders, so difficult for the authorities to recognize *homo sacer* here? The European Council Torture Committee visited the camp Sandholm in 2002 and expressed its concern regarding people held in the camp without trial, which is in conflict with the UN's principles of human rights. The Danish authorities explained the situation by emphasizing that the problem is one of capacity, adding that they 'predict' that 'tightening the immigration rules will in future deter many foreigners from coming to Denmark' so that this problem will be solved by itself (quotes are from Sørensen 2002, our translation).

Gated communities

Enter Haverleij: a stable, harmonic, safe and securitized gated community within the municipality of s'Hertogenbosch in the Netherlands. Haverleij literally constitutes an island connected to the mainland only by a bridge. It is a perfect defensible space, literally a fortress. As it is advertised, one can live there 'like a prince' (Larsen 2003). What is marketed in Haverleij is a kind of exclusive safety that can guarantee freedom from the world of (unwanted) strangers and as such Haverleij is just another materialization of the obsession with security, with the 'zeitgeist of urban restructuring' that results in the increased 'militarization' of contemporary city life (Davis 1990: 223, 232).

Whereas in the disciplinary era exception was enclosed inside the panopticon, we are now witnessing the reversal of this situation. The becoming-rule of the exception and the related process of spatial fortification have come to include today even the classical spaces of disciplinary enclosure. Rose's description of the way the old Victorian asylums have been transformed from panoptic sites to contemporary gated communities is a case in point:

> In a reversal that would be laughable if it were not so sad, these are no longer promoted as measures to secure the community outside from the inmate . . . High walls, closed circuit video cameras, security guards and the like can now be reframed and represented as measures that keep threat out rather than keep it in . . . Outside the walls, danger lurks, epitomized by the image of the madman.
>
> (Rose 1999: 248–9)

Herein we have the underlying fantasy of the contemporary urban elite: the city is an unpredictable and dangerous site of survival. Seen from Haverleij, the outside, the 'urban jungle', is a zone of indistinction where terror reigns and *homo sacer* engages in a struggle for survival. It is thus small wonder that Haverleij is keen on marketing a safety characteristic of those good old 'bygone times' (Larsen 2003; see also http://haverleij.nl).

This nostalgia is, of course, not specific to Haverleij but a general characteristic of the environments built by 'New Urbanism' or neo-traditionalism such as Disney's Celebration in Florida (see MacCannell 1999). Such spaces are designed as a genuine *Gesamtkunstwerk* – as fantasy spaces with detailed plans for all aspects of a perfect micro-society, including even the colour of curtains in the homes. Disney's Celebration seeks to re-create the image of the nineteenth-century American city: an imaginary space in which there did not exist antagonisms and safety did not constitute an urgent concern. According to the Disney Foundation, the target is to make the town 'feel like it has a tradition, even though it doesn't' (ibid.: 116). The nostalgia for safety is nowhere as evident as Celebration's logo:

> Celebration's copyrighted logo is pure kitsch: 'a little girl with a ponytail riding a bicycle past a picket fence under a spreading oak tree as her little dog chases along behind.' The entire ensemble is symptomatic of an unavowered desire to rewind the life of the people from the present back to 1945 and replay it as if it had not been lived under threat of nuclear annihilation. The Celebration logo reproduces the opening scene of the infamous 1950s civil defense film 'Duck and Cover': a boy happily riding his bike past picket fences in Anytown, US is hit by a nuclear blast. The phrase 'a sense of' – as in 'a sense of

security', 'a sense of community', 'a sense of family values', 'a sense of involvement', 'a sense of mutual interdependence' – forcefully reminds us of the impossibility of living 'as if' the last fifty years could be erased from collective memory. Yet this impossible desire is precisely the aim of neo-traditionalism.

(ibid.: 108)

In the nuclear age, fear reigned, making personal safety an urgent concern. Today, the fear of the atomic bomb is absent and instead the threat of terror is spreading throughout most Western societies. This is the background against which gated communities are emerging as secure but de-politicized enclaves (Rasmussen 2003: 5). To explain the strict regulation practised in Celebration, a board member says: 'I'm convinced these controls are actually liberating to people. It makes them feel their investment is safe' (MacCannell 1999: 112). However, this 'liberation', or the illusion of safety, comes with a high price. The perceived pressures and threats from the outside are translated into a demand for conformity on the inside. Those who complain about the practice of management are quickly labelled the 'Negatives' and are encouraged by the Disney Concern to leave (ibid.). This 'fifth column', the vocal 'Negatives', are even offered a release from their contracts on the condition that an agreement is signed in which they promise 'never to reveal their reasons for leaving Celebration' (ibid.: 113).

In Celebration nothing accidental is allowed to happen; concomitantly, the environment is standardized as much as possible. Its car dependency prevents accidental meetings on the street, and the homes are designed in a panoptic style (ibid.: 113–14). Moving into Celebration one buys not only a house but a lifestyle: the inhabitants are not allowed to change the colour of their house, the way their gardens are organized, or hang other curtains, or to decide where to park their cars. In Celebration everything is private, even the town hall, and Disney Concern decides which political propaganda should be allowed in the city (Rasmussen 2003: 6). Indeed, Celebration is a kind of 'heterotopia' of purification, which forms 'another space, another real space, as perfect, as meticulous and well-arranged as ours is disordered, ill-conceived and in a sketchy state' (Foucault 1997: 356).

As such, Celebration epitomizes the contemporary dilemmas cities face, which are, as identified by Sennett: dilemmas of citizenship, of the public realm and of attachment to the city (see Sennett 2000: 27). Marketing not only property but also 'access' to a securitized lifestyle, most gated communities have literally no public spaces; indeed, they are spaces in which some basic citizenship rights such as freedom of movement are denied outright (see Rifkin 2000: 114–33). Threatening the idea of the common good and violating the rights based on citizenship, such communities often 'act *in opposition* to the interests of the wider community' (Bell, quoted in Amin and Thrift 2002: 139). In contrast to the idea of the *polis*, that there is something in common shared by the citizens, gated communities are part and parcel of a process of privatization, 'which in turn is linked to a growing skepticism about government's ability to police streets, stabilize neighborhoods and property values, and generally look after the public realm' (Dillon 1994: 11). Consequently, the emerging 'vigilantopolis' (Davis 1999: 391) resembles a juridical zone of indistinction which is both inside and outside the city. It is telling in this context that some of them deliberately assert the view that 'civilians can deal with crime more easily because we are not hampered by constitutional restrictions like the police. We can slam and jam' (E. Michael, quoted in ibid.: 391). Indeed, gated communities constitute 'a gang way of looking at life, the institutionalization of turf. And if it goes on indefinitely, and gets intensified, it practically means the end of civilization' (Jane Jacobs, quoted in Dillon 1994: 12).

With their technologies of pre-emptive social filtering, inward-looking architectural design, biased premium infrastructure links (e.g. special transportation and virtual networks excluding others) and privatized governance regimes, gated communities constitute a new type of localization essentially different from what is traditionally understood by 'city'; they demonstrate, rather, how the 'city' is 'splintered' today (see Graham and Marvin 2001). What characterizes this process of 'splintering' is, first, the increasing 'unbundling' or fragmentation of the standardized welfare state infrastructures of the Fordist era through the processes of privatization and, second, the selective 're-bundling' of the fragments through advanced premium networked infrastructures, a context in which mobility is an essential concept:

> Rush hour. Roads choked, cars packed bumper to bumper. São Paulo's motorists are going nowhere fast. . . . But high above them, the city's elite swoop through the skies in helicopters, impervious to the anarchy unfolding beneath them. Despite the costs involved, helicopter taxis are fast becoming one of the most popular means of getting around Brazil's most populous city.
>
> (Wheatley 2001: 50)

Indeed, with helicopters constituting a sort of smooth space elevated above the street level, São Paulo reminds us of *Bladerunner*'s LA. The helicopter is a powerful object that translates wealth and mobility into each other and thus it is increasingly employed by the urban elite to commute between enclaves of work and residence (see Graham and Marvin 2001: 283). In effect, helipads are increasingly in-built standard features of São Paulo's gated communities to hinder the intrusion of territory into their non-places. This escape from the constraints of place is experienced as freedom (Augé 1995: 116). The helicopter can go as far as the securitized enclaves, abandoning the in-between places whenever it is necessary. Hence the relationship between the gated communities and the ('rest' of the) city becomes one of 'indifference':

'The new global elite . . . avoids the urban political realm. It wants to operate in the city, but not rule it; it composes a regime of power without responsibility' (Sennett 2000: 27). The waste product of this extra-territoriality provided by technologies of mobility that can globally connect the securitized enclaves is the dis-connection of the abandoned spaces (see Bauman 2003).

The rebundled or reordered fragments establish, however, not a 'city'; what we get instead is fragments: governmental districts, cultural centres, office parks, gated communities, ghettos, etc., and hybrids such as themed shopping malls, the airport retail area, etc. The unbundled fragments producing an incoherent overall structure:

> can exist only when they are connected to the networked infra-structures that allow them to sustain their necessary or desired socioeconomic connections with spaces and people in more or less distanced elsewheres . . . Thus networked infrastructure becomes directly embroiled in the secessionary process, supporting the material construction of partitioned urban environments.
>
> (Graham and Marvin 2001: 228)

Our point is that the background against which this development can take place is the logic of exception. The solipsistic enclaves of the under-theorized splintering city are, in other words, camps. Moreover, there is a crucial link in this respect between desired and undesired camps, between voluntary and forced segregation:

> Refugee camps and the *nowherevilles* share the intended, in-built, pre-programmed transience. Both installations are conceived and planned as a hole in time as much as in space, a temporary suspension of territorial ascription and the time sequence. But the faces they show to their respective users/inmates sharply differ. The two kinds of extraterritoriality are sedimented, so to speak, on the opposite poles of globalization. The first offers transience as a facility chosen at will, the second makes it permanent and irrevocable, an ineluctable fate: a difference not unlike the one that separates the two outfits of secure permanence – the gated communities of the discriminating rich and the ghettos of the discriminated poor. And the causes of difference are also similar: closely guarded and watched entries and wide open exits on one side of the opposition, and largely indiscriminate entry but tightly sealed exits on the other. It is the locking of the exits in particular that perpetuates the state of transience without replacing it with permanence. In refugee camps time is suspended; it is time, but not history.
>
> (Bauman 2002: 114)

Aiming no longer at disciplinary confinement but also exclusion, our society seems to be producing two kinds of camps: those voluntary camps where the entry is blocked but the exit is free, and those where the entry is free but the exit is blocked. Some camps are designed to keep people (outcasts) 'out', some to keep people (inmates) 'in'. In both cases the principle is founded on the distribution of (the possibilities of) entry and exit. As such, contemporary camps function as two horizons that attract or repel the consumer-citizens/ denizens who do not know if they will go 'up' (gated community) or 'down' (detention centre). And there is nothing that automatically leads the majority from one extreme to the other, which materializes the *Unsicherheit*, or fragility, that pertains to 'liquid modernity' (Bauman 2002). This suspension, and the insecurities and uncertainties that follow, are part and parcel of the functioning of the camp in that it compels people to recognize power as potentiality (of abandonment). In this process there does not emerge a new, another, 'model' of the city on the basis of the idea of the camp in the sense that the 'existing' or real situations could be taken as divergences from or 'exceptions' to the model.

The becoming-rule of exception basically refers to a kind of spatiality suspended in-between 'exclusion' and 'inclusion'. As Bauman reminds us in this context, occupying such indistinct zones historically has been the privilege of pariah groups such as *les malheureux* of the eighteenth century, *les misérables* of the nineteenth century and now *the refugees* (2003: 129–30). Indeed, the exclusionary aspects of the camp can be likened to the expulsion of the poor in early modern Europe where the poor were liable to expulsion outside their home parishes because relief was normally restricted to the local poor. The 'ghetto' of the poor, likewise, historically has condensed what the city is not, a negativity that emerges through the relational logic of dichotomic differences between order and disorder, normality and perversion, the law and unlaw (despotism), etc.

What the logic of exception can add to this is the awareness that the dichotomic difference should not be treated merely as a difference between elements within the same symbolic economy. Rather, the 'other', e.g. the ghetto, signifies what is prior to difference (see Grosrichard 1998). The difference that matters here is that of between difference and the lack of difference. As such the 'ghetto' is beyond the symbolic order: constituting a 'fantasy space' in the Lacanian sense; it resembles a kind of 'state of nature'. Not an empirical space but a space constructed through the logic of exception. Yet, its stuff is material, e.g. signifiers, buildings, etc., and as such the fantasy space belongs to the symbolic register (cf. Lacan 1977: 146–78). In other words, fantasy has a spectral structure in which reality and fantasy become indistinct categories through a discursive representation of a space beyond the symbolic.

What can be said about the 'end of the city' in this context? As mentioned before, historically the city has been imagined as an enclosed space surrounded by 'walls' demarcating the limits of inclusion and exclusion (Virilio 1997). Enclosure establishes a distinction between the *polis* and (the state of) nature. Yet the transition from nature (the real) to the *polis* (the symbolic) is not clean-cut and it is here we must look for the ideological fantasies that sustain urban reality: in fact 'the circle of reality can be closed only by means of an uncanny spectral supplement' (Žižek 1994: 21). Then, urban reality presents itself via its failed symbolization and it can never be a Whole. It is precisely this lack that is foreclosed through urban fantasies based on the reduction of exception to an anomaly, and it is precisely through these fantasies that the Real returns in the form of an abject or object of desire (camp as the detention centre or the gated community), constructing a scheme in which the lack in the urban 'reality' (the symbolic order) can be filled and the city can be experienced as an imaginary whole with fixed coordinates.

The end of the city

In what sense, then, does the camp signal the 'end' of the city? The first answer to this question is that the city has never existed as a whole; it has always been held together by the exception. The idea of an 'ordered' city is thus fundamentally nostalgic, the very symptom of which is the camp. The fantasy created thus is: if the hole (the camp) did not exist, the city would have been a whole. The camp in this sense is the 'contingent' space that hinders the urban order that would have been if, that is, the camp did not exist. What this fantasy hides is of course that the camp is a 'necessary' effect of existing power relations. And precisely as such, the camp participates actively in the construction of the contemporary urban reality. Paradoxically, thus, the camp is what holds the city together: thanks to it, one can fantasize a non-antagonistic city! Thus, a radical position against the idea of the camp as an anomaly is indeed to say that the camp does not exist: the city is always already antagonistic; it is an antagonism.

This is not the whole story, though. Inasmuch as politics is the ability to debate and the capability to change the frames of the political debates and struggle on the basis of conflict, the camp means that power can escape the agora, that there is an essential link between increasing mobility and the splintering city. Seen from the perspective of mobility, the city is no longer founded on the inside–outside divide (see Chapter 3). The world of 'camping' is a world, in which power is nomadic. Post-panoptic power is able to 'travel light', finds engagement neither necessary nor desirable, and speed is fast becoming the paramount factor of stratification and domination (Bauman 2000: 150–1). If 'hit and run' is the logic that makes people obey today, to be in the right camp means to be in a position to run at short notice. Political conflict requires time and engagement, that is, dialogue; yet nomadic power can bypass the agora. Power moves to the 'space of flows'; politics, the agora, remains incessantly local (Castells 1996). Thus, although thirty years ago he defended 'disorder' against panoptic enclosures of the 'ordered' city in *The Uses of Disorder*, Sennett can argue today that we have to revise our 'fear of discipline', that the contemporary city also needs 'disciplinary spaces' – 'spaces of democracy' (1999: 278). The reason why an urban anarchist starts talking about the necessity of disciplinary spaces, or about the necessity of, yes, order, is of course mobility, or rather, its power of transcending politics. Speed enables power to escape the agora, the political space, in which private fears are translated into 'political' issues (Bauman 1999: 87).

To the extent that this is the case, the mobile elite seems to be elevated above the existing modes of dispute and conflict which Boltanski and Thévenot (1991) call 'regimes of justification' or 'cities' (*cités*). The inhabitants of the voluntary camps often need not and do not justify their actions with reference to a principle of equivalence and an assumption of common humanity. Rather, their behavioural principle seems to be non-equivalence and non-commitment to the 'common good', be it 'society', 'justice', or a locality. On the other hand, though, the camp means an increasing distance between knowledge and action; thus knowing more and more (about suffering in the camp Woomera, for instance) is in no way a guarantee for an ethical and political action (see Boltanski 1999).

Hardt and Negri make a radical attempt at a redefinition of the common good in *Empire*, which seeks to formulate an immanent critique of liquid capitalism. Within Empire, there emerge significant new questions regarding the common good. The public–private divide is crucial in this context in that capitalism historically relies on expropriation and privatization of what is common. In fact, in Empire, 'the public is dissolved, privatized, even as a concept' (Hardt and Negri 2000: 301). Yet, it is not necessary to weep over the destruction of this immanent relation between the public and the common by the transcendent power of private property; rather, one should focus on how the common operates today. Today the common good is a network phenomenon: markets are assuming the form of networks, ownership is progressively replaced by access, and the exchange of property is giving way to connections between servers and clients in networks (Rifkin 2000: 4–5). In the imperialist era, social wealth was transferred from 'outside' while sovereignty emerged 'inside'; in Empire, this divide is no longer operational, and the nature of both labour and accumulated wealth is changing. Thus 'common good' comes to involve social networks, communication, information and affective networks, while, at the same time, social labour is progressively becoming more immaterial, producing and reproducing all aspects of the social (Hardt and Negri 2000: 258).

This brings us to the question of resistance. If there is 'no return from the camps' to politics in the classical sense (see Agamben 1998: 188), how are resistance to and emancipation from the camp possible? In this context the concept of multitude is significant because if the naked body of the *homo sacer* is the negative limit of humanity and its passivity, its positive, and productive, limit is the multitude (see Hardt and Negri 2000: 366; see also Chapter 7). Having no spatial or temporal boundaries, Empire adopts biopolitics as its context and recognizes society as a realm of biopower (ibid.: 23–4, 195). Significantly in this respect, and against the idea that global capital increasingly escapes political regulation, Hardt and Negri argue that global capital can be global only because a global political-institutional apparatus supports it. 'Empire' is precisely the link between this apparatus and global capital, signifying at once the formal juridical sovereignty and the sovereignty of capital, its content. Empire is 'a machine for universal integration' (ibid.: 198) and it is in this horizontal world that the multitude stands in opposition to Empire without transcendent mediating institutions (ibid.: 393). As such, the multitude is the fundamental creative force that keeps Empire and capital afloat. It is the living material and immaterial labour that sets capital in motion, not the other way around; the 'final word on power is that *resistance comes first*' (Deleuze 1988: 89). In short, then, the concept of the multitude enables an approach that can incorporate indistinction and the naked body in a productive way. Let us, at this point, return to the protests that emerged at Woomera in April 2002. The detention centre was one of the central focuses of the 'Woomera 2002' protests and the protests draw on the logic of indistinction and the 'whatever', trying to build a 'body without organs', a multitude:

At brief moments at Woomera2002, our bodies came together with a consistent intensity to form bodies without organs and machines of struggle. At those points, dead ideology ceased to matter. Concepts always matter, but the illusion that we were going to convince people of ideas first, which would then lead to homogeneous action, was broken. The distinction between these things became untenable, and predictable rhetoric about 'us' 'locking up Ruddock' and 'freeing the refugees' evaporated as we enacted concepts together. Concepts like freedom. Concepts that were uncoded by liberal, or social democratic, or socialist, or whatever ideology.

(Desert Storm 2002)

However, 'resistance comes first' means that there is no simple dichotomy between power and resistance, or between one form of camp (e.g. detention centre) and another (e.g. the 'sanctuary' as 'a strategic reinscription of the sacred space of the church as a defence against the sovereign power of the state' – Walters 2002: 287). The problem of resistance against the camp is not a problem of building another camp but 'how to determine the enemy against which to rebel' (Hardt and Negri 2000: 211). Contemporary urbanism has transformed the processes of 'control' (in contrast to 'discipline') into a form of sociality through a discontinuous space of interacting and heterogeneous differences. In this process the camp seems to become a space of negotiation and the proliferation of heterogeneous insides and outsides.

Acknowledgments

Parts of this chapter were previously published in *Citizenship Studies* 8(1): 83–106 (2004). Used with permission. Available on www.tandf.co.uk/journals.

5

FROM RAPE WARS TO THE PARTY ZONE

Although it has been an integral aspect of warfare throughout history, organized rape is often regarded as an anomaly. There is also an obvious reason for this: in 'normal' war, one army confronts another in the conquest or defense of a territory; in contrast, war rape is based on an asymmetrical strategy through which the enemy soldier attacks a civilian woman (not another male soldier) and does so only indirectly with the aim of holding or taking a territory. As such, rape becomes a weapon of (asymmetric) war with the aim of inflicting traumas and destroying social bonds. War rape is a weapon of individual and social abjection, not 'just' a deplorable casualty of war provoked by soldiers' spontaneous frustrations. And the logic at work in this process, we would argue, is the logic of the camp.

Initially we focus on the process of abjection itself. We expand on two basic forms of abjection, pollution and shame/guilt, relating both to war rape. We then further differentiate between shame and guilt: whereas guilt can be verbalized and can perform as an element in a brotherhood of guilt, shame cannot, which is why it often results in traumas. War both creates and destroys communities (of the perpetrators and the victims respectively) through the transformation of the citizen into a naked body, and, in this sense, war is a continuation of biopolitics by other means. However, as we discussed earlier, camps come in twos. In this respect we ask what might be the mirror image of the negativity of war rape. With Foucault, one needs to detect power in its positivity; precisely, one is captured by power in the flight, at the moment when one imagines one is liberated. In this context, it is important to recall that rape or other transgressive acts fascinate because they are not allowed. What we want to add to this picture is a kind of hedonism enjoyed on a massive scale: the party tourism, which we analyse as a symmetrical zone of indistinction, in which voluntary reduction of the citizen to the hedonistic 'party animal' is experienced positively, or, as a liberation from the daily routine of the 'city' or civilization. Our point is to show that party tourism, one of the most romanticized and commercialized 'freedoms' of our time, functions according to the logic of exception.

War rape

Recently, rape was used strategically in Former Yugoslavia and in civil wars in Rwanda, Liberia, Uganda and Sudan. We focus here on Bosnia between 1992 and 1994. Most studies of war rape focus either on the woman as victim or on the soldier as aggressor. The case of Bosnia, however, presents a significantly more complex picture. Regarding victimhood, for instance, in some cases family members were forced to rape one another or to witness a family member being raped. On the side of the aggressor, there is evidence to suggest that rape was used as a rite of initiation. Being forced to rape, soldiers or fellow Serbs were forced into a brotherhood of guilt. Those who refused were humiliated and in some cases castrated or even killed. In Bosnia, rape was used to re-segregate hitherto intermingled groups: Serbs, Muslims and Croats. Even in cases where rape is enforced by a third party, both victims and perpetrators find it difficult to co-exist after the event (Askin 1997: 292).

During the war in Bosnia a considerable number of rapes were reported. A rough estimate is that between 20,000 (European Community figures) and 50,000 (the Sarajevo State Commission for Investigation of War Crimes) rape victims exist (Salzman 1998: 363; Fisher 1996: 91; Jones 1994: 117). Some were raped in their own houses, others in brothels, and still others in rape camps. Particularly horrifying is the practice of forced impregnation that occurred in some rape camps set up in Brcko, Dboj, Foca, Gorazde, Kalinobik, Vesegrad, Keatern, Luka, Manjaca, Osmarka and Tronopolje (Skejlsbæk 2001: 220). That is, in stark contrast to the common assumption that it is a spontaneous crime, rape is rational and necessitates much planning. Thus women in some camps were continuously raped until a doctor or a gynaecologist established pregnancy (Fisher 1996: 112) and held in captivity until abortion was no longer possible (Salzman 1998: 359; Sofos 1996: 86). This practice can be seen as an extremely cruel form of torture (Nikolic-Rastanovic 1996: 202) or as an integral part of strategic ethnic cleansing. Thus, it is claimed that although camps were set up and controlled by paramilitary forces, the political leadership in Beograd was secretly condoning it (Fisher 1996: 108). Further, patterns of rape strongly suggest that a systematic rape policy existed (UN 1994: 59).

In understanding how rape became a crucial signifier in the Bosnian war, we need to go back to the 1980s. One of the first cases of 'rape' that had political consequences was the reported rape of Djordje Martinovic. Martinovic was admitted to the hospital in Kosovo with splinters of glass in his anus, claiming that that Albanian men had raped him with a bottle (Bracewell 2000: 563). This was not true; he made the unfortunate sexual experiment himself. Nonetheless, the story quickly became instrumental in political propaganda. A petition signed by Serbian intellectuals thus read: 'the case of Djordje Martinovic has become that of the entire Serb nation in Kosovo' (petition on Djordje Martinovic, in ibid.: 571). As Martinovic was 'raped', so was the

Serbian nation. Serbs could no longer feel safe in their own land (in Serb mythology Kosovo is considered the cradle of Serbia). Hence two clearly demarcated camps were being created: one Serb and one Albanian. This demarcation was later reapplied in Bosnia, though with the focus shifting from propaganda to actual war, a war of words that paved the way for a war of bodies. And in contrast to the case of Kosovo, the war was not fought between two parties. Rather, it created two parties, two essentialized groups, and gave their boundaries a hitherto unknown rigidity. A war, which included rape, was waged against the Muslims to prevent them from degrading Serbian women: aggressor and victim swapped places. Scenes of rape were even shown on Serbian TV. The scenes actually depicted Muslim women being raped but the voices were overdubbed to create the impression that these victims were Serbs (Salzman 1998: 353; Goldstein 2001: 354). The general atmosphere was captured in Milovan Milutinovic's text 'Laying Violent hands on the Serbian Woman', which appeared during the war:

> By order of the Islamic fundamentalists from Sarajevo, healthy Serbian women from 17 to 40 years of age are being separated out and subjected to special treatment. According to their sick plans going back many years, these women have to be impregnated by orthodox Islamic seeds in order to raise a generation of janissaries on the territories they surely consider to be theirs, the Islamic republic. In other words, a fourfold crime is to be committed against the Serbian woman: to remove her from her own family, to impregnate her by undesirable seeds, to make her bear a stranger and then to take even him away from her.
>
> (quoted in Gutman 1993: x)

According to the genetic myth underlying this text, if an Albanian male rapes a Serbian woman who then becomes pregnant and gives birth, then the child would be considered Albanian, even though genetically speaking it is 'half Serb' (Sofos 1996: 86). Women are thus reduced to incubators, ensuring the reproduction of male genes (Salzman 1998: 365). This patriarchal ideology played a crucial role when rape was turned into a weapon; raping them, one was forcing Muslim women to give birth to 'Chetnik' babies, who would later kill them (ibid.: 359; Fisher 1996: 111–13). This strategy is of course only successful if the victim shares the patriarchal ideology. The fact that Catholic and Muslim women refer to their foetuses as 'filth' or 'that thing' or 'it' seems to indicate that this was in fact the case (Salzman 1998: 365).

War rape has a biopolitical purpose to destroy an ethnic group by killing it, to prevent its reproduction or to disorganize it, infecting it, removing it from its home soil. Significantly in this context, the RAM plan from 1991, which was authored by Serbian officers and which might be taken as a manual for the ethnic cleansing of Bosnia, recommends that the army strike 'where the religious and social structure is most fragile', that is, against women, adolescents and children. Women are excellent targets for ethnic destruction due to their symbolic position (Seifert 1994: 62–3). In Bosnia, to this effect, rape was deliberately staged in some cases by forcing family members and other inhabitants of the town to watch or carry out acts of rape (Pettman 1996: 190; Askin 1997: 271; Salzman 1998: 359). This aesthetization/theatricalization of rape was geared to increase the feeling of impotence in the Bosnian men by representing the Serbs as sexually superior, the Bosnian men's 'role' being that of impotent men unable to protect their women. Hence some of them were forced to wear women's clothes (Goldstein 2001: 357). In several cases men were literally castrated (ibid.; Askin 1997: 271). The rape of women, and thereby the impotence of their men to protect them, stand as a symbol of a defeated community. To understand the effects of this strategy, we need to investigate the way rape and abjection link together.

Biopolitics of rape

The rape victim often perceives herself as an abject, as a 'dirty', morally inferior person. The penetration inflicts upon the victim a stigma, which cannot be effaced. But abjection has a communal aspect as well: the victim is excluded by neighbours and by family members. In a sense, therefore, the victim suffers twice: first, by being raped and, second, by being condemned (Kesic 2002: 316). Further, in the case of forced pregnancy, the mother might see her child as an abject: as an alien and disgusting object, which occupies a zone of indistinction between inside (the child is never hers) and outside (she feels polluted by it). It should be noted that the 'abject' is not merely the pathological. Abject threatens normality, but it is more than the photographic negative of an order created through the differentiation between the normal and the pathological. Rather, it is inscribed in a primordial chaos, marked by a primary indistinctness or formlessness. Before differentiation, ordering is a relation to lack of distinction. The abject is, in other words, not a pole in distinctions but indistinction itself.

The abject is an object that provokes disgust, and the reaction towards it is guided by a distinction between purity and impurity. However, seemingly impure objects are not avoided in all cultures and some objects are considered impure only when they appear as being out of place (e.g. the soup in the beard or the hair in the soup). Further, in some traditions, filth can be elevated into a sign of spiritual purity as is the case for the hermit. So, why does the abject provoke corporeal responses of a bodily and reflex-like character? According to Bataille (1993: 23), the abject is a sign of a prior animal existence that threatens our identity as humans. The prohibition against eating flesh from a pig, for instance, thus upholds a distinction between the animalistic and the human. Humans achieve form in distancing themselves from animal immanence. Thus, the distinction between purity and impurity is secondary. The most basic attribute of the abject is its formlessness. What makes the abject uncanny is that it is both human and inhuman, both interior and exterior, both repelling and fascinating. We have form on one side and the lack of it on the other (Kristeva 1982: 65). The abject is without form, indistinct, and here lies its danger. The abject is what crosses boundaries of 'distinct' entities or territories, e.g. the body (ibid.: 75). Abjection is about indistinction. By the same token, the practice of avoiding the abject serves to uphold a distinction, a culture or a tradition.

Like the object of desire, the abject requires libidinal and cultural investment. In Freud's vocabulary, the object is totem and the abject taboo. The object and abject are, in themselves, nothing; only when they are *posited* as objects or abjects of desire do they achieve their extraordinary status. The concept of 'extimity', coined by Miller (1989) to describe objects of desire, is equally useful to describe the abject. Being wanted but not possessed, the object of desire belongs to an external reality. However, as something desired, it also belongs to the interior. Objects of desire are thus given by the logic of a lack. The abject is, on the contrary, always in surplus, there is 'always too much' of the abject. The urge is therefore to get rid of it, which is as impossible as obtaining *the* object of desire.

Concomitantly, cultures, traditions and communities are as much defined by what they reject as by what they elevate. Rites of pollution uphold and support a social structure. Rape pollution aims to strengthen a patriarchal structure (see Salzman 1998: 367). In this context the woman is considered as wealth in need of protection. Indeed, etymologically speaking rape is derived from the Latin 'rapere', which means 'to steal, seize or carry away' (Macnamara 2002: 2). The rapist steals, so to speak, wealth that belongs to another man. All rites of pollution thus have a positive counterpart transforming the object under threat into wealth (Kristeva 1982: 65; Bataille 1993: 46). Under this logic, war rape seeks to devalue the woman as an object of desire, turning her into an abject. That is, strategic rape attacks not only the victim but also aims to dissolve the social structure of the attacked group. It taints its ethnic stock.

Shame

In most, if not all, religions, humanity is given as a double immanence in relation to both the lowest (animalism) and the highest (religion). 'Man' can either fall into animalism (that is, become abject) or can rise above the human realm towards the Gods. Dirt, filth and blood indicate remoteness to the divine realm. That is, in religious discourse, the distinction between holiness and fallenness intertwines with a distinction between purity and impurity. In this respect Kristeva mentions three kinds of abjected objects in a biblical context: abdominal food, excremental matter and menstrual blood (1982: 71). It might, however, be more useful for us to operate with a distinction between abjection from outside and from inside. Excrement and equivalents (decay, infection, disease, corpse, etc.) are dangers to identity coming from the outside, while menstrual blood is a danger coming from within. Indeed, this distinction overlaps with the portrait of abjection found in the the Old Testament and the New Testament, respectively. The Old Testament gives a number of prescriptions on what to consider pure or impure. Simply to avoid abjected matter is of course the easiest way to retain purity, and if pollution should occur, a vast number of cleansing rites are to be found; of these, sacrifice is the most common. Abjection is described as pollution or contamination, that is, seen as something that does not affect the subject in any fundamental way. In the New Testament the distinction between purity and impurity is reversed. Sin is attributed to all believers. Instead of holiness gained through a constant avoidance of abjected matter, we find here confessions through which sin (abjection) is elevated into a sign of faith. Abjection is internalized. It comes no longer from the outside but from within (ibid.: 114).

In relation to these two forms of abjection, rape can certainly be understood as primary pollution, that is, as pollution from without; an enemy penetrates the body of the victim. We are so far in the domain of the Old Testament. However, there is no rite for purification here, which is usually the case regarding pollution from without. The feeling of shame indicates that rape also follows the path of secondary abjection. As such, rape becomes an attribute that denigrates the person in question (otherwise the victims would not feel ashamed), which brings us to the New Testament. But again there is something that does not fit into the picture: rape cannot be elevated to a sign of faith through confession. Rape pollution resists conversion into language. Thus, rape is a hybrid of the two forms of abjection.

We can now further differentiate the secondary form of abjection into sin and shame. From the perspective of the perpetrator, rape serves as an initiation ritual and as the sign of one's fidelity to the cause, e.g. of a gang, an army or a nation. From the perspective of the victim, the same act often resists translation into language and thus cannot serve as the basis of the formation of a social bond. To understand this traumatic impact, one must understand the metaphorical overlapping of the bodily and psychic interiors. The body's interiority is seen, at least in Western culture, as its most private and intimate part. 'The vagina is a gateway inside, the gate to the woman's soul by which act of entry property in her body is claimed' (Miller 1997: 102). At the same time, however, everything that leaves this interior is considered filthy (with tears being the exception that proves the rule). This ambivalence emerges because substances are not impure in themselves but become so in crossing the border between inside and outside; hence no abject without a blurred distinction.

Rape is the border-crossing practice *per se*, transforming one's inner being into an abject (see Seifert 1994: 55). In Lacanian psychoanalysis, the interior is purely residual: it is the unconscious. The unconscious is what remains when all symbolical attachments are removed: I am always more than my job, more than my family ties, my nationality, etc. Thus, the interior of the body metaphorically stands for that which is always more. Violence is to invade the interior, to fill it. In the interior everything becomes abject, because nothing properly belongs there.

Shame is produced through a border-crossing act by which the subject works as the agent of its own desubjectivation, its own oblivion as a subject (Agamben 1999b: 106ff.). Thus, shame is directly linked to the concept of sin (and guilt), that is, internalized pollution, something one is responsible for, and which therefore affects one more deeply. However, unlike sin, shame resists verbalization, it cannot be elevated into a sign of faith or belonging. The notion of 'forced choice', which blurs the distinction between the guilty and the not guilty, is significant is this respect. The sexualized violence against Bosnians forced them into a grey zone in which ethical purity is impossible. For instance, victims were often forced to transgress the prohibitions against murder or incest. A father was forced to rape his daughter or a son his mother. Prisoners were forced to perform oral sex on each other; internees were forced to bite off each other's testicles, etc. (Human Rights Watch 1993: 216–19, 339; Stigelmayer 1994: 137; Askin 1997: 271, n. 893). In all these cases, the victims had actively participated in a perverse ritual aiming to destroy their dignity and feeling of moral worth. That is, the victims are made to feel complicit in their own torture.

Perversion as social bond

How does the logic of abjection work on the side of the perpetrator? Does he feel shame or does the transgression function as part and parcel of the creation of a brotherhood in guilt? Significantly in this context, during the war, all laws were suspended and everybody, including the paramilitary groups, was given the opportunity to behave as a sovereign:

> [T]he West which perceives Milošević as a kind of tyrant doesn't see the perverse, liberating aspect of Milošević. What Milošević did was to open up what even Tijanic calls a 'permanent carnival': nothing functions in Serbia! Everyone can steal! Everyone can cheat! You can go on TV and spit on Western leaders! You can kill! You can smuggle! Again, we are back at Bakhtin. All Serbia is an eternal carnival now. This is the crucial thing people do not get here; it's not simply some kind of 'dark terror,' but a kind of false, explosive liberation.
>
> (Žižek and Hanlon 2001: 19)

The war allowed soldiers to enter an 'exceptional' space which was made possible by Milošević, and which made rape, burglary and other crimes possible and acceptable. Thus, concepts such as carnival or festival capture something essential about the behaviour of Serb paramilitary troops in Bosnia. Bataille's festival, for instance, is a state of exception (see Bataille 1993: 124). One of his examples is that of the Hawaiian islands, where the death of the king signaled a period in which all prohibitions were lifted: 'No sooner is the event announced than men rush in from all quarters, killing everything in front of them, raping and pillaging to beat the devil' (ibid.: 89). This lasted until the king's body turned into a hard and incorruptible skeleton. Then a new king was introduced and order restored (ibid.). The festival, thus, did not threaten the royal power. Rather, it served as an outlet, allowing people to partake in it. As such, the festival represents a reactionary state of exception, an attempt to strengthen and legitimize the grip of the game rather than changing its rules. In this sense the 'festival of the king's death' is perfectly legal, that is, authorized by the law itself through a regular self-suspension (ibid.: 129).

Like Bataille's festival, the festival in Bosnia was not spontaneous. Milosevic allowed the paramilitary groups to share his power in return for unlimited 'love' and loyalty. And the same logic was repeated at lower levels. Being forced to transgress a taboo, the soldiers became like clay in the hands of their leaders. The aim was to baptize a brotherhood in guilt. In this context, rape became a sign of social solidarity and refusing to join the others in rape was regarded as a sign of non-commitment; in rape 'a man seals his allegiance in atrocity' (Morrow 1993). Abjection thus works on both sides. War rape is a double-edged sword. For the victim, abjection has a destructive impact because it cannot be verbalized, and on the side of the offender, it works to create a strong symbolic bond, a brotherhood in abjection or in guilt. In this context, rape was used as a rite of initiation, which made men true Serbs, implying the rejection of cultural interaction in any form. Forcing individuals to transgress norms is also to force them to choose sides. Either they were Serbs, Croats or Muslims. No other option existed. Some neighbours even became enemies overnight.

There can be a brotherhood in guilt, but never a sisterhood in shame. The first kind of abjection produces 'sin' (guilt), the second, shame. However, the distinction between sin and shame can easily dissolve. What within a closed community of soldiers is understood as guilt (as a transgression which proves one's manhood and loyalty) is transformed into shame as soon as the soldier leaves this community. Inside Serbia, the paramilitary groups were heroes, outside they were seen as perverts.

To sum up our argument so far, the body cannot be understood in isolation from other territories (see Douglas 1966: 122). As land is penetrated by enemy troops, so is the body. The biopolitics of rape is, in other words, that of the camp. As such, rape camps illuminate some important aspects of contemporary 'post-modern' warfare: the importance of asymmetry, the paradoxes of identity formation, and finally some preliminaries on the way the body can be used in inflicting traumas. One is thus tempted to label the rape camp as pharmaceutic. Like the pharmakon, defined as poison and remedy at the same time, the biopolitics of rape destroys/poisons the enemy's body politics and constitutes/remedies 'ours'. Interestingly, however, in its Latin use, the pharmakon is not just a remedy or a poison but also a scapegoat. The *pharmakos* is typically a stranger, which symbolizes a perceived threat against a community (George 2002: 169–70). In this sense the *pharmakos* refers to that which, later on in Roman law, became *homo sacer*.

What is significant so far is that, from the perspective of the victim, the biopolitical abandonment in the rape camp is experienced as 'poison', as naked repression. Is it, then, possible to find camps in which abandonment is experienced more as 'remedy' than as poison? This question gives a significant twist to the story of rape camps and brings us to party tourism, the positivity of which mirrors the negativity of war rape. Indeed, as we argue in the following, party tourism exemplifies the opposite extreme of the rape camp. The rape camp is a zone of indistinction, in which the victim is reduced to *homo sacer*. Similarly, the party zone reduces the tourist to a 'party animal', which is experienced positively, as freedom. Indeed, the truth of the camp is this twinning of repression and liberation. The obvious negativity of the first is what makes it difficult to see the logic of the camp in the seductive positivity of the latter. Let us now move to Ibiza and Faliraki to substantiate this claim.

Welcome to Gomorrah

> Four in the morning . . . Beer bottles smash on to the pavement but the human swarm hears nothing over the music pounding from the bars. The doors of the Nightlife disco open and two young men barrel past the bouncers, vomit smeared on their bare chests. They embrace, then wrestle, then soil each other's hair. Five teenage girls watch and applaud until one is grabbed by a bouncer and carried on his shoulders up the steps. One of her friends lunges to try and pull down the exposed knickers. The bouncer whirls and his captive's knee-high white boots catch the lunger in the face. She howls . . .
>
> (Carroll 1998)

Enter the party zone: Ibiza, 'the loud, drunk, brash Gomorrah of the Med' (Barrett 1998), where, as a consequence of excessive activity, a journalist from the local paper, *Diario Ibiza*, branded its tourists 'animals', while the UK's official representative on the island called them 'degenerates, out of control', and a local hotel receptionist found it more appropriate to point out that the tourists 'behave like pigs, they respect nothing' (quoted in Carroll 1998). In response, the clubbers say: 'The island has a unique atmosphere. We have tried other places, such as Portugal and Cyprus. But nowhere else gives you the freedom to misbehave' (quoted in Hopkins 1999). From the point of view of the clubbers, that is, Ibiza is a post-Oedipal social space in which there is no law (and thus no 'misbehaviour') and in which the only prohibition is the 'prohibition to prohibit' (see Virilio 2002: 2).

Ibiza has been transformed from a 'paradise island' for alternative holidays in the 1960s, first into a bastion of package tourism and then into a clubbers' Mecca of unchallenged hedonism through the late 1980s and the 1990s. Its transformation is part of a global process and thus it is not alone in marketing excess. Already in the early 1990s, other similar tourist destinations flourished in competition with Ibiza. Faliraki, Rhodes, for instance, has become just another 'Gomorrah of the Med', where wild life comes out to play in a hedonistic cocktail of sun, sea, music, cheap alcohol and drugs, sex, and expectation of excess:

> The girl on the podium in Ziggy's and Charlie's bar is surrounded by half a dozen drunken lads and she is dancing for them. Suddenly, she lifts the bottom of her shorts away and shows them her crotch. She laughs, they laugh. Just another night in Faliraki . . . Here, there are bars called Climax and Big Peckers and clubs called G-Spot and Sinners . . . Here, girls bare their breasts and gangs of boys sometimes walk naked up the street.
>
> (Gillan 2002)

One should add to this picture a large amount of alcohol and drugs, reported and unreported rape incidents, and other forms of excessive violence such as street fights among people who claim 'We're on holiday and we want to have fun' (quoted in Velidakis and Harris 2002). Anything goes in Faliraki. It is, very much like Fitzgerald's Riviera, a hedonistic zone of exception where 'people do exactly what they [are] tempted to do and pay no penalty for it' (Fitzgerald, quoted in Littlewood 2001: 205). Which is perhaps also the secret behind the TV documentaries, like *Club Reps*, that advertised non-places such as Faliraki, creating a demand and thus contributing decisively to their success, and behind the 'voracious' tour industry that manipulates the 'ordinary kids' visiting Ibiza (Carroll 1998), while non-Spanish detectives 'have watched in bewilderment, trying to fathom how the drugs trade has flourished unchecked and why their Ibizan counterparts have had such miserable luck trying to identify the ringleaders of the £200 million industry' (Hopkins 1999).

With its orgiastic hedonism appealing to young tourists who 'go crazy' away from home, and with its tour operators who take commission not only from the hotels but also from bars and discos, while vouchers, excursions, flyers and discounts are being used to push the tourists into bars and keep them there, the party island Ibiza is a spectacle of excess. It is the clubbers' idea of paradise ('great music, cheap drugs and high expectations of casual sex'). But also the effect of Mayhem, 'the hedonistic hell' in which excess flourishes, fuelled by an unchecked drug trade, mostly ecstasy but also cocaine and speed (ibid.). Ritzer and Liska argue that tourism in general tends to become an ecstatic form today (see 1997: 108–9): 'And that was what they all wanted, a drug: the slow water, a drug; the sun, a drug; jazz, a drug; cigarettes, cocktails, ices, vermouth. To be drugged! Enjoyment! Enjoyment!' (D.H. Lawrence, quoted in Littlewood 2001: 201)

While the body as an object of fascination (e.g. the tourist having sex in public) and the body as abject (e.g. the tourist vomiting in public) become indistinguishable, what Baudrillard (1990) termed 'the obscene' becomes total, for there is no longer any appeal to any value or depth. 'The quality proper to any body that spins until all sense is lost, and then shines forth in its pure and empty form' (ibid.: 9). In the Ibiza scenes described above the body is naked, metamorphosed into pure enjoyment and excess. Having left the social origin, stripped of former identities, the tourist occupies, or fantasizes to occupy, a sort of state of nature, in which tourists 'behave – literally – like escaped convicts' (Houellebecq 2002: 27). As is written in bold letters on t-shirts sold in Ibiza: 'Good girls go to heaven; bad girls go to Ibiza'.

It is important, however, to bear in mind that this 'state of nature' does not exist prior to 'civilization'. Voluntarily *aban*doning civilization, the 'exceptional' life of the party tourist is not simply external to civilization. Rather, the tourist/bandit occupies a threshold in which life and law, outside and inside, civilization and state of nature become indistinct. And then again, the production of abandonment is bare life. In this regard, the 'naked' tourist borders on *homo sacer* or his recent incarnations, some of which are 'the man without qualities' (Musil 1996), 'the man without content' (Agamben 1999b), 'the man without limits' (Virilio 2002: 10) and 'the man with no bonds' (Bauman 2003: vii).

Let us, to clarify this metamorphosis of man and animal, nature and politics, mention *Bisclavret*, one of Marie de France's plays, which discloses the werewolf's particular location in the zone of indistinction between nature and politics, animal world and human world. It tells of a baron who once a week is transformed into a werewolf (bisclavret) and, after hiding his clothes, lives in the forest preying on other animals and stealing. His wife suspects something and persuades him to confess his secret and to reveal where he hides his clothes, even though he is aware that he would remain a wolf forever if he lost his clothes or were caught putting them on. With the help of her lover, the woman takes the clothes from the place where he hid them, and he remains a wolf forever:

> What is essential here is the detail . . . of the temporary character of the metamorphosis, which is tied to the possibility of setting aside and secretly putting on human clothes again. The transformation into a werewolf corresponds perfectly to the state of exception, during which (necessarily limited) time the city is dissolved and men enter into a zone in which they are no longer distinct from beasts. The story also shows the necessity of particular formalities marking the entry

into – or the exit from – the zone of indistinction between the animal and the human (which corresponds to the clear proclamation of the state of exception as formally distinct from the rule).

(Agamben 1998: 107)

It is significant in this context that 'club-goers in Ibiza and Faliraki tend to be ordinary, well brought-up youngsters' (Barrett 1998). They become, metaphorically and literally, naked bodies, in Ibiza. Only when they are 'caught' naked, e.g. arrested or fined by local authorities, do they oppose their nakedness and being labelled 'holiday hooligans'. Thus, 'I am not a lout but a public school-educated university student', said Simon Topp, who was told by local authorities in Faliraki to pack his bags for exposing his bottom in the street five hours after he arrived on Rhodes (quoted in *The Guardian*, 6 July 2002). What is really at issue here is of course the biopolitical relation between the citizen and his body, a relationship, in which the tourist becomes *homo sacer*.

The tourist camp

I no longer want to worship anything but the sun. Have you noticed the sun detests thought . . .
(Oscar Wilde, quoted in Littlewood 2001: 190)

Going abroad purely for pleasure, bypassing other places in between, and abandoning himself to sun, the tourist enters an enclosed, exceptional and 'duty-free' (Augé 1995: 101) zone 'taken outside' home, everyday routine and familiar social/moral contexts. In the words of Club Med: 'No constraint, no obligation. Barefoot, dressed in shorts, a sarong, bathing trunks if you like, you completely forget so-called civilised life' (quoted in Littlewood 2001: 210). As an 'antidote to civilization' Club Med sells places 'where one could strip off not just clothes but everything that locked one into a public role' (ibid.: 211). Indeed, free from the constraints of place, the traveller's space is 'the archetype of non-place', which, in the manner of a 'parenthesis' (Augé 1995: 111), or an attractor, excludes and includes an increasing number of people:

A person entering the space of non-place is relieved of his usual determinants. He becomes no more than what he does or experiences in the role of passenger, customer or . . . Perhaps he is still weighed down by the previous day's worries, the next day's concerns; but he is distanced from them temporarily by the environment of the moment. Subjected to a gentle form of possession, to which he surrenders himself with more or less talent or conviction, he tastes for a while – like anyone who is possessed – the passive joys of identity-loss, and the more active pleasure of role-playing.

(ibid.: 103)

In the previous chapter, we called this 'exceptional' space, or non-place, 'camp' and emphasized the paradoxical relationship between inclusion and exclusion that accounts for its ex-territoriality. What can be added in our present context is that increasing mobility, of which tourism is a significant part, means that the populations' 'ontological status as legal subjects is suspended' (Butler 2000: 81). It does not mean that passports are no longer produced at the strictly policed borders. Despite the borders, increasing mobility creates zones of indistinction, into which people can 'exempt' themselves from their usual identities or territories – a process which promises a paradoxical form of belonging in the shape of abandonment and which is experienced as 'freedom'. The tourist's life in Ibiza and Faliraki is a 'camp life' in this sense.

Importantly in this respect, as is the case with the werewolf, there are important 'formalities' regarding such camps, based on a range of prescriptive, prohibitive and informative instructions. These formalities endeavour to keep the 'city' at bay: urban gloom versus the holiday resort, the dark city versus the sun, *bios* versus *zoē*, citizen versus the naked body. In this sense, the tourist site is a camp, a world 'in which the goal is to enjoy whatever is free' (sun, sea, bodies), a world, which is 'anti-intellectual, physical, almost animal' (Littlewood 2001: 199).

In Ibiza, in Faliraki, or in the Club Med, simple natural life (*zoē*) excluded from the *polis* is no longer confined to the *oikos*, the private sphere. Rather, the private and the public enter into a zone of indiscernibility in the serenity of the metamorphosis from the citizen into 'almost animal'. Hence the references 'dark skin', 'simplicity', 'primitive sexuality' and other racial assumptions as to the savage and the sensual, 'amoral' and 'permissive' aspects of enjoyment 'outside' daily routine and so on must be reconsidered in the context of the liberation of *zoē*, bare life, from *bios*, the *polis*.

As we already mentioned, what is characteristic of modernity is not only the capture of *zoē* in the *polis* but also the fact that its increasing coincidence with the polis as exception everywhere tends to become the rule (Agamben 1998: 9). 'In contrasting the "beautiful day" (*euēmeria*) of simple life with the "great difficulty" of political *bios*, Aristotle may have given the most beautiful formulation to the aporia that lies at the foundation of Western politics' (ibid.: 11). This aporia – the convergence between the biopolitics of totalitarianism (abandonment to violence and death) and mass hedonism (abandonment to sun, sea, sex and drugs) – is the hidden link between the concentration camp and the Club Med, a link which is mentioned by Littlewood in *Sultry Climates* but, we believe, must be recontextualized in relation to the idea of camp:

In the spring of 1950 Gérard Blitz put up an advertisement in the Paris metro which showed simply the sun, the sea and his telephone number. This was the start of the Club Méditerranée, which across the next four decades grew into the largest holiday resort company in the world. Blitz, a diamond-cutter from Belgium in prewar days, had been running a rehabilitation centre for the survivors of concentration camps and was convinced that sport and relaxation in the sun help people to put behind them the experiences of the war. What he set out to do was to extend this prescription to population at large. The Club Méditerranée was in this sense, like so many impulses towards the sun, an outcome of war. (In more ways than one – the first Club Med village, on Majorca, consisted chiefly of army surplus tents furnished with military cots.)

(Littlewood 2001: 208)

Club Med aimed to market an atmosphere of leisure and pleasure in its enclosed sites around the Mediterranean where sun and sea were assured and where it 'established a reputation for excellent food, accompanied by unlimited wine'. Inside these sites, money was substituted with beads, and holidaymakers were expected to use first names or the informal and intimate '*tu*' form in their interactions, and the commodified nature of the club sociality was veiled by a language-use referring to the staff as 'gentils organisateurs' and the clients as 'gentils members'; 'more specifically, the Club adopted Polynesian-style thatched huts as its standard architecture and the sarong as its preferred form of dress' (ibid.: 209).

In short, the Club Med re-formulated the idea of the camp, tailoring it to the imaginary, symbolic and real enjoyment of the holidaymaker. In this, the identity of the tourist is stripped of its public connotations and his desire is moved by the promise of an eroticized, corporeal, 'animal' world, experienced as freedom from the 'city': the dark, routinized, disciplinary 'iron cage' of the citizen. If bare life is invented in colonies and came back to Europe in the form of concentration camps (see Bauman 2002: 109), it now enters the heart of the consumer society, which gives an interesting twist and content to the moral argument that tourism 'must not be separated from its colonial legacy' (Kaplan 1996: 63). The camp as a (non)place of consumerism works as catharsis of *homo sacer*'s desire and fantasies.

The Carnival

If one considers spectacular tourist sites as holy places, cultural artifacts as religious fetish, and souvenirs as relics, there is something quasi-religious to tourism. On the other hand, says Littlewood, tourism sets up, against the religion of the spirit, an 'anti-religion of the senses' characterized by the supremacy of the senses and the primacy of enjoyment: a 'coded promise of sexual adventure' (2001: 193, 210). However, this apparent contradiction dissolves and the double excess, that there are both quasi-religious and anti-religious aspects to tourism, makes sense once one considers tourism as a phenomenon located in a zone of indistinction between and thus beyond the religious and the profane. After all, the 'sacred' dimension of *homo sacer* is not located within the religious domain (Agamben 1998: 106). What confronts us in Ibiza and Faliraki is a life that as such is exposed in a profane and banal way. This brings us to Sade.

As Agamben notes, the biopolitical element is explicit in Sade's work, where the *theatrum politicum* is staged as 'a theatre of bare life', in which the physical body appears, through sexuality, as a pure political element, and the *maisons* where everybody can publicly summon any other body so as to force him to satisfy his own desires come to appear as 'the political realm par excellence' (ibid.: 134).

> Sade's modernity does not consist in his having foreseen the unpolit-ical primacy of sexuality in our unpolitical age. On the contrary, Sade is as contemporary as he is because of his incomparable presentation of the absolutely political (that is, 'biopolitical') meaning of sexuality and physiological life itself. Like the concentration camps of our century, the totalitarian character of the organization of life in Silling's castle – with its meticulous regulations that do not spare any aspect of physiological life (not even the digestive function, which is obses-sively codified and publicized) – has its root in the fact that what is proposed here for the first time is a normal and collective (and hence political) organization of human life founded solely on bare life.
>
> (ibid.: 135)

While the public and the private, *bios* and bare life, become interchangeable, the bed takes the place of the city. The significance of sex and party tourism lies in this swap. Further, when the city is transformed into a hedonistic consumer product (the tourist camp), assuming the status of an object of desire, we encounter the Sadist face of marketing too. The Sadean maxim of unconstrained enjoyment ('I have the right to enjoy your body, and you have the equal right to enjoy mine') is adopted today by the tourism industry in its assertion that it gives people what they desire, a move in which it only takes one step from marketing excess 'to "marketing" as forced enjoyment' (MacCannell 2000: 69). The 'party animals' are thus expected to sheepishly follow the club rep, who knows what they desire, from bar to bar. In other words, the demand of unlimited enjoyment depends upon the existence of a 'victim' granting the Sadean pervert his license (ibid.: 70):

> Interviewed for a BBC series broadcast in 1996, the [Club Med's] Director of Development, 'Dudule', explained, 'The Club's philosophy is that everyone must find a way to be free in his mind, in his body and with other people. One can be natural and do things one would not do in everyday life.' In the vocabulary of tourism, any mention of freedom is likely to contain a coded promise of sexual adventure. Dudule's sub-Gidean philosophy of naturalness and personal freedom

reflects the Club's image as a place of sexual liberation, where erotic adventure can be taken for granted. In a world given over to play rather than work, to the physical rather than the intellectual, to the natural rather than the socially conditioned, where the body, tended and displayed with narcissistic concern, is the focus of so much attention, sexual preoccupations are bound to be close to the surface. . . . Small wonder that, according to Ellen Furlough, 'Club Med villages came to have a reputation as places with 'an erotic morality' involving many 'brief encounters'.

(Littlewood 2001: 210)

As a 'festival', or 'carnival', life in the holiday resort consists of a kind of potlatch, an opportunity to become naked, that is, to get rid of one's markers of identity. Nakedness is in this respect decisive, for it presents a contrast to 'self-possession'; in stripping naked:

bodies open out to a state of continuity through secret channels that give us a feeling of obscenity. Obscenity is our name for the uneasiness which upsets the physical state associated with self-possession, with the possession of a recognized and stable individuality.

(Bataille 2001: 17–18)

However, the 'festival' generated in the holiday resort is not spontaneous. The rules are suspended rather than destroyed. The 'transgression' of the holiday-maker completes the rule by transcending it (ibid.: 63). Or, in other words, the 'orgy of sun, sea and sex' implies not only a revolt from but also an affirmation of the daily norms (Littlewood 2001: 213–14).

Moreover, we should not be misled by the appearance of a return by man to nature. It is such a return, no doubt, but only in one sense. Since man has uprooted himself from nature, that being who returns to it is still uprooted, he is an uprooted being who suddenly goes back toward that from which he is uprooted, from which he has not ceased to uproot himself. The first uprooting is not obliterated: when men, in the course of the festival, give free play to the impulses they refuse in profane times, these impulses have a meaning in the context of the human world: they are meaningful only in that context. In any case, these impulses cannot be mistaken for those of animals.

(Bataille 1993: 90)

So how do we interpret this strange desire acted out in festival? How can 'becoming animal' be interpreted if it is always mediated by human 'law'? Human beings are, under the influence of two simultaneous emotions, both fascinated and terrified, by nature. Indeed, this strange double economy of desire and disgust, of object and abject, or of transgression and confirmation, is the underlying matrix of the tourist camp. It is by oscillating between the two poles that the tourist becomes a 'party animal'. However, the limited potential of this oscillation necessitates taking issue with the contemporary valorization of transgression.

Biopolitics of transgression

Bech's (1999) *Leisure Pursuit* might be illustrative in this context. He shows how the transgressive lifestyles of homosexuals are today spreading to the wider society. Basically, modern life conditions – such as urbanism, lack of norms, unsafety and insecurity related to identities, the problematization of gender, aesthetization of identities, surveillance and discipline, and so on – form the background of homosexuals' lifeworlds. In a sense, therefore, the 'homosexual' is a real abstraction: in the realization of certain erotic preferences

> one cannot avoid becoming involved in this form of existence to some extent, irrespective of one's background and affiliations in terms of class, race, etc. This is partly because such a realization brings one into close contact with the very same conditions of which the homosexual form of life is a result and to which it is an answer.
>
> (ibid.: 63)

Party tourism can along these lines be seen as a typical leisure pursuit. As Littlewood shows, even though official narrations of tourism have excluded the issue of eroticism as a differentiated, intolerable deviance from mainstream tourism (e.g. 'sex tourism') and have adopted it 'as a lightning conductor for guilt that might otherwise taint the rest of society', and even though the tourists themselves have, as a rule, 'presented their travels as a cultural narrative rather than a sexual one', since the first half of the twentieth century the sexual dimension of tourism has come on open display through consumer hedonism (2001: 4–6, 205). Indeed, it is as if sex tourism is there to create the illusion that the rest of tourism is sex-free.

If erotic desire is part and parcel of the processes that have installed tourism as a carnivalesque practice, this is precisely where the camp, proving a perfect device (of transgression) for both expressing and containing people's discontents with the contemporary world, comes into play. And herein lies the problem with Bech's understanding of the homosexual as *avant-garde* (1999: 64) and other celebrations of transgression. First, the concept of *avant-garde* is obscure in a condition in which the exception is generalized; when the lifestyle of the *avant-garde* is generalized, then the *avant-garde* cannot remain an exception. Second, the idea of a generalized transgression is impossible to sustain, not only because this would mean the becoming rule of transgression,

117

but also because the idea of leisure cannot be sustained without that of work. The pursuit of leisure necessitates a notion of the dullness of (one's own or others') everyday life, at least at the level of fantasy. The pleasure of eroticism, homosexual or other, consists in breaking a taboo, which is acknowledged in breaking; the rule works because it is broken. And third, breaking or transgressing the norm is not necessarily an emancipatory move. If, for instance, in the contemporary 'reflexive' society, the symbolic authorities are in retreat, this means that the standard situation of the disciplinary subject is reversed (see Žižek 1999a). The problem of authority in this context is not that of the symbolic authority that forbids enjoyment but that of the superego, of the obscene authority that enjoins one to enjoy (e.g. in Ibiza).

Hence the social bond today often materializes itself in arenas for acting out transgressive scenarios. The normalized and law-abiding subject is haunted by a spectral double, by a subject that materializes the will to transgress the law in perverse enjoyment. If the subject, as Freud claims, internalizes social norms through a superego, one should add that this superego itself is split into two distinct but interrelated figures of the law, between the two figures of the father. First, the father of the law, of the symbolic order, castrating the subject through the law and language, and second, the obscene father, commanding no less than transgression and enjoyment. Whereas the first authority simply prohibits, 'Don't!', the latter says: 'You may!' (2000: 132). However, because the transgressor needs a law to transgress, and because the law is not destroyed but rather confirmed through the act of transgression, any attempt at balancing these two functions is doomed to be fragile. And an important tendency related to the generalization of the logic of the camp is the disturbance of this fragile balance. We are witnessing the demise of symbolic efficiency, or, the fall of Oedipus (1999: 322–34). Foucault's disciplinary society was about the reproduction of power through 'strategies without subject'. Today we are confronted with the exact opposite situation, subjects caught in the consequences of their actions without a master that regulates their interactions (ibid.: 340). This is a scenario in which transgression does not result in freedom but in new, and even more rigid, authority structures, in which *perversion* is *père-version*, the version of the father: in the post-Oedipal era, the dominant mode of subjectivity is no longer the disciplinary subject of normalization but the 'polymorphously perverse' subject following the command to enjoy (ibid.: 248):

> With the full deployment of capitalism, especially today's 'late capitalism,' it is the predominant 'normal' life itself that, in a way, gets 'carnivalized,' with its constant self-revolutionizing, its reversals, crises, reinventions, so that it is the critique of capitalism, from a 'stable' ethical position, that more and more appears today as an exception.
>
> (Žižek and Daly 2004: 213)

118

Let us, at this point, ask: does the sexualized 'naked body' of party tourism, as it is so often supposed, really disturb the social order? As Foucault remarks, what makes any form of sexuality 'disturbing' is not the sexual act itself but the 'mode of life' related to it (Foucault 2001: 298). A relationship is not merely about its sexual consummation but about generating a mode of life that 'can yield a culture and an ethics' (ibid.: 300). Significantly in our context, the 'mode of life' is precisely what the tourist so eagerly escapes from in the pursuit of erotic freedom in the 'camp'. Which is also the point at which the tourist's body attains its true biopolitical quality:

> Like the concepts of sex and sexuality, the concept of the 'body' too is always already a biopolitical body and bare life, and nothing in it or the economy of its pleasure seems to allow us to find solid ground on which to oppose the demands of sovereign power.
>
> (Agamben 1998: 187)

Neither sex nor the naked body is 'outside' the reach of power. Thus the attempt to locate liberation in the liberation of the body is doomed to be ineffective. The 'freedom' of the tourist opens up for the inscription of life within power, founding the very power from which the tourist tries to liberate himself, hence extending the range of the biopolitical paradigm. When bare life becomes both the object of power and the subject of emancipation, transgression understood as the liberation of *zoē* from the *polis* (e.g. Reichian sexual liberation) becomes meaningless (see ibid.: 10).

Occasional belongings

What happens when the 'werewolf' becomes 'human' again, and at what cost? Here is an account of how a love story ends on returning home from Ibiza.

> It 'appens all the time. It's obvious if you think about it. Because we work 'ere we get blasé about the place. But to the majority of the Brits it's a million miles away from their real world. Sure, while they're 'ere it seems as if love will find a way, but at the end of the day they go 'ome, back to their normal lives. When some of 'em think of what they've done or the people they've turned into on holiday it scares the fuckin' shit out of 'em. All they want to do is scurry back to their comfort zones, and if that includes an old boyfriend then tough titty.
>
> (Butts 1997: 106)

What is surprising here is of course that it should be surprising that the bonds developed on holiday are short-lived. In that sense, Ibiza is not atypical (outside) but rather typical (inside) of the wider society. Thus, the denizens of liquid modernity, says Bauman, are unbound – they are the 'men with no bonds'. For the same reason they must connect. 'None of the connections . . . are, however, guaranteed to last. Anyway, they need to be loosely tied, so that they can be untied again' (Bauman 2003: vii). In a liquid social space, one feels compelled to keep one's distance as one 'relates', without making commitments; relations thus incarnate both instantaneity and disposability (ibid.: 21). One needs to be able to fall out of love as quickly as one falls in love. Which is symptomatic of the logic of 'networking':

> Unlike 'relations', 'kinships', 'partnerships', and similar notions that make salient the mutual engagement while excluding or passing over in silence its opposite, the disengagement, 'network' stands for a matrix for simultaneous connecting and disconnecting . . . In a network, connecting and disconnecting are equally legitimate choices, enjoy the same status and carry the same importance.
>
> (ibid.: xii)

It is no coincidence that in Ibiza, what Giddens (1992) called 'pure relationship', relations without bonding, is infinitely easier to attain in that relations are maintained only in so far as those who 'relate' derive enough satisfaction from the relation, and can be terminated at will – they are, in Bauman's words, 'communities of occasion' (2003: 34, 91). And to be sure, 'pure relationship' is ambiguous in that it both fascinates and frightens the holidaymakers when they 'think of what they've done or the people they've turned into on holiday it scares the fuckin' shit out of 'em' (Butts 1997: 106).

It is significant, though, that this is experienced as freedom in Ibiza and Faliraki, as a becoming-Don-Juan of the ordinary person. Who was Don Juan, if not the *avant-garde*, the libertine who denigrated the tradition, ignored the social bond and insulted the religion? Don Juan did not even weave his seductions into lies that he knew the women he targeted would like to hear; he did not hide the fact that he was immoral and he did not make a secret out of his disloyalty – he knew not only how to seduce but also how to dispose himself of the women he seduced, always following the call of the next opportunity. And, above all, he did not take the law seriously, which is what more than anything else made him a seductive figure. However, seen from another angle, Don Juan's inability to bond was fundamentally a sign of his impotency (Žižek 1991: 114). And from this perspective Don Juan does not seem to be a libertine but a victim, a slave of his list of 'victories', who are reduced to names in a book his servant was writing. Indeed, in Ibiza today the 'chaos' which Don Juan stands for seems to have been 'normalized' as transgression has become a rule, a social demand.

When everybody becomes a Don Juan, however, waste, not only of objects but also of subjects, piles up. Occasional communities and their exceptional belongings are as much about disposal as about bonding, as much about anxiety as about enjoyment. Or, like Derrida's pharmakon, as much poison as antidote. If human waste is the other name of *homo sacer*, Ibiza and Faliraki are indeed as much dumping grounds as settings of late modern youth's 'sentimental education'.

6

FROM TERROR TO THE
POLITICS OF SECURITY

Imagine, my shadow has become mad, he thinks that he is the human being and that I – just imagine – that I am his shadow!

(Andersen 1965: 193)

It is well known that the USA has historically been associated with terrorism when terror served its own interests. Even Bin Laden was created by the CIA and, for a long time, literally followed his masters like a shadow, especially during the Afghan war of 1979–92, a time when 'networks of terror' and the White House did not call each other 'evil' or 'devil' yet. Later, however, the shadow somehow 'fell out' and went his own way, but then unexpectedly revisited his old masters on 9/11. The tables were now turned and, with the 'war against terror', the master started to follow his old slave/shadow, Bin Laden. Following one's own shadow, however, one becomes a shadow oneself: a shadow of the shadow. It is indeed as if the logic of the war against terror is already predicted in H.C. Andersen's short story *The Shadow*! A man loses his shadow in 'a warm country'. Upon returning, he continues his life without his shadow. One day, however, and without warning, the shadow knocks on his door. 'Nay, is it really you?' the man says, surprised, 'it is most remarkable.' 'Tell me what I have to pay,' says the shadow in turn, 'for I don't like to be in any sort of debt.' This is the first step through which the slave/shadow in the story is transformed into an agent of humiliation, into a master: 'The worst thing for global power is not to be attacked or destroyed, but to be humiliated. And it was humiliated by September 11 because the terrorists inflicted something on it then that it cannot return' (Baudrillard 2003: 101). But the real revenge of the shadow in Andersen consists not in merely surprising or humiliating the man but in convincing him to travel with him to seek 'knowledge' (power?) in other countries (imperialism?). That is, making him a shadow of a shadow. And herein lies Bin Laden's real victory: turning the war against terror into his own shadow, thus creating a zone of indistinction between action and reaction, in which terror and the war against terror justify

122

each other. The alienation at work here reveals a paradoxical relationship between fundamentalist terror, which reduces all politics to religion, and the politics of security, which reduces all politics to security as a 'moral duty'. In this relationship, security and religion become indistinct and security tends to become a new religion, or, better yet, a new fundamentalism. We are facing, in other words, a twin threat: terrorism *and* the politics of security. Whichever twin wins, politics loses.

For all the hostility between them, fundamentalism and the politics of security share the logic of the camp: a homology in which convergence and divergence, similarity and difference become indistinguishable. The politics of security speaks in absolutes. So does fundamentalism. Like fundamentalism, the politics of security has its own priests with indisputable authority to interpret current affairs and to decide how the script must be implemented. Religion consecrates certain objects, endows them with a divine aura, and makes their defence an obligation for the faithful. So does the politics of security, sanctifying 9/11 and sublimating the defence of a 'way of life' at the expense of politics and dialogue.

Fundamentalism

Modernity, modernization and modernism would, according to classical sociology, lead to mass secularism and, by the same token, to the disappearance of religion and myths before the global tendency of detraditionalization. On the contrary, we are today witnessing a massive proliferation of traditions, but with a decisive difference: today's traditions have to contemplate and defend themselves in an awareness that there exist other ways of being and acting (Giddens 1994: 83). That is, traditions are becoming more and more reflexive. Conversely, in this perspective, if a tradition insists on its own ritual truth by refusing the dialogue to explain itself, then we are dealing with 'fundamental-ism', a tradition that defends itself in the traditional way. Hence for Giddens, for example, fundamentalism is a defence of tradition as such, a doctrinaire manner of refusing negotiation to protect a principle (ibid.: 85).

So far so good, but this perspective misses a crucial difference between an orthodox belief as such and fundamentalism, which emphasizes that fidelity to a principle is not enough; something 'more' is necessary. Indeed, in search of this 'more', the fundamentalist stance explicitly distances itself not only from unbelievers but also from those 'lukewarm' believers who are not prepared to do everything to fulfill God's will. Thus, fundamentalism 'considers those who advocate moderation, understanding, or dialogue to be even more detrimental to the cause than the "real" enemy' (Belge 2001: 3). The lukewarm believers postpone the inevitable clash between believers and unbelievers and therefore let the right moment for victory pass. True faith, on the other hand, allows for superior insight and urges one to act on behalf of God and other believers. Thus, fundamentalism considers itself the 'vanguard of faith', targeting both the immediate enemy and guiding the 'mass' of lukewarm believers (Moussalli 1999: 38; Münkler 2002: 70–1).

Islamic fundamentalism perceives Islam to be 'more' than a religion, as 'a political ideology which should be integrated into all aspects of society' (Roy, O: 2001). At first sight, therefore, it makes sense to contrast fundamentalism and secularism: the latter denies religion any space in the political realm and the first rejects the distinction between the political and the religious life altogether. This distinction is highly problematical though. Secularism is originally a religious concept; the idea of separating the state and the church contained in Lutheran Protestantism. Nevertheless, over time the religious connotations of secularism have been eroded and the present use of the concept is culturally, rather than religiously, embedded. A more serious problem, however, stems from the concept of fundamentalism, which signifies an extreme distortion of religious faith. The problem with this understanding of fundamentalism is its political use, which cannot perceive or accept that a certain dose of fundamentalism or lack of reflexivity is present in all religions. To imagine a religion that is not conservative, fundamentalist, dogmatist or orthodox is to imagine a religion without religion.

In this respect, Kierkegaard's thoughts on the nature of belief (as a Christian philosopher!) is relevant. He distinguishes between three stages of belief (the aesthetic, the ethical and the religious) in a hierarchical way. Significantly, the movement from the ethical to the religious stage has the character of a leap: one has to be within a religious discourse to accept its validity; one cannot enter a religious discourse through the work of reason and reflexively judge religious beliefs as true or false (Kierkegaard 1962a: 80–90, 224–47). The same goes for religious experience: one cannot feel the magic of religion without already being religious. The one who needs proof of the existence of God does not truly believe, or, more accurately, does not have faith. Kierkegaard's argument here involves a short-circuit between faith and knowledge. Faith must have the character of knowing. In believing, I am certain that God exists. But although I know that God exists, he remains only partially known; uncertainty, too, is absolutely necessary. Religion thus involves 'fear and trembling', without which the believers would be reduced to puppets in a mechanical universe (Kierkegaard 1962b: 7, 111). God's withdrawal makes human freedom and faith possible.

Following this, it is easy to distinguish totalitarianism and fundamentalism. While totalitarianism refers to a world-view in which everything fits together and negativity is denied or projected onto an enemy, fundamentalism refers to an equally all-encompassing world-view, which is, however, always to be doubted: there is always a distinction between man's limited insight and God's superior insight and will. The difference between fundamentalism and totalitarianism is thus the absence of a true transcendence within a totalitarian world-view. The Nazi ideology, for instance, refers to a divine kingdom (the Reich of a Thousand Years), which can be realized on earth. Along the same lines, the divine power to distinguish between good and evil was assumed by the Nazis, whose Final Solution became the equivalent of the concept of judgment day (Rogozinski 1993). In contrast, the Kierkegaardian 'leap' signifies the uncertainty of faith, which is founded in a groundless decision. It is the declaration of faith that founds faith, or, in other words, its logic is a performative logic involving the conversion of socio-cultural necessity into subjective faith by the subject itself. Sociologically speaking, religion differs from other social systems by dealing with and accepting this *abyss* of faith. Religion interprets contingency not merely as unfulfilled opportunities, overload of information, risk, etc., but as transcendence (Luhmann 1992). Religion actively embraces the constitutive abyss (God, the law, etc.) and engages in a transcendental justification.

Terror

At this point, we need another conceptual distinction, one between fundamentalism and terror. One can be a fundamentalist without being a terrorist and a terrorist without being a fundamentalist. But fundamentalism and terror can co-exist when fundamentalist values, objects or practices are defended by violent means. Significantly in this context, both Bin Laden and Bush go further than just holding certain values, objects and practices sacred. Like Bin Laden, Bush is prepared to use whatever means is required to protect his values (including torture, imprisonment without a trial and 'collateral damage' on a massive scale). Let us return to Kierkegaard, the philosopher of fundamentalism, for clarification.

In the first of his three stages mentioned above, consciousness is described as 'aesthetic' and characterized by the absence of moral standards and by a desire to enjoy different emotional and sensuous experiences (Kierkegaard 1962c). Kierkegaard's example is Don Juan, who sees freedom as the absence of law and strives for a bad (i.e. non-religious) infinity. In contrast, Socrates, the tragic hero, is an example of ethical consciousness for he is prepared to sacrifice impulses and desires in the confrontation with the moral law. The hero's consciousness is purified by following the law. But in the third stage, one acknowledges that the moral law cannot be fulfilled, or, in theological terms, that one is a sinner. One accepts that one is separated from God and that the moral law can only serve as an approximation of the highest good. It is this recognition of sin and separation that serves as a foundation of faith. Abraham is therefore Kierkegaard's real hero of faith. His readiness to sacrifice his only son, as an act of madness, exemplifies the essence of faith and confirms the supremacy of God's authority. Importantly in this respect, however, Abraham does not pretend to have understood God's will. His act of sacrifice 'bridges' the earthly and the divine but does so without annihilating the distance. God does not reason or negotiate with Abraham; he demands, Abraham obeys.

Hence the distinction between the ethical and the religious: whereas ethics is given as a taxonomy that can be known through reason, religion means accepting a God whose will remains unknowable. No true faith can persist without accepting this uncertainty as its paradoxical ground. Thus, faith can 'bridge' the human and the divine only temporarily; it continuously needs to be reaffirmed. For this reason, Kierkegaard describes religion as a suspension of the ethical (1962b: 51–62). The willingness to commit an immoral act serves as a proof of faith. And herein lies the link between religion and terror. Terror breaks the moral law in a way similar to Abraham's act against the imperative not to kill. In fact, it is perfectly plausible to suggest that terrorists are well aware that what they are doing is morally wrong (see Juergensmeyer 2000).

Religious terror nevertheless cancels the distance between the divine and earthly realms in search of certainty, or, politically speaking, in search of final victory. The gap is no longer mediated but traversed. The human and divine are reduced to elements on the same continuum. Thus, terrorists can conflate the personal, political and cosmic levels, while the struggle for one's faith, political violence, and the cosmic battle between good and evil interchangeably support one another (see ibid.: 145–63). Significantly in this respect, characterizing the earthly realm by fallen-ness, devilish desires, by evil and the chaotic state of nature, the 'vanguard' of faith takes upon itself the political task of re-installing order where it thinks disorder reigns, empowering good where it thinks there is evil and encouraging faith where it thinks there is none. The terrorist, in other words, situates himself on the side of order (by obeying the divine commands), on the side of peace (by fighting for it), and on the side of good (by trying to represent it). Following this logic, terror is not war but a response to war. 'The world is at war', Bin Laden claimed in February 1998 in response to the American involvement in the Middle East (quoted in ibid.: 145). Fundamentalism paradoxically perceives terror, a strategy of chaos, as a necessary evil to establish divine order on earth.

Jihad

Uncertainty about one's faith is a defining aspect of Islam just as fear and trembling for Kierkegaard define a proper Christian attitude towards faith. This interpretation is justified with reference to the distinction between two forms of *jihad* in Islamic theology: *jihad al akbar* (the greater *jihad*) and *jihad al-asghar* (the lesser *jihad*). Whereas the greater *jihad* is the existential struggle in the context of one's faith, the lesser *jihad* is the struggle for self-preservation and self-defence (Firestone 1999: 17; Noor 2001). Not only is *jihad al-asgar* a secondary form, it is also strictly regulated with ethical sanctions and prerogatives such as the prohibition against killing women and children and destroying harvest and livestock. A further restriction is that *jihad* cannot be waged for the sake of territorial expansion (Noor 2001).

This existentialist understanding of *jihad* differs greatly from the way the phenomenon is portrayed in the metaphor 'clash of civilizations'. The key figures here are Barber (1996) and Huntington (1997), both re-popularized by 9/11. But something essential is missing in both views of the 'clash'. Barber fails to see that religion does matter on the American side; Huntington searches for religion in the wrong place. Both understand American power as being essentially different from and opposed to Islamic fundamentalism. America is either understood as a secular regime obsessed with brands, goods and consumerist culture (Barber) or as a humanistic version of the Christian faith (Huntington): it is, in both cases, a civilized, non-antagonistic, and non-crusading civilization that counters a barbaric version of Islam. *Jihad* becomes, in this context, short-hand for 'atavistic politics of retribalization, balkanization, fanaticism, and tyrannical paternalism – a largely pathological orientation associated with violence, intolerance, and little respect for human life' (Euben 2002: 6). Barber, for instance, is aware that this version of a bloody holy war on behalf of a partisan identity is a highly selective one, but he still uses it to organize his argument, which reifies and de-historicizes the concept of *jihad* and erases its contradictions and ambivalences (ibid.: 8; Johnson 1997: vii). Barber fails to see that the very concept of *jihad* is what is at stake in the struggle between Muslim democrats and fundamentalist terrorists (Hefner 2001; Johnson 1997: 36). The clash 'between' silences, the clash 'within'.

However, things are more complicated than distinguishing between a proper and an excessive understanding of *jihad*. The conflict is not just one between different interpretations of Qur'anic verses but equally one of emphasizing different parts of the Qur'an. Euben distinguishes between the parts dealing with Muhammad's early life in Mecca where *jihad* is equated with the persuasion of non-Muslims, and the Medina period where *jihad* is the '*jihad* of the sword'. It goes without saying that the moderate Islamists take the early verses as the primary ones, while the radicals focus on the later ones. In both cases, however, *jihad* expresses an encounter between Muslims and non-Muslims, between *dar al-Islam* (abode of Islam) and *dar al-harb* (abode of war) (Euben 2002: 13).

Dar al-Islam basically means the territory in which Islamic law reigns supreme. Hence it is a territory of peace although the existence of apostasy, dissent, schism, rebellion, robbery and the like is admitted (Johnson 1997: 67). *Dar al-harb*, on the contrary, is a 'law-less' territory characterized by a permanent state of war. The divine commands are not heard and the result is eternal human strife (ibid.: 48–9). *Dar al-harb* is not merely characterized by conflict (in contrast to the *umma*, the Muslim community regardless of race, ethnicity, nationality, etc.). It is also perpetually in conflict with the *dar al-Islam* (ibid.: 51). Following this, *jihad* to the radicals is the relation between the Muslim and non-Muslim world rather than a way of relating to one's faith. Important in this context is the concept of *tawhid*, that is, the monotheist doctrine that there is only one God: Allah. For radicals such as Abu A'la al-Mawdudi (1903–77) and Sayyid Qutb (1906–66), this basically implies a demand for *jihad* against all non-Islamic systems (Moussalli 1999: 27). *Tawhid* calls for an Islamic revolution and cancels any possibility of dialogue or compromise (ibid.: 35).

Jihad to the neo-fundamentalists also signifies an internal relation among the Muslims themselves, that between those of true faith and those who open their doors to foreign corruption and thus betray the essence of faith, that is, the lukewarm believers (Euben 2002: 14). The Qur'anic concept of *al-jahiliyya* (paganism) is here given a new interpretation. Originally, it was taken to mean an ignorance of Islam in areas unaware of the Prophet's revelations. However, Mawdudi and Qutb take the concept to apply to a 'condition' rather than a particular historical period. Whenever there is an ignorant deviance from the path of true Islam (*al-hakimiyya* or the divine rule), there is a condition of *al-jahiliyya* (Moussalli 1999: 27). Human beings have diverted from the divine law and replaced it with paganism, nationalism, materialism and abstract philosophy (ibid.: 24). *Al-jahiliyya*, in other words, condenses the ills of modernity (Euben 2002: 15):

> Humanity today is living in a large brothel! One has only to glance at its press, films, fashion shows, beauty contests, ballrooms, wine bars, and broadcasting stations! Or observe its mad lust for naked flesh, provocative postures, and sick, suggestive statements in literature, the arts and the mass media! And add to all this the system of usury which fuels man's voracity for money and engenders vile methods for its accumulation and investment, in addition to fraud, trickery, and blackmail dressed up in the garb of law.
> (Al-Mawdudi, quoted in Ruthven 2001: 3)

The cure is to eradicate evil through *jihad*. It is important to emphasize here the shift from a legal to a moral discourse. Islamic fundamentalists take the distinction between the *dar al-Islam* and the *dar al-harb* as a distinction between good and evil and not as a legal distinction (Johnson 1997: 68). The Western Crusader spirit renders the peace of the *dar al-Islam* impossible. Evil is everywhere. As a consequence, Qutb transcendentalizes the *umma*, which no longer designates the existing Muslim world but instead an a-historical potentiality waiting to be actualized, or, in Qutb's words, 'a demand of the present and a hope for the future' (quoted in Euben 2002: 18).

Bin Laden

The similarity between Al-Mawdudi, Qutb and Bin Laden's discourse is not a coincidence. Bin Laden studied under the guidance of Qutb's brother Muhammad (Ruthven 2001: 4). Joining this radical group, he saw himself as a representative of the whole Muslim community. Because it is a 'decentralized' religion with no supreme leader, Islam is full of self-proclaimed leaders (Noor 2001). Bin Laden became one of them by constructing his 'Disneyland Islam' (Al-Qattan 2001). Literally attempting to resemble the prophet, he has forsaken his hometown in trying to escape the infidels and the unfaithful members of his tribe. Like the prophet's flight, his has been 'arduous and perilous' (Gerecht 2002). And he adopted the usual fundamentalist strategy of purification, staging a return: thus:

> Mohammad's Cave at Hira, where he received the first revelations, is echoed by the image of Bin Laden emerging from another cave; the dress-code, the archaic language, the strange sexual politics where Bin Laden marries his son to his companion's teenage daughter – all these vulgarities are supposed to bring us back to a primordial state of 'true', 'real' Islam.
>
> (Al-Qattan 2001)

The ideological fantasy at work here is not just the purity of faith but also the expectation that Bin Laden, just as the Prophet Muhammad, will be victorious (ibid.). Finally, like the Prophet, Bin Laden claims that he has not chosen this mission out of any personal consideration (Bin Laden 2001c). He was 'chosen' by Allah (Bin Laden and Miller 2001).

Bin Laden's faith consists in *jihad* against Americans (ibid.). *Jihad* is a 'religious duty' (Ghaith 2001). And the person guided by God is never misguided (Bin Laden 2001b). Hence there is no sign of uncertainty in Bin Laden's discourse: 'We have done what God has ordered us to do. God called on us for "*jihad*" and we complied' (2002a). Apart from God's orders, the attacks are justified with reference to American hostilities: 'What America is tasting now is something insignificant compared to what we have tasted for scores of years' (2001a). 'Whoever has destroyed our villages and towns, then we have the right to destroy their villages and towns . . . whoever has killed our civilians, then we have the right to kill theirs' (2002b). Allah permits revenge when attacked. America 'does not distinguish between infants and military', claims Bin Laden, referring to Nagasaki (Bin Laden and Miller 2001) and feels justified in doing neither. Americans and their allies are the biggest 'gangsters and butchers' of this age (Bin Laden 2002a). Bin Laden's actions, on the other hand, consist only of 'reactions' (ibid.). 'This is a defensive *jihad*' (2001c). Indeed, one is tempted to claim that an elective affinity is today emerging between 'pre-emptive' war against terror and 'defensive' terror, between reaction-as-action and action-as-reaction.

In his 'defensive' strategy, Bin Laden needs the figure of Western imperialism characterized by grave moral depravation. One has to choose sides in this struggle between religion and infidelity, morality and depravation. Equally worrying, however, is the behaviour of the Islamic leaders who have 'anesthetized the Islamic nation to prevent it from carrying out the duty of *jihad'* (2001b). They are hypocrites who imitate the West's paganism and blasphemy. The suicide attackers, in stark contrast, are the 'vanguards of Islam', true martyrs (2001a). Suicide, however, is strictly forbidden in Islam. Bin Laden's plea for martyrdom is thus not based on the Qur'an but on the writings of Abdullah Azzam, his mentor, and Tamim Al-Adarni, Azzam's right-hand man. In this context martyrs are promised a heavenly reward in the form of a multitude of sexually willing virgins who after each intercourse miraculously regain their virginity. Such 'kitsch' invites commentary on the economy of desire that sustains it, but suffice it to mention here that the man who travelled through the world to recruit martyrs never became one himself. Of all places, Al-Adarni died of a heart attack in Disney World (Kermani 2002: 8).

To sum up, then, Bin Laden's rhetoric is part of a radical militant fundamentalism and his world is one in a state of war. The hostile West (the *dar al-harb*) is attacking the peaceful *umma* that he claims to represent. The Islamic world (the *dar al-Islam*) is, however, in a state of decline (due to *al-jahiliyya*). Terror, against this background, is what counters the foreign Crusaders and awakens the anaesthetized. Which is the task of the vanguard. Let us now re-use the same framework to analyse Bush's rhetoric.

Bush

The concept of holy war has long been rejected as a threat to civilization (Johnson 1997: 15). At least, this is what the modern West likes to believe. In this perspective, acts of terror are the only 'wars' left for religion. However, in the war against terror, religion has been strongly emphasized:

> And we're thankful to God, who turned suffering into strength, and grief into grace. Offering thanks in the midst of tragedy is an American tradition, perhaps because, in times of testing, our dependence on God is so clear . . . Lincoln asked God to heal the wounds of the nation and to restore it, as soon as it may be consistent with the divine purposes, to the full enjoyment of peace, harmony, tranquility. We pray for this goal, and we work for it.
>
> (Bush 2001h)

Bush claimed that the American nation is 'one Nation under God' (2001c) and on the day of the attack cited Psalm 23: 'Even though I walk through the valley of the shadow of death, I fear no evil, for You are with me' (2001a). Nevertheless, Bush's religiosity differs from Bin Laden's. Bush's Christianity is a kind of private background morality, which finds its way into the public discourse only in times of emergency. Bin Laden's is a cosmology, which serves as the background for everything he thinks and does. The fundamentalism of Bush is elsewhere, in his emphasis on absolute values such as freedom, democracy and free enterprise, values defended because they are 'right and true for all people everywhere' (2002a). Hence, it has today become legitimate to kill in the name of democracy. 'Freedom is the non-negotiable demand of human dignity; the birthright of every person – in every civilization' (ibid.). Conditions might be unfavourable for the spread of these values: war, terror, dictatorships, poverty and disease. When these obstacles are removed, liberalism will reign supreme: 'The great struggles of the twentieth century between liberty and totalitarianism ended with a decisive victory for the forces of freedom – and a single sustainable model for national success: freedom, democracy, and free enterprise' (ibid.).

The USA is the 'vanguard' of freedom and liberty (ibid.). Its cause is larger than its self-defence (Bush 2002b). Indeed, the USA was attacked not as the USA but as the vanguard of universal freedom, which America symbolizes (Bush 2001e). The USA incarnates 'the collective will of the world' (Bush 2001f). Hence, every freedom-loving nation should stand by the side of the USA (Bush 2001b). There is in this sense no 'clash' of civilizations; the Muslims of the world 'deserve the same freedoms and opportunities as people in every nation. And their governments should listen to them' (ibid.). Governments are thus free to choose what is right for them: liberalism.

Interestingly, this vanguard position is contrasted not only to terror but also to Europe, the 'lukewarm believer' in liberalism without the willingness to do what it takes to defend it. 'Americans are from Mars and Europeans are from Venus' (Kagan 2002: 3). Hence the 'lack of European support' for the second Iraqi war, a perception according to which the USA consists of the true idealists, in contrast to the Europeans who are acting in self-interest (see ibid.: 26, 11–15). The Europeans are unwilling to pay the price even of their own peace, i.e. in Bosnia; they rely instead on the USA for their own safety (ibid.: 24). In other words, the very condition of possibility for the European/Kantian position is a Hobbesian world order provided by the USA:

> Although the United States has played the critical role in bringing in this Kantian paradise, and still plays a key role in making that paradise possible, it cannot enter this paradise itself. It mans the walls but cannot walk through the gate. The United States, with all its vast power, remains stuck in history, left to deal with the Saddams and the ayatollahs, the Kim Jong Ils and the Jiang Zemins, leaving the happy benefits to others.
>
> (ibid.: 25)

The USA acts as a Leviathan whose power assures peace according to the logic of exception. The 'responsibility' of the USA as vanguard is thus clear, and it is no less than 'to rid the world of evil' (Bush 2001d). And again, in this struggle between good and evil, there is no middle ground; one is 'either with Us or against Us' (Bush 2001f).

The end of the 'enemy'

Unsurprisingly, though, this moralistic discourse makes war more, not less, probable. It resembles an attempt to eat the last cannibal. Tellingly in this respect, the war against terror is a new kind of war, not for territory but for 'universal values' such as humanitarianism (Virilio 2002: 43). The other side of this humanitarian ideology is the reduction of the enemy to the non-human (see Schmitt 1985b: 72–3). 'Having become the sole reference . . . the human now reigns alone, but it no longer has any ultimate rationale. No longer having any enemy, it generates one from within, and secretes all kinds of inhuman metastases' (Baudrillard 2003: 93). Hence the war against terror defines the terrorist not as an enemy who deserves respect, but as an abstract, spectral evil to be exterminated. In this sense, the war against terror is not a Clausewitzian war: one does not make treaties with evil or try to adjust one's conduct to make them like oneself; one does not try to see the world from their position; and one does not attempt to negotiate with them or reason with them; 'you behave with them in the same manner that you would deal with a fatal epidemic – you try to wipe it out' (Harris 2002). For Bush it is 'enough to know that evil, like goodness, exists. And in the terrorists, evil has found a willing servant' (Bush 2001g). Paradoxically, however, this reduction of the enemy to 'evil' exposes a fundamental political inability in the West:

> Two philosophical references immediately impose themselves apropos [the] ideological antagonism between the Western consumerist way of life and Muslim radicalism: Hegel and Nietzsche. Is this antagonism not the one between what Nietzsche called 'passive' and 'active' nihilism? We in the West are the Nietzschean Last Men, immersed in stupid daily pleasures, while the Muslim radicals are ready to risk everything . . . Furthermore, if we look at this opposition through the lens of the Hegelian struggle between Master and Servant, we cannot avoid a paradox: although we in the West are perceived as exploiting masters, it is we who occupy the position of the Servant who, since he clings to life and its pleasures, is unable to risk his life (recall Colin Powell's notion of a high-tech war with no human casualties), while the poor Muslim radicals are Masters ready to risk their life.
>
> (Žižek 2002: 40–1)

Sacrificing the most sacred of the sacred, human life, the 9/11 suicides articulate a new, postmodern challenge to the consumer society, in which to die for a cause is unimaginable. The consumer society cannot, in other words, speak the 'language of the evil' (Baudrillard 1993: 81–8). In a sense, therefore, 9/11 proved Schmitt right in his juxtaposition of the state of exception to the liberal parliamentary rule. He saw the latter as a form of hyper-politics, in which everything is politicized but only in a non-committal way and without real consequences. In other words, liberalism forgets that Leviathan always stood against Behemoth, that the political is conditioned by a permanent struggle between order and chaos (Schmitt 1996: 21). Hence Schmitt was sceptical of international law for it criminalized the enemy. With the disappearance of the 'enemy', the political disappears too. When the enemy is stripped of legitimacy, war turns into 'police action', 'humanitarian intervention', 'peace-keeping action', or, in extreme cases, mass extermination. Hence in the 'war' against terror:

> We cannot even imagine a neutral humanitarian organization like the Red Cross mediating between the warring parties, organizing the exchange of prisoners, and so on: one side in the conflict (the US-dominated global force) already assumes the role of the Red Cross – it perceives itself not as one of the warring sides, but as a mediating agent of peace and global order crushing particular rebellions and, simultaneously, providing humanitarian aid to the 'local populations'. Perhaps, the ultimate image of the treatment of the 'local population' as *homo sacer* is that of the American war plane flying above Afghanistan – one is never sure what it will drop, bombs or food parcels.
>
> (Žižek 2002: 93–4)

The de-legitimization of the enemy is perhaps most clearly reflected in the way the USA has treated the inmates in Camp Delta, Guantanamo Bay, which we discussed in Chapter 1. Camp Delta reduces the inmates to *homines sacri* deliberately abandoning them to inhuman conditions in a legal limbo. Moreover, their containment is not seen as a punishment but as a pre-emptive action to make it impossible for them to plan and implement terror actions. That is, one is detained not with reference to a past crime but with reference to future eventuality, which, given that the American administration expects the war to last for decades, means almost permanent abandonment.

Terror and exception

According to Schmitt, the state is not only threatened from outside by international law, but also from inside by the 'partisan war'. With the deterioration of the state's sovereignty, the partisan, or the 'hero', can practically attain the role of the sovereign and restate the friend/enemy distinction instead of the state. This distinction between interior and exterior (national/international) politics on the basis of the partisan/international law seems, however, to be displaced today onto another, new and more global, distinction between two forms of post-politics: international terrorism, on the one hand, which has replaced the partisan, and the politics of security, which hides behind humanitarian paroles, on the other.

As we mentioned before, post-politics is characterized by the disavowal of the political content of political strategies and actions. Let us return, at this point, to the logic of exception. If the state of exception relates itself to the law as its suspension, declaring a state of exception is an implicit acknowledgement of the primacy of the law. Here, a state of exception is a temporally and spatially delimited situation. In this context Schmitt contrasts normal politics and politics of security, the latter being the background against which politics achieves its meaning through a recourse to the friend–enemy conflict. Following this logic in relation to terrorism, we are confronted with a choice: the genuinely political *qua* Schmitt's friend/enemy distinction, which sublimates order as an absolute value and indexes politics to the politics of security (Žižek 1999b: 18; Balakrishnan 2000: 110) on the one hand, and post-politics on the other.

However, turning Schmitt's logic against him, one could ask: is the politics of security genuinely political? Or, is it the perversion of the political? Our point is that politics of security can be elevated above politics only if it contains in itself the possibility of radical critique. However, politics of security is by definition reactionary; a state of exception is declared to save the condition of normality, that is, to avoid a true exception (Žižek 2002: 108). Which is why the state of exception is different from chaos or anarchy and characterized more by an order, even if that order is not a juridical order (Agamben 2003a: 32). This brings us to the problem with the Schmittian understanding of conflict:

> Far from simply asserting the proper dimension of the political, he adds the most cunning and radical version of the disavowal, what we are tempted to call ultra-politics: the attempt to depoliticize the conflict by bringing it to its extreme, via direct militarization of politics. In ultra-politics, the 'repressed' political returns in the guise of the attempt to resolve the deadlock of political conflict by its false radicalization – by reformulating it as a war between 'Us' and 'Them', our enemy, where there is no common ground for symbolic conflict . . . The clearest indication of this Schmittian disavowal of the political is the primacy of external politics (relations between sovereign states) over internal politics (inner social antagonisms) on which he insists: is not the relationship to an external Other as the enemy a way of disavowing the *internal* struggle which traverses the social body? In contrast to Schmitt, a leftist position should insist on the unconditional primacy of the inherent antagonism as constitutive of the political.
>
> (Žižek 1999b: 29)

This ultra-political gesture also explains the US right turn in the aftermath of 9/11 by pushing all criticism aside with reference to self-defence. It is of course legitimate to defend oneself against terror through a temporally and spatially delimited state of exception. The problem is that the exception has become permanent and global in the war for 'infinite justice'. Its beginning or end is no longer clearly marked. Further, the state of exception, including internment without trial, illegal monitoring, torture, and so on, seems to have become a system in its own right next to the legal system. The exception, in other words, has become the rule, or, by the same token, the law and its exception have become indistinct. Which is also why it is unclear whether the USA today is in a state of exception or not. On the one hand, there is a long-term war against terrorism, which legitimizes exceptions, but, on the other, society seems to function normally (see 2002: 40). Perhaps we are confronted with two types of state of exception: a national one, which the USA quickly ended, and an international one, which seems to be infinite.

The French military analyst Alain Joxe (2002) has called the USA an 'empire of disorder'. To establish mutual relations of protection and obedience, and thus take responsibility for those submitted to one's power, is the first prerogative of sovereignty (ibid.: 122–3). The USA, however, refrains from doing so. In the absence of a political strategy, the USA proclaims: 'it is an unfortunate situation but we are not imperialists' (ibid.: 44). To put it differently, the USA wants to act in a sovereign way but does not want to carry the burden of sovereignty. It is as if, for the USA, the world has become chaos, a place where the USA no longer attempts to realize political aims through negotiation or common projects. Power is no longer exercised according to a classical imperialist doctrine, but rather through a system for managing chaos (ibid.: 14, 170). Unsurprisingly, the characterization of the whole world as chaos merely legitimizes American military inventions.

As such, the 'axis of evil' also recalls Schmitt's 'amity line'. As we mentioned in Chapter 2, imperial Europe and the New World, the American colonies, constituted two different spaces: Europe, characterized by law, and the New World, characterized by the absence of law. This made the New World prone to conquest. The last word in the New World was naked power. As such, the New World was nothing else than the materialization of the state of exception as a principle. Which even 'relaxed' the relationship between European states by displacing the conflicts among them to the war against the 'barbarians' (Schmitt 1985b: 66). Hence, wrote Schmitt, the state of nature can be a no man's land but it is in no way a non-place; it can be localized somewhere, for instance, as Hobbes did, in the New World (ibid.: 64–5). Similarly, in the 'axis of evil' that is today's 'no man's land', American military actions tend to gain unlimited legitimacy to target the 'barbarians' and their 'rogue states', which are expected, by definition, to absorb every kind of violence, while it all dramatically de-politicizes and 'relaxes' the USA's internal conflicts.

Unsicherheit

When the British comedian S.B. Cohen – *Ali G* – recently crossed the Atlantic 'to help the US with some of the problems following 7/11', his deliberate confusion of 7/11 with 9/11 was found to be obscene by most critics (Bowcott 2003). But one cannot understand 9/11 (terror) except in relation to 7-eleven (globalization). After all, the 'network society' and 'terror networks' share a common logic. Terror has become reticular and 'as global an enterprise as Coke or Pepsi or Nike. At the first sign of trouble, terrorists can pull up stakes and move their "factories" from country to country in search of a better deal. Just like the multinationals' (Roy, A: 2001). To allude to the famous twist in the movie *Fight Club*, the schizophrenia at work here consists in globalization (7/11) fighting with itself (9/11), its own spectral double:

> [One] cannot resist the temptation to recall here the Freudian opposition of the public Law and its obscene superego double: along the same lines, are not 'international terrorist organizations' the obscene double of the big multinational corporations – the ultimate rhizomatic machine, omnipresent, albeit with no clear territorial base? Are they not the form in which nationalist and/or religious 'fundamentalism' accommodated itself to global capitalism?
>
> (Žižek 2001a: 38)

The most significant impact of 9/11 is not so much the physical destruction but the construction of a new network along which 'raw emotions' flow: 'grief, anger, horror, disbelief, fear, and hatred. It was as if we'd all been wired into one immense, convulsing, and reverberating neural network' (Homer-Dixon 2002). In a sense, therefore, Bin Laden has already won. His victory consists in the production of an all-consuming fear, an omni-present risk bound up with radical uncertainty. Interestingly in this respect, referring to the 'Chernobyl of terrorism', Beck (2002) extends his concept of risk – the unpredictable and unintended consequences of human action – to the attacks on the WTC. For Beck, the distinction between danger, characteristic of pre-modern and modern societies, and risk, the central aspect of the late modern risk society, refers to technological change. However, the transition from danger to risk can be linked back to the weakening of the state mentioned above. In a risk society what is missing is an authority that can symbolize what goes wrong. Risk is, in other words, the danger that cannot be symbolized (Žižek 1999a: 322–47). There is, however, a sinister solution:

> The most sinister and painful of contemporary troubles can be best collected under the rubric of *Unsicherheit* – the German term which blends together the experiences which need three English terms – uncertainty, insecurity and unsafety – to be conveyed . . . In a fast

globalizing world, where a large part of power, and the most seminal part, is taken out of politics, . . . institutions cannot do much to offer security or certainty. What they can do and what they more often than not are doing is to shift the scattered and diffusive anxiety to one ingredient of *Unsicherheit* alone – that of safety, the only field in which something can be done and be seen to be done.

(Bauman 1999: 5)

Along the same lines, the politics of security condenses the insecurity, uncertainty and unsafety caused by terrorism to the latter element, bypassing the burden of looking for political solutions to political problems (insecurity and uncertainty caused by neo-liberal globalization). What is relevant here is that, fantasizing about a 9/11 without 7/11, the politics of security reduces security to a technological issue of risk-management, a reduction based on clean-cut borders and clear-cut enemies. This simplistic tendency is perhaps best exemplified by the increased focus on immigration in the aftermath of 9/11. Pat Buchanan, for instance, demanded immediately after the attacks a temporary stop to immigration, more border control, a radical reduction in the number of visas given to those from the countries that 'support' terrorism and the expatriation of 8–11 million illegal immigrants settling in the USA (Zolberg 2001). In addition, therefore, to being the theft of welfare, asylum seekers and immigrants are now accused of participating in global terror networks (Bauman 2002: 112).

This reduction is predictable in that it builds upon a classical understanding of the 'city' with a clean-cut inside–outside distinction, or, based on the idea of entrenchment. Entrenchment is, however, not the only metaphor that structures the city (Reid 2002). The city is not only a fortress but also a market place, and in their pure forms the two metaphors refer to two incompatible principles: on the one hand, entrenchment can lead to the blockage of the flow of wealth into the city, and, on the other, a one-sided focus on the accumulation of wealth can compromise security. Therefore, the city gates historically sought not only to block movement but also to facilitate, to regulate and to control them (ibid.: 7). The 'door', in other words, 'represents how separating and connecting are only two sides of precisely the same act' and 'transcends the separation between the inner and the outer' (Simmel 1997: 67).

Today colossal numbers of people and commodities flow across borders. And the control of this flow comes at considerable costs. For instance, the proportion of containers checked increased after 9/11 from 2 percent to 10 percent, while 90 percent remain unchecked. Likewise, in all Western countries airport security has been intensified after 9/11. In the USA security services were re-nationalized (Beck 2002: 41–2). But approximately 100 million people use US airports every year and approximately 450 million enter the country over land (Zolberg 2001). It is impossible to check so many people thoroughly, and if it were possible, one can only detect a potential terrorist if he or she has already been registered for criminal acts. But suicide attackers die only once. Moreover, terror is parasitic on surprise. Thus, against expectations, it often uses each method only once. So, faced with such structural impossibilities, strengthening US security can only take place at the expense of the US economic interests.

The same dilemma surfaces in the schism between US imperial ambitions within Empire. In contrast to Empire, the decentralized and deterritorialized global capitalist network, the US political and military power can be likened to a classical case of imperialism on a global scale. The condition for US participation in the UN is its veto right. The condition for NATO is US dominance. The USA does not want an international Court of Justice, which would mean that American soldiers could be held responsible for the crimes committed while in American military service. Whereas sovereignty in global finance capitalism is diffuse, in the politico-military field it seems to be firm and robust, indivisible and well codified (e.g. the principle that a sovereign state has jurisdiction over its citizens). Sovereignty, though, is only an absolute right for certain states. In the case of Iraq and other 'rogue' states, it becomes a secondary right. The USA

> is imposing itself as the active and determining centre of the full range of world affairs, military, political, and economic. All exchanges and decisions are being forced, in effect, to pass through the US. The ultimate hubris of the US political leaders is their belief that they can . . . actually shape the global environment – an audacious extension of the old imperialist ideology of mission civilisatrice.
>
> (Hardt 2002)

The relationship between imperialism and Empire is thus a variation over the classical differentiation between the fort and the market place. Which means that the transition from imperialism to Empire is not and cannot be clean-cut. The dialectic between imperialism and Empire is rooted in the interdependency between territorialization and deterritorialization (Deleuze and Guattari 1987).

Haunting a spectre

What followed 9/11 is often interpreted as a reflection of the US ambition for global sovereignty. For Pilger (2001), for instance, the ultimate aim of the war against terror is the acceleration of Western imperial power; 9/11 was used as a pretext to attack Iraq with no satisfactory evidence for weapons of mass destruction and with no evidence of a link between al-Qaeda and the Iraqi government. In this, al-Qaeda and especially Bin Laden have become spectre-like entities that condense every threat against the USA, a master signifier of evil (Žižek 2002: 111). Sassen (2001) even compared the fundamentalist terror with plague, an epidemic that spreads quickly and without identifiable patterns. A virus destroys the network from within, causing an implosion (Baudrillard 1993: 39). Viral terror is a subterranean micro-power, which brings with it the specter of an invisible and 'immaterial' war in which

> at the level of visible material reality, nothing happens, no big explosions, and yet the known universe starts to collapse, life disintegrates ... We are entering a new era of paranoiac warfare in which the biggest task will be to identify the enemy and his weapons.
>
> (Žižek 2002: 25)

The difference between a state of war and a state of exception is significant here. War does not necessarily mean the suspension of national law. The state of exception must be understood as a re-introduction of the distinction between the internal and the external inside the territory of the state, as an upgrading of the political (in the sense of performative use of power) at the expense of the law. In the state of exception the state can relate itself to its own citizens as if they were the enemy. Hostility is, for Schmitt, not natural but political. Potentially everybody can become enemy. The enemy is therefore by definition indefinite and invisible (ibid.: 110). Hence the state's 'pointing out' the enemy is a relieving act: it takes upon itself the burden and identifies an external enemy, thus reducing the complexity of the economy of fear. The state of exception marks the opposite movement by reinstalling fear within the subjects. People start suspecting their neighbours and the indistinction of the enemy provokes anxiety:

> They [the terrorists] have even – and this is the height of cunning – used the banality of American everyday life as cover and camouflage. Sleeping in their suburbs, reading and studying with their families, before activating themselves suddenly like time bombs. The faultless mastery of this clandestine style of operation is almost as terroristic as the spectacular act of September 11, since it casts suspicion on any and every individual.
>
> (Baudrillard 2002: 20)

Consequently, security becomes an increasingly significant concern outweighing democratic participation, a situation, in which the citizens fear not the security state but its absence. Which is, precisely, another face of post-politics: the political is pushed, as in Schmitt's analysis of the Weimar years, from the state to the individual level. In a contemporary sociological terminology, politics is individualized and identifying friend and foe has become an individual task. The individualist 'hero' is, again, Schmitt's partisan, who can elevate himself to the position of the sovereign.

Significantly in this context, the difference between 'normal' politics and the politics of security is not a question of intensity or differences of scale. Rather, as we mentioned before, it is a distinction between two kinds of politics: between politics proper and post-politics. The politics of security belongs to the second form. The major distinction here is not between those who claim that the situation is safe and those who claim it is not, but between those who appeal to the logic of security and those who do not. Security, therefore, should not be contrasted to insecurity but rather to a-security. 'Transcending a security problem, politicizing a problem, can therefore not happen through thematization in terms of security, only away from it' (Wæver 1997: 22–3).

The appeal to security is a gesture of withdrawal of certain questions from the political agenda. Post-politics suffocates deliberative politics. In this context the 'war' against terror is no longer merely a 'continuation of politics by other means'; rather, it overrides politics. As with the fundamentalist, winning becomes the superior goal of the war against terror, even when it conflicts with its initial goals. The aspiration to 'protect our freedoms' is pushed to the margins by the logic of victory or defeat (see Laustsen and Wæver 2000: 164). Thus, the war against terror paradoxically destroys what it aims to preserve: democracy and freedom. And security creates its twin: insecurity. To securitize an issue is also to create a danger.

It is worthwhile to recall the strategy of pre-emption at this point. In the ordered world of sovereign states, deterrence worked as the primary means to achieve security. But it no longer does so. Terrorists are not deterred, and they use other strategies, including wanton destruction and the targeting of innocents, implying that one cannot allow the enemy to strike first. Hence, 'to forestall or prevent such hostile acts by our adversaries, the United States will, if necessary, act pre-emptively' (Bush 2002a). Perhaps, however, the real motive behind this new doctrine is to keep the US capacity for deterrence intact. The strategy of pre-emption is primarily focused on removing any nuclear threat towards the USA (Falk 2002).

> At West Point, Bush declared with moral fervor that 'our enemies . . . have been caught seeking these terrible weapons.' It never occurs to our leaders that these weapons are no less terrible when in the hands of the United States, especially when their use is explicitly contemplated as a sensible policy option.
>
> (ibid.)

In fact, it might be that parts of the Islamic world are as scared by what they see as a violent fundamentalism as the USA is of them. Which brings us back to the perfect parallelism in the images of war against terror and in the fears sustaining them: Bush's war resembles a *jihad*, a war legitimized with a reference to higher values. And, as is the case with Bin Laden's discourse, Bush's version of *jihad* is one that marginalizes critical reflection. Liberalism, and especially freedom, is Bush's doxa, or, *tawhid*. It is a value elevated above criticism and questioning, a timeless truth. However, due to rogue states, terrorists and the like, the world is in a state of chaos. As in Bin Laden's discourse, an abode of war confronts an abode of peace. The only difference is that this abode of war, the *dar al-harb*, for Bush is the East and for Bin Laden the West. The West for Bush stands for peace, while for Bin Laden it is the East. However, in both cases there is a condition of *Al-jahiliya*. Not everybody is ready to accept and support the leadership of Bush/Laden. Bin Laden blames Muslim leaders, Bush European leaders. Both feel urged to act as a vanguard of faith.

Independence Day

> People have often asked: 'What could unite the world?' And the answer sometimes given is: 'An attack from Mars.' In a sense, that was just what happened on September the 11th: an attack from our 'inner Mars'. It worked as predicted. For some time, at least, the warring camps and nations of the world united against the common foe of global terrorism.
>
> (Beck 2002: 39)

It seems to us that Roland Emmerich's *Independence Day* (1996) is *the* film on 9/11. The Earth is attacked by hostile powers from outer space. The gigantic space ship approaching the Earth is an evil empire inhabited by aliens/nomads, who move from planet to planet and exploit their resources. They are prepared to annihilate human beings to realize their aim. The attack is initiated in a series of big cities, and the American Airforce fast and resolutely counter-attacks the space ship. However, protected by an electro-magnetic shield, the alien ship turns out to be indestructible. The rescuer is a scientist (David), who discovers a strange signal emanating from the space ship. It turns out to be a counting-down mechanism. Time to attack approaches, and Washington is the target. The residents of the White House are evacuated to an underground military bunker. It turns out that the bunker contains a research centre for outer space. It includes a UFO that had crashed in an American desert. All of which had naturally been top secret before the aliens' arrival. Meanwhile, David's father-in-law happens to warn him against catching a cold when he sees him sitting on the floor. This of course triggers the redeeming idea: the virus. David develops a virus that can penetrate the protective shield of the space ships. If this works, that is, if their protective shield can be destroyed, the aliens can also be attacked with conventional weapons. The plan is to contaminate the aliens' network with the virus. Having no choice, the president accepts the plan and contacts the other nations that without hesitation 'unite' against the enemy.

The film seems to have anticipated the American reaction to September 11. Evil alien powers attack the house of God and their actions are totally unexplainable. The film never attributes to the aliens a depth in the form of an insight, ability, motives or emotions. Further, they are invincible; their networked weaponry is infinitely superior to what is available on Earth. The only choice: us or them, Good or Evil. As the sublime incarnation of humanity the USA gathers a world-encompassing alliance for the war against the enemy. Such a reading, however, is slightly boring and, what is worse, reifying. It is much more interesting to play with the basic assumption of the film, that it is narrated from an American perspective. What if we saw the hostile space ship as a metaphorical description of a global American empire, which suffocates the local life forms in consumerism and indifference? Is it so clean-cut a matter to decide what Good and Evil consist of?

We deliberately excluded a point in our narration of the plot. After the protective shield of the alien ship is penetrated, there emerges an intense battle between American fighter-planes and the aliens. Towards the end of the film every American fighter gets shot down, except one. When the last fighter is to fire its missiles, it turns out that the missiles cannot be detonated. Then its pilot chooses to lead the fighter against the target, transforming his plane into a missile and himself into a suicide attacker. What if the 9/11 pilots conceived of their acts as such heroic gestures whose aim was to destroy the empire of evil? The movie condenses the self-conception of the terrorists.

Throughout this chapter we showed that terror and its adversary mirror each other. We have two networks that stand against, mimic and justify each other. We have two camps, each of which claims to be good and to fight evil. And we have two strategies, which dissolves the democratic habitus in a post-political condition. Thus Bin Laden's construction of the 'Americans' perfectly mirrors Bush's representation of Al-Qaeda, and the rhetoric of the extermination of evil is what unites the two poles in spite of asymmetries (Johnson 2002: 223). A mental experiment might be helpful in this context. What if we universalize the right the USA proclaims for itself? What if Israel claimed the same right against the Palestinians, and India against Pakistan (Žižek 2002: 125–6)? Žižek mentions one of Bush's speeches where he refers to a letter written by a 7-year-old girl whose father is a fighter pilot in Afghanistan. In the letter she says that even though she loves her father, she is ready to sacrifice him for his fatherland. The question is how we would react if we on TV saw an Arabic Muslim girl who, in front of the camera, claims that she will sacrifice her father in the war against America. We need not think very long to establish that the scene would be received as an expression of fundamentalism or a morbid form of propaganda. The Muslim fundamentalists can even exploit their own children without hesitation (ibid.: 43).

The point of such a dialectic reversal is not to make excuses for terrorism. As Rushdie writes, and at this point we agree, fundamentalists seek more than demolishing skyscrapers: they are the enemies of freedom of expression, democracy, the right to vote, Jews, men without a beard, homosexuals, women's rights, secularism, dance, and so on (Rushdie 2001). It is, however, central also to insist that the Western tradition is one of democracy and criticism. Rather than undermining democracy in the war against terrorism, we must support it; and rather than keeping away from criticizing Bush's international policies in the name of patriotism and unity of the nation, we must criticize it mercilessly (Kellner 2002: 154–5). 'Independence' could refer to independence in the classical Kantian sense, namely as *Selbstdenken*: independent thinking. The ultimate catastrophe is the simple and simplifying distinction between good and evil, a rhetoric that basically copies the terrorist rhetoric (Zulaika 2002: 198) and makes it impossible to think independently. It is in this sense that the dominant paranoid perspective transforms the terrorists into abstract and irrational agents, pushing aside every explanation that refers to social conditions as an indirect support for terrorism (Žižek 2002: 33).

To conclude, terrorism is basically a mirror to understand the contemporary post-political society. Terror is, of course, uncanny and horrible. This, however, should not divert our focus from social change. It is said that frogs are unable to sense small changes in temperature. If they are put in an open pot and placed on a heater, they will normally jump out. But if the temperature is increased only slowly, they will be boiled alive. This story condenses in a nutshell the true danger of 'camping' in the form of securitization. The ultimate danger here is not the denial of fundamental rights and freedoms but our indifference towards these changes. While extreme right-wing opinions on immigration pervade most political parties today, one can reasonably fear that some of the radical opinions characterizing the war against terror (e.g. the acceptance of torture) will further disseminate. Clausewitz wrote that war is a continuation of politics by other means. Terror is the continuation of post-politics by other means (see Baudrillard 2002: 34; Bauman 2002: 94).

Acknowledgment

Parts of this chapter were previously published in *Alternatives* 29(1): 89–113 (2004). Copyright © Lynne Rienner Publishers. Used with permission.

Part III

CONSEQUENCES

7

SOCIOLOGY AFTER THE CAMP

Ours is, as we have argued throughout this book, a society in which exception is the rule, a society in which the logic of the camp is generalized. And it is impossible to understand the contemporary society without considering this. In a sense, therefore, the camp remains an acid test for social theory. If what the politics of modernity repressed was the camp as exception (see Bauman 1989), what today's post-politics represses is the camp that has become the rule.

There is a significant difference between old and new camps, though. What made the first camps disturbing was their politicization of life and death through a scientific rationality. They were, in Arendt's (1973) words, 'experimental laboratories' in which the limits of de-humanization were tested on those exempted from society. What makes today's camps disturbing, in turn, is the subtle interplay between exemption and self-exemption. The contemporary camps constitute a different kind of 'laboratory', a laboratory of disengagement, in which the limits of social (non)relationality and (self-) exemption are tested. We are witnessing today the rise and rise of not only compulsory but also voluntary 'camping'. And significantly, contemporary camps seem to come in twins, not as identical but rather as non-identical twins, revealing not a perfect symmetry but rather an ambivalent disparity. Hence the homology, the similarity in difference, between, say, refugee camps and gated communities, which share the logic of exception on the basis of inequality, expressing convergence and divergence simultaneously in a twilight zone that cannot be contained within the 'city'.

The contemporary camp signifies a new dream of community that offers a paradoxical ideal of belonging on the basis of not belonging, a community, in which undoing the social bond functions as *the* bond. Some abandon 'society', and some are abandoned by it. However, all are painfully or joyfully aware that (self-)exemption is the new game in town, the stake of which is the power to escape or disengage, to 'travel light' (Bauman 2000: 58). That is, the new game is as much about nonrelating as relating; (self-)exemption is not merely another type of social relation based on the logic of 'distinction', which, for instance, emerges when the 'elite' (e.g. 'high culture') distantiate themselves from the 'mass' (e.g. 'low culture') all the while both parties share the same social space (see Bourdieu 1989). What is at stake with today's camp is the constitution of the social space itself. In fact, it is this significance of the camp as the shadowy double, or the unconscious, of the social that sociology fails to illuminate today because it still perceives the camp as an anomaly. To understand the camp as the rule, however, we must first see sociology from another perspective. Thus we focus here on some central sociological assumptions, which make the camp imperceptible. Then we ask what difference the camp makes for sociology.

(In)difference

We argued that we live in an increasingly fragmented, 'splintering' society in which distinctions (between culture and nature, biology and politics, law and transgression, mobility and immobility, reality and representation, inside and outside . . .) tend to disappear in a zone of indistinction. But what is the conceptual and ontological status of 'indistinction'? Does it mean the disappearance of difference as such? At first sight it seems that the concept of indistinction is opposed to difference, that the camp is a de-differentiation machine, which creates a flattened world devoid of difference. That is, however, not the case. What needs to be clarified here is, first, the difference between indistinction and the absence of difference and, second, the status of indifference in relation to an ontology of difference. Our starting point is the two different understandings of difference, as negative and positive difference, which also point towards two different understandings of the camp.

First, difference can be taken merely as a negative difference, as difference between beings. As such, difference refers to a distinction between already differentiated identities (such as sexual, racial or cultural difference), that is, differences already mediated by representation. In the essentialist perspective, for instance, identities are distinct from each other. Or, alternatively, in the structuralist perspective, difference becomes an element of a system of relations (e.g. between the same and the other), a reduction which can only take place if we imagine difference as something imposed on, that is, something that follows, an initial situation, which lacks difference and form (Colebrook 2002: 34).

In this perspective the social, too, constitutes an already differentiated or stratified world that emerged from an undifferentiated mass, for instance, Hobbes's 'state of nature'. Here it is assumed that social *organ*ization chronologically follows an undifferentiated mass, a 'body without organs' (see Deleuze and Guattari 1987). Lacking form and organization, this body is an image of 'the zero degree of difference. Pure chaos, the undifferentiated reality' (Callinicos 1982: 94–5). This state, however, is produced or imagined from within the social. In other words, systems of difference do not differentiate an already given undifferentiated organism (see Deleuze and Guattari 1983:

327–8). The body without organs is constructed retroactively; first, after its construction it is imagined as the origin of the social or as its ultimate remainder, as what remains of the social when everything is taken away.

Similarly, the image of *homo sacer*, the paradigmatic subject of the sociology of the post-political society, is a formless and indistinct identity, the 'human as such'. That is, a fetish modelled on the image of the body without organs. With *homo sacer* as a transcendent point of reference, real differences among human beings are reduced to negative differences that originate from a homogeneous, indistinct ground zero of humanity. To arrive at positive differences, however, we need to undertake a 'reversal' according to which being can be seen as becoming and identity can be understood in terms of difference (Deleuze 1994: 40).

That is, we need an ontology in which difference becomes the ground of being, in which repetition of difference is the only form of identity, becoming is the only form of being (ibid.: 41). Repetition here consists of conceiving indistinction (the same) on the basis of the different. Difference, then, ceases to be a difference between distinct identities but becomes a process of differentiation (ibid.: 56). Following this, the chronology of the relationship between the distinct/different and the indistinct/undifferentiated must be reversed: organization (language, strata, social machines) is what reduces difference. Through organizing, that is, slowing down and 'selecting' differences from the flow of difference, life, we constitute distinct zones within difference (Colebrook 2002: 38). It is not an undifferentiated ground zero that precedes the social; on the contrary, it is the flow of positive differences that are imperceptible and not yet organized into distinct identities (or negative differences).

Indistinction refers to the process in which the binary organization of the strata on the basis of negative differences is undone. It presupposes a previous process of differentiation of social formations and shows that their binary divisions no longer work. What disappears or becomes indistinct in this process is negative, not positive, difference. In other words, the logic of the camp is based on 'the cancelling out of differences in quantities' (Deleuze 1983: 46).

Difference, however, surpasses negative difference. In fact, the camp can be seen as a (positive) difference-machine in the Deleuzian sense. As such, the camp signifies the logic through which the contemporary society has transformed the processes of post-panoptic 'control' into a form of sociality in a discontinuous space of positive differences that interact with one another in multiple ways. This mechanical character of the camp also explains why the creation of spaces of indistinction is a differential process and why we are witnessing differing constellations of the *dispositifs* of discipline, control and terror in each camp. Thus different camp-machines co-exist, overlap and clash, containing within themselves elements of one another, while they are coded, decoded and recoded differently (e.g. in terms of class, race, sex, crime record, age, consumption patterns, and so on) allowing for the proliferation of heterogeneous insides and outsides, of belongings and enclosures.

To put it differently, although the camp is born in a zone of indistinction there are differences between camps and redifferentiations can follow dedifferentiation. Hence even though the logic of the camp (and its blindness to difference) potentially include everybody in a generalized smooth space of indistinction (e.g. through universal 'human rights'), differences denied from the domain of politics re-emerge as 'cultural differences' and are managed through mobile and hybrid camp-machines that replace the disciplinary enclosures (see Hardt and Negri 2000: 199). Such proliferation of quantitative differences without political consequence reiterates rather than destabilizes already existing or new differentiations (Braidotti 2004).

In short, the logic of the camp can successfully combine the different moments of undifferentiation, differentiation and administration in different contexts. To sum up, then, we are speaking of two kinds of indistinction. First, the kind of indistinction that chracterizes the flux (of positive difference) that precedes the social, which should not be confused with the state of nature, and second, the indistinction in the sense of the de-differentiation of negative differences. What we have then is, first, a pure flow of intensive, positive differences. From this 'chaos', social assemblages and territorializations are organized; distinctions, or, stratifications, emerge. Then these distinctions dissolve in a zone of indistintion (the camp), and each camp is fetishized as a residue, a remainder *vis-à-vis* the city. However, indistinction can be followed by further differentiation (e.g. the camp-machine). Hence the camp must not be thought of as an identity but also as a virtual difference that differs from itself, a potentiality not necessarily actualized into distinct and determined forms. The 'real' camp is not necessarily an actual substance; rather, we start from the virtual (that is, real but not actual), from the immanent plane of positive differences. In this sense the camp can be understood in terms of the Deleuzian 'series':

> Each series tells a story: not different points of view on the same story, like the different points of view on the town we find in Leibniz, but completely distinct stories which unfold simultaneously . . . Each series explicates and develops itself, but *in* its difference from the other series which it implicates and which implicate it, which it envelops and which envelop it.
>
> (Deleuze 1994: 123–4)

Seen in this way, every camp relates to other camps that, as difference-machines, further differenciate it. Thus each camp, being already an (in)difference, must be understood in a variable relation with other (in)differences.

Homo sacer and multitude as twins

The twinning of the empirical camps has a theoretical counterpart in *homo sacer* and the *multitude* on the basis of some significant homologies. The concept of *multitude* refers to a network of individuals who are productive, creative, hybrid and nomadic subjectivities without forming a 'people', to a 'universal nomadism' formed in constellations of events and transindividual singularities that cannot be flattened onto systemic logics (Hardt and Negri 2000: 60–1; Virno 2004: 21–6). The sociality of the *multitude* consists of a horizontal network of mobile, transindividual connections, a productive field of force. As such, as the immanent source of all social production, the *multitude* is the double of *homo sacer*. If the naked life of *homo sacer* is the negative limit of the human togetherness and is constituted through human passivity, *multitude* signifies the potentiality of naked life, the 'power that naked life could become' (Hardt and Negri 2000: 366).

Both concepts directly relate to biopolitics and thus to the direct investment of life by power and capital. They constitute as such a twinned answer to the question of subjectivity in biopolitics. Whereas *multitude* refers to biopolitical subjectivation, *homo sacer* defines the contours of desubjectivation. The terrain of biopolitics is the 'no man's land' between this double movement, between identity and nonidentity, a zone of indistinction in which 'identification takes place only on the threshold of absolute desubjectivation' and in which every subjectification risks being subjected to the state (Agamben 2004a: 116–17).

Just as the principal raw material of *homo sacer* is flesh, the *multitude* is a *multitude* of bodies: 'there is no possibility for a body to be alone' (Negri 2003b: 3). Both concepts seek to define the remainder of 'people' (see ibid.: 1); *multitude* and *homo sacer* are basically what is left when the unity of 'people' dissolves. Whereas 'people' refers to homogeneity and identity by excluding its outside, *multitude* and *homo sacer* are deterritorialized concepts that bear an indistinct and inclusive relation to their outside. In this sense, both concepts signify a body without organs. However, there is also a difference. *Multitude* refers to a process in which the production of active differences disorganizes the 'people' into an intensive and substantive multiplicity; *homo sacer*, in contrast, refers to the production of passive or negative differences out of active differences. The idea of 'man', or the 'human being as such', for instance, is produced in the form of a basic distinction from which all other differences emerge. That is, naked 'life' of *homo sacer* is perceived as an origin, as a ground zero, which then takes different 'forms'. In a transcendent twist, one differentiated element (*homo sacer*) becomes the starting point of all differences.

In this sense *homo sacer* is the fetish that illuminates the illusion of transcendence and as such Agamben's concept *homo sacer* seems to remain at the level of an undifferentiated ontology, 'the indifferent background against which all perspectives are neutralized and discoloured in order to be brought back to an ontology that is incapable of producing meaning in non-discursive means' (Negri 2003a: 1). In this ontology, which is indifferent to antagonisms, the state of exception and constituent power (*potenza*) become indistinguishable. While *bios* is reduced to an indistinct *zoē*, everything becomes indexed onto a totalitarian horizon (ibid.: 2). At this point, however, Agamben seems to move in a Spinozist/Deleuzian direction by internally traversing the biopolitical rather than observing it from an outside position, a gesture, which 'goes beyond the state of exception by going though it' (ibid.). In this movement, *homo sacer* is unfolded, turning from inert biopolitical material into an active and creative agency, into the *multitude*, or a 'coming community'.

As twins, the concepts of *multitude* and *homo sacer* cannot be separated from each other. Where the one attracts, the other repels, and vice versa. And one never knows whether, when, where and, ultimately, why one belongs to the *multitude* or is reduced to *homo sacer*. That is, we are confronted here with a fundamental ambivalence. *Homo sacer* and the *multitude* are the two extreme horizons for the contemporary processes of (de)subjectivation that attract or repel the consumers/denizens of 'liquid modernity' and the *Unsicherheit* it produces, and, even worse, there is nothing, no secure guide, that automatically leads the majority from one extreme to the other (Bauman 1999; 2000). This suspension between the two opposing lines of (de)subjectivation transforms the global populations into a vast, planetary petty bourgeoisie 'in which all the old social classes are dissolved' (Agamben 1993: 62).

For this vast petty bourgeoisie, which emerged as a grey zone in between the proletariat and bourgeoisie and then became generalized, stable identities and differences (e.g. between languages, ways of life, traditions) tend to lose their meaning, and diversity is reduced to a post-political spectacle of negative differences without consequence. The 'ultimate frustration of individuality' in such a society consists in being reduced to *homo sacer* (ibid.: 64–5). If, on the other hand, individuality can untie the grip of passive differences, there opens up the possibility of a sociality that consists of a 'singularity without identity', a community without essentialized subjects (ibid.: 65). In a sense, therefore, the chance of *homo sacer* is to become *multitude*, or, the becoming *multitude* of *homo sacer* is the chance of biopolitics.

Decisive in this context is the idea of an 'inessential commonality': singularities connect and communicate without sharing an identity, an essence, which can unite them (ibid.: 18). Singularity must be understood as a 'whatever', that is, as 'the thing *with all its properties*, none of which, however, constitutes difference' (ibid.: 19). The reference here is to Spinoza, for whom all bodies share in common the attribute of extension and yet this commonality cannot constitute the essence or the difference of the single case. Whatever is the indifference between the general and the particular, between the generic and the individual (ibid.: 48), a mode of individuation that does not proceed from form, identity or subject, a multiplicity of the rhizome type that escapes stratification or organization (ibid.: 17). It is 'a set of speeds and slownesses between unformed particles, a set of nonsubjectified affects' (Deleuze and Guattari 1987: 262).

The novelty of the politics of the *multitude* or 'whatever' singularity is that it is not a struggle for the control of the state but rather a 'struggle between the State and the non-State (humanity)' (Agamben 1993: 85). This disjunction, however, does not have anything to do with a simplistic affirmation of the 'social' as against the state because, possessing no identity and no bond of belonging, singularities do not come from and cannot form a *societas*. 'What the State cannot tolerate in any way, however, is that the singularities form a community without affirming an identity, that humans co-belong without any representable condition of belonging' (ibid.: 86). Singularity is the enemy of the state. Hence the state attempts to capture the singularity, to represent it, because presence without representation is irrelevant and threatening to the state, which is, indeed, the real scandal hidden behind 'the hypocritical dogma of the sacredness of human life' (ibid.). Following this, if *homo sacer* is a transcendent political figure born out of such hypocrisy, the *multitude* could be said to be its immanent double. If, through the production of *homo sacer* power takes life as its object, through the singularity of the *multitude* 'life becomes resistance to power' (Deleuze 1988: 92). In other words, resistance to biopower is the power of life, a vital power that cannot be contained within particular *dispositifs* or strategies such as discipline, control or terror. If power is based on the capturing of the singularities and locking them into identities, the *multitude* is the name of the refusal to disappear into the 'apparatuses of capture'.

This refusal is what explains the nomadism of the *multitude*. *Multitude* is what deviates, however slowly, from fixation or linear movement (Deleuze and Guattari 1987: 371). It is by deviation and not necessarily by physical movement that singularities create another space. Hence the defining characteristic of the nomad is not sheer movement but the 'refusal to disappear' (Deleuze 1995: 138). In a similar way, Bauman's 'exile' seems to be the *aliquid* of 'liquid modernity'. Hence the distinguishing mark of the 'exile' is not sheer physical movement but 'the refusal to be integrated', a kind of 'spiritual' exercise. The exile is the one who is determined to remain 'nonsocialized', as a singularity that is present but not represented, '*in*, but not *of* the place'. The exile only accepts relation in the form of a nonrelation, integration through the condition of non-integration (Bauman 2000: 207–9).

Nonrelation or non-integration is a precondition to become a part of the *multitude*. That is, membership of *multitude* takes place not by adding but by subtracting. The *multitude* must disorganize itself in relation to the social strata. It is in this sense a line of flight, a nonrelation (Deleuze and Guattari 1987: 149–66). That is, the *multitude* is a form of disorganization, a nomadic 'war machine' defined by its singularity, its exteriority to the state and the society. The *multitude* is that which cannot be contained in the striated, rigidly segmented social space; it consists of flows (speed), operates in a smooth (nomadic) space, and unties the social bond (codes) in multiplicity. 'War' here must be understood as a mechanism against social organization: 'just as Hobbes saw clearly that *the State was against war, so war is against the State*, and makes it impossible' (ibid.: 357). A war machine as an assemblage that has as its object not war – war is only 'the supplement' of the war machine – but the constitution of a creative line of flight. War is simply 'a social state that wards off the State' (ibid.: 417), not necessarily violence.

But there is no guarantee that the *multitude* automatically continues folding along new deterritorializations and novel, rhizomatic connections. The line of flight always confronts some potentital dangers, which are fourfold: fear, clarity, power and passion for abolition (ibid.: 227–31). First, the fear of destratification may cause a search for security and can make stratification seem attractive. In this case, the *multitude* is reterritorialized and turns into a stratified (Freudian) mass. The second danger is less obvious and more interesting. Clarity arises when one attains a perception of the molecular texture of the social. What used to be compact and unified seems now to be leaking, a texture that enables indistinctions, overlappings, migrations, hybridizations. Clarity fascinates. Through clarity the *multitude* does not merely reproduce the dangers of the rigid in a miniature scale; moreover, it may become a transgressive delirium, a microfascism (ibid.: 228).

The third danger emanates from the rhizomatic or nomadic character of power itself. That is, a simplistic dichotomy between a nomadic, molecular *multitude* and a static, molar power is naïve. Power itself can go nomadic. Such nomadic power, characteristic of control society for instance, can capture and stabilize the movements of the *multitude*. Power itself is not creative but it is always immersed in a web of creative lines of flight. In this respect what makes power dangerous is its impotence. Hence it 'will always want to stop the lines of flight' (ibid.: 229). This 'impotence', however, is paradoxical in that it is also power's potentiality, that is, its capacity to suspend itself or to apply in no longer applying or actualizing itself (Agamben 1998: 28). Which is why one is often captured by power on flight, at the moment when one thinks one has escaped or is 'liberated'.

And finally, the *multitude* has itself as a danger. A line of flight can lose its creative potentials and become a line of death 'turning to destruction, abolition pure and simple, the passion for abolition' (Deleuze and Guattari 1987: 229). If clarity produces a microfascism of the *multitude*, the passion for abolition takes microfascism further by transforming the *multitude* into *homines sacri*: a line of flight that desires its own death. At this point, at which escape borders on death, war (destruction) ceases to be a supplement for the war machine and becomes its main object. Now, in a zone of indistinction, war and war machine coincide, or, become indistinguishable. 'To create', writes Bauman, 'always means breaking a rule. . . . For the exile, breaking rules is not a matter of free choice, but an eventuality that cannot be avoided' (2000: 208). When, in turn, breaking the rule itself becomes a rule, the line of flight cannot avoid suffocation. Hence engagement is as necessary as disengagement for the 'exile' (ibid.) and hence a 'minimal subject', from which one can extract assemblages, is as necessary as undoing the social bond (Deleuze and Guattari 1987: 270).

So, the 'planetary petty bourgeoisie' is an ambivalent and essentially open-ended concept. Oscillating, or suspended, between flight and death, it has in its horizon two extreme forms of (de)subjectivation: the *multitude* and *homo sacer*. But how can nonrelation or non-integration to the state or society ('flight') have a political relevance? Is flight a post-political solution to a political problem? The answer to this question lies in the virtuality of flight: 'a flight which would not imply evasion, a movement on the spot, in the situation itself' (Agamben 2004a: 121). The true nomads are those who follow 'a line of flight on the spot', true nomadism is 'motionless travel' (Deleuze and Parnet 1987: 38–9), 'spiritual rather than physical mobility' (Bauman 2000: 209). It is against this background that one can link flight (non-integration to the society) and the political (changing the society), revolt and revolution.

Historically speaking, anarchism has theorized revolt as an individual act of subtraction or nonrelation; revolution, on the other hand, aims at breaking down institutions to collectively re-establish new ones. We have, so to speak, two ontologies: the first ontology of becoming leads to the politics of flight, while the other understands the political in the classical sense, as something transcendent to the social. The task today is to think both gestures together in an ambivalent zone 'between the line of flight as a gesture of revolt and a purely political line' (Agamben 2004a: 121). The task, in other words, is to bridge singularity (flight) and collectivity (politics), linking presentation and representation together. Politics (the 'party', the 'agora') is necessary to transcend the singularity and, by the same token, singularity ('class', 'flight') is indispensable for the production of revolts and other individual experiences that can be translated into a political language (see Bauman 1999: 87; Agamben 2004a). Let us, at this point, focus on the category of nonrelation as a paradoxical but sociologically decisive category.

The paradox of nonrelation

Sociology has always known of paradoxes of inclusion and exclusion. There is, for instance, no possibility of including some elements in a social group without excluding some others. Further, in a differentiated society the difference between 'inclusion' and 'exclusion' can never be decided once and for all. Thus persons can simultaneously belong to different systems, and as social hybrids, be included in some systems while being excluded by others (Luhmann 1995).

There remains, however, a serious problem here, which relates to the possibility of simultaneous inclusion and exclusion in the same system. The problem here is not so much the co-existence of inclusion and exclusion but the paradoxical yet constitutive relation between them, which is also a relation between nonrelation and relation, between unbonding and bonding. As we argued before, power does not distinguish between inside and outside, or, between inclusion and exclusion. Power emerges as a potentiality, which excludes in including, includes in excluding (Agamben 1998: 50). In other words, power is a power not to pass from virtuality into actuality. Hence, ontologically speaking, power is 'always double' (ibid.: 47). The twinning we get here is that of between the potential (virtual) and the actual. At the limit, 'pure potentiality and pure actuality are indistinguishable, and the sovereign is precisely this zone of indistinction' (ibid.). And logically, if virtuality never fully passes into actuality, and if in this sense the social has the form of exception, we must think beyond the concept of relation. Which is also to say that the existing sociological category of 'relation' is not sufficient to understand the camp. The camp as a sociological object necessitates a new, paradoxical conception of relationality. In the lack of a better concept we call this paradoxical relationality 'nonrelation'.

Then let us ask: how can sociology suspend itself, its own relationality, and open a zone in which it can relate to its own limit, to its own shadowy, transcendent moment? This question, which is the political and ethical mystery of sociology, revolves around the category of (non)relation. And perhaps the best place to look for an answer is Bourdieu's 'relational sociology' characterized by the primacy of relations between agent and structure, actor and system, and so on. In Bourdieu, a relational analysis involves a twinning that consists in a simultaneous mapping of the class structure of the relations between different positions occupied by agents and mapping out the dispositions, the habitus, or position-takings of the agents, which are the practices realized in the framework of the given positions in a field (Bourdieu and Wacquant 1992: 105). Since positions and position-takings are like 'two translations' of the same phenomenon, they are analysed together. This, however, is not all. Agents can compete in conformity with the rules of the game 'but they can also get in it to transform, partially or completely, the immanent rules of the game' (ibid.: 99).

Hence the field of power and the field of politics are not to be confused, a distinction, which, in our terminology, corresponds to that of between the political and (post-)politics. When the players change the game, this involves, a kind of social 'event' that has the form of exception. Changing the game is suspending the (social) relation, for the change does not belong to the game itself. It is a nonrelation (the state of exception) that makes relation (the rule of the game) possible.

What is more interesting, however, Bourdieu's suspension of his own 'game', sociology, through the logic of exception. In an interview (Pécseli 1995: 10–11), Bourdieu says that he is under certain circumstances willing to transgress the 'limits' of sociology, even if it might seem naïve to other experienced sociologists. He felt challenged to do so, for instance, during an interview he was himself conducting for *The Weight of the World* (Bourdieu *et al.* 1999):

The respondent was a woman in the most miserable situation one can imagine. She was young and had fallen as deep as one can. There was something pathetic about her. Her extreme pain moved me. As a sociologist one can always identify with the respondents and feel empathy for them, and I left for a moment my task and asked her questions such as: what can I do for you? Do you have a brother or a sister? Who can help you?

> (Bourdieu, quoted in Pécseli 1995: 11; our translation)

Bourdieu here cuts the flow and suspends the interview. This is precisely the ethical-political moment of sociology in creating its own exception. And significantly, regarding this suspension Bourdieu refers to Spinoza's 'intellectual love':

Thus, at the risk of shocking both the rigorous methodologist and the inspired hermeneutic scholar, I would say that the interview can be considered a sort of *spiritual exercise* that, through *forgetfulness of self*, aims at a true *conversion of the way we look* at other people in the ordinary circumstances of life. The welcoming disposition, which leads one to make the respondent's problems one's own, the capacity to take that person and understand them just as they are in their distinctive necessity, is a sort of *intellectual love*: a gaze that consents to necessity in the manner of the 'intellectual love of God,' that is, of the natural order, which Spinoza held to be the supreme form of knowledge.

> (Bourdieu 1999: 614)

'Intellectual love' emerges here in the form of an epistemological break that can be located within Spinoza's hierarchy of three forms of knowledge. The first, and the lowest, form of knowledge (imagination) consists in inadequate and vague ideas acquired on the basis of the perception of singular objects through chance encounters. The second kind, which corresponds to reason, is 'a knowledge of common notions and through common notions' (Deleuze 1990: 290), a knowledge, through which what is singular is positioned in relation to other singularities and structures through common categories. And, finally, the third and highest form of knowledge is intuitive knowledge, which dissolves any relation to time and space for it perceives things as singular events outside time and space, e.g. the sum of the angles of a triangle is always and everywhere 180° (Albertsen 2003: 8).

The third kind of knowledge is not possible without the second. However, it goes beyond the relationality characteristic of the second form of knowledge in that it revolves around a singularity which expresses the One, that is, the univocality of substance that is the cause of the singular. The attributes of things are no longer perceived merely as common properties but 'as what constitutes the singular essence of divine substance, and as what contains all the particular essences of its modes' (Deleuze 1990: 300). Singularity reveals God's essence. As such, Spinoza's third kind of knowledge is necessarily intellectual love of eternity (God, that is, nature). In this sense the decisive difference between the second and third kinds of knowledge is that the third kind of knowledge focuses on ideas defined by their singularity, and to the extent it does so it becomes nonrelational with respect to the second form of knowledge. It is a nonrelational gesture that does not precede relationality (as is the case with the first kind of knowledge) but follows it.

The 'limit' at which Bourdieu asks his respondent 'what can I do for you?' is the point of an epistemological break between the second to third forms of knowledge. Spinoza's three forms of knowledge translate in Bourdieu into phenomenology, objectivation and praxeology (Albertsen 2003: 9). The first explicates the primary experiences of the social world; the second illuminates the relations between objective positions; and the third links these positions with the singular dispositions of the actors. Intellectual love emerges in this context when Bourdieu is surprised by the moment of love, or when he, driven to the limit of sociology, is forced to take an ethical position. In this ambivalent zone in between sociology and philosophy, Bourdieu can understand the individual as a singularity, which gives a nonrelational twist to his relational sociology. Here, singularity is no longer merely part of a positional network of relations.

To put it differently, only at the second level of knowledge the singular 'habitus' can be perceived as an outcome of 'class' and the social is understood as a structured relational network that produces the positions, which the individuals take. To use Bourdieu's own terminology, the transition from the second to the third kind of knowledge is a transition from the positionality of habitus to the singularity of habitus, which also signals a shift in emphasis from 'distinction' to 'indistinction' (e.g. between sociology and politics/ethics). Regarding the 'relationality' characteristic of the second form of knowledge, Bourdieu's self-suspension (of sociology) takes the paradoxical form of a 'non-relation': an intellectual approach to the social world that is aware of the social conditions of singular events.

Nevertheless, in a Spinozist framework, nonrelationality is itself a form of relationality. With submission to necessity, there emerges a new relation, a relation of love. In its individuality, singularity expresses *conatus*, the substance as such, and in this sense it is non-related. But singularity is at the same time a point of passage for every relation. In a Spinozist world everything is a 'line', a relation. In this light, nonrelation (line of flight) is a hyper-relation.

In a similar way, Agamben's whatever singularities constitute relations (a coming community) without however being represented as such, that is, as actual relations in the form of class, sex, us–them relations, and so on. In fact, this suspension of the actual is what makes pure relationality possible. Thus, in whatever singularities the common and the proper, *genius* and individual, coincide (Agamben 1993: 18–20). The reason why such singularities cannot be represented is that they are too common, 'gemein', that they are simply taken for granted (Bolt 2003: 26). Love is a good example again. It is not directed towards a property of the loved one (e.g. being blond) but, at the same time, it does not ignore such properties in the name of a dull, universal love: 'the lover wants the loved one *with all of its predicates*, its being such as it is. The lover desires the *as* only insofar as it is *such*' (Agamben 1993: 2). Again, whatever singularity (the lovable) is a passage between the common and the proper, the virtual (the totality of possibilities) and the actual. As such singularity is part of a totality.

To return to Bourdieu, 'intellectual love' is nonrelational in the sense that it can perceive singularities (the dispositions of the respondent) outside the actual time and space constraints (of positions), disengaging them from their social network. Bourdieu cuts off such relations to be able to detect the singularity of the respondent. What is tricky here, however, is that this nonrelation, the understanding of things as being outside time and space, paradoxically takes 'the whole world as a background' for all possible immanent interactions (Albertsen 1995). In a sense, therefore, singularity is what makes it possible for nonrelations to produce hyperrelations. For the same reason, the relationship between singularity and substance in Spinoza is characterized by indifference between being and becoming 'according to which being is said of becoming, identity of that which is different, the one of the multiple, etc.' (Deleuze 1994: 40). Spinoza's monist substance is that which returns in singularity, or, the being of becoming. In other words, the necessity of differentiation in singularity (becoming) can only take place in a relational, positional network (the One, univocity, the 'great chain of being'). Without the first we collapse into a simplistic phenomenology that cannot relate the singular to any positional network; without the latter we end up in a New Age type of distorted Spinozism without the notion of differentiation or singularity.

Exception as nonrelation

Can singularity be a pure non-relation? Can one, unlike Spinoza, imagine a singularity without a concept of God (nature)? Badiou's attempt to formulate a concept of singularity, which is not captured in a relational network, or which is fully transcendent to the world, is interesting in this context. Whereas for Spinoza and Deleuze, singularity is hyper-relationality, for Badiou, singularity is totally nonrelational in the sense that, as an event, it does not belong to the set or context of a given world. Whereas in Deleuze transcendence is immanent (or hyper-relational), in Badiou, it remains transcendent (not relational or hyper-relational). Hence the two kinds of singularities: Deleuze's immanent Sense-Event and Badiou's transcendent Truth-Event.

Badiou's is a specific theory of nonrelation, in which the basic idea is the rejection of relation. Every social event is built upon the premise of disengagement from the prescriptions of relation; the true social act is 'excepted' from the social and, consequently, it no longer brings together 'but separates' (Badiou, quoted in Hallward 2003: 27). In Badiou's ontology, which adopts mathematics as its basis, a set is not determined by the relations between its elements; membership and inclusion are different things. Indeed, this distinction between membership (or belonging) and inclusion is one of the most important distinctions for this theory.

Belonging is axiomatic in the sense that it has nothing to do with the intrinsic characteristics of the elements that relate to each other (ibid.: 84–5). A set is defined as any collection of dispersed multiplicities, also called elements or members. Ontologically speaking, everything is a set because everything is a multiple. 'To exist is to be an element of' (Badiou, quoted in ibid.: 84). Thus any term is itself a set and at the same time 'belongs' to a set. A term (which is also a set) is said to be 'included' in another set when all of its own members or elements are also members of that set. When this is the case, the first set is said to be a 'subset' of the second set. For instance all the subsets of 'students', 'workers', 'employers', etc., can be said to be different subsets of a set, e.g. the 'nation', while, at the same time, their intrinsic characteristics remain indifferent to different relations.

What is significant here from our point of view is the possibility of membership without inclusion and inclusion without membership. A term, which is not included in a set, may be a member of it. Or, a term, which is not a member of a set, may be included in it. Translated into a sociological framework, Badiou's distinction between membership and inclusion refer to presentation (e.g. membership of a society or a situation) and representation (inclusion or being represented in the state). There are, then, the following three possibilities: a term is defined as being 'normal' if it is both a member of and included in a situation; 'excrescent' if it is included or represented without membership/presentation; and 'singular' if it is present without being represented, or a member without being included.

'Excrescent' emerges due to an excess, due to the fact that not all subsets can belong to a set because the number of possible relations between the elements of a set, that is, the number of its subsets, is necessarily greater than the number of the elements of the set. Hence there is always an actual excess of subsets over sets, of inclusion over membership. In any set there will be at least one element to which nothing belongs, a nondecomposable term, the basic element of a situation in the sense that it makes all belonging possible (ibid.: 88–9). In this sense the number zero, for instance, is an excrescent: it is included but does not have an objective counterpart, thus ceasing to exist or 'belong'. It can only be represented as a lack. As such, nevertheless, it lays the foundation for all sets of numbers. Zero is involved in all rows of numbers even though it is literally not there, making possible 'the unlimited production of new multiplicities, all drawn from a void' (Badiou, quoted in ibid.: 104).

In this sense 'ideology' is nothing else than the repression of an excrescent element in any situation. What is excluded from membership, the excrescent, paradoxically makes 'belonging' possible (or holds 'society' together) by creating a consistency, a founded set, out of dispersed multiplicities. The notion of ideology is relevant here. Ideology is the point at which the void, the inherent antagonism of the social, is displaced onto a paradoxical object, the excrescent. Only afterwards, through a retroactive illusion, it appears as if the excrescent is what makes the social antagonistic. In this way, transposing the inherent antagonism in the heart of the social onto an excrescent figure, ideology generates the illusion of wholeness, of universality in the form of its opposite (the excrescent). For instance the 'Jew' in the Nazi discourse signifies excrescence in the sense of being 'included' (represented) in the situation without belonging (presence). As such, it gives the Nazi ideology its consistency, holding it together, like a knot at which different ways of argumentation meet one another. Hence the ethical and sociological answer to the Nazi discourse is to say that 'the Jew does not exist', it is only a representation: if we suspend the functioning of the excrescent element, the efficiency of the entire ideology is deconstructed (Žižek 1999a: 175–6).

Inversely, the 'Jew' in the concentration camp seems to be a 'body without word', a biopolitical member of the situation without being included in it. Also *homo sacer*'s twin, the multitude, whose singularity cannot be included by the state, exemplifies Badiou's third case, singularity, or, membership without inclusion. The multitude is *within* Empire but its nomadism, the real force of productivity and creativity behind the 'empty', 'parasitical machine' of Empire, cannot be represented as such (see Hardt and Negri 2000: 60–1, 103).

What is interesting here is to ask how the concept of exception relates to Badiou's scheme. As Agamben (1998: 24–5) points out, at first sight, exception seems to fall into the category of singularity. However, what defines sovereign power is exactly its inclusion of its outside by no longer applying to it. In other words, it represents singularity as such, as singularity, or as something unrepresentable. That which cannot be included is included as an exception. Including, paradoxically, membership itself in the situation, the exception generates a zone of indistinction between excrescence and singularity: 'the exception is what cannot be included in the whole of which it is a member and cannot be a member of the whole in which it is always already included' (ibid.: 25). The exception signals the crisis of the distinction and the correspondence between membership and inclusion.

The contemporary experience of the camp is the experience of exception precisely in this sense, an experience of occupying the gray zone between excrescence and singularity. This experience of a suspension or oscillation between two horizons: between representation without presentation and presentation without representation. The paradigmatic subject of the camp, therefore, is simultaneously the subject of total representation, a 'word without body', and of biopolitics, a 'body without words'. The task of sociology, one could say, is to give word, to 'politicize' this oscillation between life as spectacle and naked life, which is so far experienced individually, and in some cases as privilege.

The new terrain of sociology, by the same token, must be this zone of indiscernibility, in which the society of spectacle and biopolitics overlap, a zone in which *homo sacer* as a fetishized image of the 'human as such' (that is, as a representation without presentation since life without form is not possible) and the *multitude* (presentation without representation) meet each other. Exception is precisely what signifies the impossibility of automatically distinguishing *homo sacer* from *multitude* insofar as spectacle-ization and biopolitics overlap in control societies. For instance, to the state *multitude* appears as excrescence, whereas to the humanitarian ideology *homines sacri* appear as *multitude*. The separation of the two, that is, or the basis of nonrelationship through which the multitude can emancipate itself from the fate of *homo sacer*, is the political challenge of our time. The political task, in other words, is to imagine a radical critique of power that can go beyond the category of relation, including the pure relation characteristic of the ban(opticon).

Justification, critique and the camp

What is most disturbing regarding the contemporary camp is that it can effortlessly escape critique. This becomes visible if we ask how the camp is legitimized. In this context the 'sociology of criticism' can support a 'critical sociology' of the camp. Focusing on the first, Boltanski and Thévenot (1991) argue that critique is based on justification and justifications can only be criticized on the basis of other justifications. Justification and critique take place in those critical moments in which agents express discontent. In such moments people engage in public dispute and critique by referring to *regimes of justification*. Boltanski and Thévenot register six such regimes (of inspiration, opinion, domesticity, civility, market and industry) each with their own criteria of validity and internal consistency.

What is interesting in our context is the difficulty of formulating a critique of the camp from within these six regimes. The 'regime of inspiration', for instance, is characterized by the grandeur of inspiration, spontaneity, creativity and movement. Inspiration is about transgressing oneself (Boltanski and Thévenot 1991: 200–5). Here concepts such as mobility and nomadism are associated with resistance to and emancipation from the sedentary power. What is seen as static is criticized with reference to what is creative, dynamic and flexible. The problem, however, is that such critique takes the disciplinary society for granted. To be sure, discipline was an 'anti-nomadic technique' (Foucault 1991: 218) but, as we discussed before, the contemporary society itself operates according to the logic of nomadism. Ours is a 'nomad capitalism' (Williams 1989: 124), which justifies itself with reference to aesthetic inspiration: 'Be Inspired', as a Siemens ad reads. Meanwhile, capitalists themselves boast in new ways – 'I am such a nomad, I am such a tramp' (A. Roddick, the owner of *Body Shop*, quoted in Kaplan 1995: 54) – and a new capitalist discourse based on metaphors of mobility promotes the flexible organizational forms that can 'go with the flow' (Thrift 1997: 39). In a nutshell, today 'we are witnessing the revenge of nomadism over the principle of territoriality and settlement' (Bauman 2000: 13). Deleuze and Guattari had complained, 'history is always written from the sedentary point of view' (1987: 23) – but today exception is the rule. In today's camps we are 'condemned to nomadism, at the very moment that we think we can make displacement the most effective means of subversion' (Lotringer and Virilio 1997: 74).

As with aesthetic critique, a social critique from within Boltanski and Thévenot's 'civic regime' seems toothless *vis-à-vis* contemporary camps. The camp is the enemy of politics. Democracy, reflection and dialogue require concentration and slowness, but the camp makes social interaction and engagement impossible. The camp is post-political precisely because it can escape the agora, the political space, in which the translation of private fears into political issues can take place (Bauman 1999: 87). Or better, the camp is beyond politics. Its power can sail away from the citizen's democratic control, disappearing into the space of flows. As such, the camp transcends the horizon of justification. Camping elites are not limited by a principle of equivalence or an assumption of common humanity. Rather, their behaviour is character- ized by non-commitment to any 'common good', be it society, justice or a territoriality. In liquid modernity, the threat is to be left alone, to remain tied to the ground (Bauman 2000).

Hence the twin faces of the contemporary camp: ex-territoriality and absolute confinement. Confinement here does not become panoptic, though. Panopticism was based on mutual engagement, the co-presence of power holders and those subjected to power (ibid.: 10). The camp does away with this. Inasmuch as conflict and criticism require relation, the camp is a non-relation and plays on absence rather than co-presence. Which is why camps may seem so arrogant, and civic critique so ineffectual, hopeless, inconse-quential and irrelevant.

In fact, the same type of argument could be reiterated regarding the remaining four regimes of justification. For instance: the camp is efficient; the camp sells; the camp is a successful symbol of recognition and distinction; and it can promise a new dream of belonging. These characteristics make the camp compatible with the grandeurs of the industrial, market, opinion and domestic regimes of justification. And then again, in each case, the camp can transcend criticism because, from the point of view of justification and critique, the camp is what it is: violence.

What is significant here is that in all the six regimes of justification 'violence is kept at bay' (Boltanski 1999: 67–8). Boltanski and Thévenot (2000: 361) suggest that there is a regime of violence, which is beyond any principle of equivalence, a regime that is located at the 'limits' of justice/justification (ibid.). That is, violence is an exception that transgresses the limits of justification. Likewise, a regime of love is beyond the rule of equivalence. Decisive regarding 'love' here is the distinction between ethics as a codex and ethics as ambivalence (see Bauman 1993: 8). The first seeks to formulate a rule-set for being *with* the other; the latter is about being *for* the other. Such unconditional responsibility, the 'authentic relationship' (Levinas 1985: 87–8), paradoxically emerges in the form of a nonrelation: the suspension of being with (the social) in the perspective of infinity. Unconditional responsibility (love) in this sense borders on an exceptional situation, a shock, which resembles sobering up from the intoxication of being (see Bauman 1998a: 16).

Then, love and violence meet here as two forms of exception with respect to justification and critique, simply because they both refer to situations characterized by non-equivalence. So to speak, they are the two extremes in which normality is suspended or transgressed without the cover of justification.

Let us, at this point return to our example from Bourdieu where self-suspension of sociology becomes the source of intellectual love, or, freedom. Bourdieu offers the respondents an exceptional situation for communication, freed from the given, to make it possible for them 'to testify, to make themselves heard, to carry their experience over from the private to the public sphere' (Bourdieu *et al*. 1999: 615). The 'testimony' here builds upon the paradoxical logic of relation in which only a non-relation allows for a relation through which emerges an 'extra-ordinary discourse, which might never have been spoken, but which was already there, merely awaiting the conditions for its actualization' (ibid.: 614). In a sense, therefore, Bourdieu's method becomes a transcendental empiricism, which simultaneously focuses on the actual (the network of the interview) and the virtual (real but not yet actual).

And precisely at this point the idea of exception in Bourdieu seems to divide itself into two: Spinoza's intellectual love, on the one hand, and sovereign violence, on the other. Violence here is not symbolic violence. Rather, it is the constitutive violence that aims at changing the rules of the game. Bourdieu refers in this context to his interviews with members of the Front National, which 'bear numerous traces of the respondents' attempts to master the constraints contained within the situation by showing that they are capable of taking in hand their own objectification' (ibid.: 615–16). In this case it is not Bourdieu but his respondents who 'nonrelate' to the game. On the basis of this duality, Bourdieu concludes that every investigation is 'situated between two extremes doubtless never completely attained: total overlap between investigator and respondent, where nothing can be said because nothing can be questioned, everything goes without saying; and total divergence, where understanding and trust would be impossible' (ibid.: 602). The division here, we want to add, is not only between violence and love as two different forms of exception. Both violence and love further divide into two and thus produce further cases of twinning. Significantly in this respect, Benjamin was the first to divide Schmitt's concept of exception, producing a remainder of it. For Schmitt, as already mentioned, exception is a limit concept that presupposes a 'normal' situation as its background. The state of exception aims at the preservation of this normality with extraordinary means. However,

> if the 'decision' [to declare the state of exception] is so radically independent of the norm, as Schmitt claims, it is difficult to see how this decision to suspend the law itself can be justified, since every justification takes place with reference to a norm.
>
> (Eriksen 1998: 253; our translation)

What is tricky here is that in creating a state of exception the state refers to its *right* to self-preservation, and this invites a paradox: even though exception is a situation in which the law is suspended, Schmitt can speak of a *right* to suspend the law. In other words, Schmitt's project is to legitimize the state of exception, or, to normalize what is exceptional (ibid.).

Which brings us to Benjamin. To be sure, Benjamin was in many ways inspired by Schmitt's methodological extremism, even though his own project was opposed to Schmitt's. Whereas Schmitt wanted to legitimize Nazi power, Benjamin criticized it. Schmitt was conservative, Benjamin revolutionary. Indeed, this tension found its best expression in their understanding of sovereignty. Hence to Schmitt's exception Benjamin opposed the suspension of suspension, a 'real' exception, or better, an exception to exception itself. What is decisive here is the notion that, when generalized, exception loses its status as a limit of normality:

> The tradition of the oppressed teaches us that the 'state of emergency' in which we live is not the exception but the rule. We must attain to a conception of history that is in keeping with this insight. Then we shall clearly realize that it is our task to bring about a real state of emergency, and this will improve our position in the struggle against Fascism.
>
> (Benjamin 1992: 248–9)

Whereas in Schmitt exception is the political kernel of the law, it becomes divine justice in Benjamin. And then we are confronted with the difference between two exceptions: Schmitt's exception is nothing else than an attempt at avoiding the 'real' exception, the revolution, or, the divine justice. Benjamin's exception, in stark contrast, suspends the relationality between the law and its suspension in 'a zone of anomy dominated by pure violence with no legal cover' (Agamben 2003b: 33).

Along the same lines, there seems to exist a division within love itself, that is, between love as a radical exception and love as an institutionalized, commodified and mediatized version of exception, which suspends daily reality only to conserve it. In this latter sense, love resembles a permitted exception that has become a norm, or, as Beck and Beck-Gernsheim (1999) characterize romantic love: a 'normal chaos'. Drawing on the Calvinist motif of sacrifice, they argue that 'romantic love' has taken the place of religion in today's individualized society. Interestingly, romantic love as such is an exceptional situation – the 'law-givers are the lovers themselves' – whose self-referentiality excludes the idea of justice (ibid.: 181, 192). Consequently, 'abandoning one's own children for someone else is not a breach of love but a proof of it; idealizing love means pledging to break with all false forms of it' (ibid.: 174).

However, there is something fundamentalist about this romantic ambition of sacrifice, the ambition 'to break with all false forms' of love. To clarify this, we can refer back to Kierkegaard's interpretetion of Abraham's sacrifice. Even though Abraham sacrifices his own son, he remains uncertain as to God's will and he reaffirms the distance between the divine and the worldy. That is, Abraham sacrifices the idea of sacrifice itself; moving beyond the idea of exchange, without any expectation of return, his sacrifice does not bring with it any certainty as to God's will or Abraham's position in the socio-symbolic order. 'Romantic love' in Beck and Beck-Gernsheim's sense, on the other hand, is a promise of certainty, an 'alternative to doubt' (ibid.: 192). Thus Beck and Beck-Gernsheim characterize it as a 'religion without churches' (ibid.: 177). In our terminology, however, such love is closer in its *modus operandi* to fundamentalism than religion as such (see Chapter 6).

Both forms of love feed upon the suspension of normality, but one of them does this by turning exception into a norm, perhaps only to avoid its twin, a real exception. What is more interesting, however, is that insofar as exception divides itself into two, one conservative, the other radical exceptions, it can also return to the domain of justification. To discuss this, we first need to discuss the 'new spirit of capitalism' (Boltanski and Chiapello 1999).

Is the camp the 'new spirit of capitalism'?

It seems to us that, insofar as the camp builds upon positive power and, by the same token, insofar as it needs and seeks justification, it can find it with reference to a new, emerging regime of justification, based on a compromise between three hitherto distinct regimes of justification and critique: the aesthetic, the industrial and the market regimes (see Baltanski and Chiapello 1999). Indeed, the logic of indistinction seems to have permeated regimes of justification. Thus, aesthetic creativity, industrialist productivity, and the market's grandeur, willingness to take risks, are no longer exclusive worlds. Boltanski and Chiapello call this new compromise 'project regime', a new regime of justification and critique emerging as a zone of de-differentiation between three previously differentiated regimes of justification. Hence, the new spirit of capitalism is a 'monstrous hybrid', a 'leftist capitalism' (ibid.: 290). This hybrid, indistinct regime is perfectly in tune with the logic of networking. Its grandeur is connectionism, that is, always being on the move towards a new project and living a life of simultaneous and successive projects.

In this world, a pre-established habitus is no longer desirable: the 'grand person is mobile. Nothing must disturb his displacements' (ibid.: 168, 183; Albertsen and Diken 2001: 19–20). In other words, the 'project regime' turns nomadism (exception) into a rule, perversion into law.

Indeed 'capitalist society never stops internalizing a revolutionary war-machine' (Deleuze 2004: 161). The development of the project regime confirms that critique is not a peripheral activity; it contributes to the power it criticizes. In other words, power can capture, assimilate and accommodate critique. Any critique of power is thus constantly confronted with the danger of being appropriated by power and thus becoming dysfunctional. Which is, for instance, what happened to the 'aesthetic citique' of capitalism through the concept of 'nomadism', in which, according to Boltanski and Chiapello, the 'new spirit of capitalism' finds a new form of justification.

Hence today aesthetic critique seems to have liquefied into a post-Fordist normative regime of justification, which promotes creativity, flexibility and difference. Indeed, one is tempted to see Spinoza as the grammatician of the project regime because most of his themes (anti-teleology, anti-dialectic, multitude, the plane of immanence occupied by bodies and souls, power as potentiality, the destruction of the subject, and so on) converge with the characteristics of the new, post-Fordist spirit of capitalism (Illuminati 2003: 317). Similarly, Žižek characterizes Deleuze as 'the ideologist of late capitalism' (2003: 184).

The problem here is twofold. The first relates to the nature of exception, the second to the nature of critique. Regarding the first, it is necessary to relate normalization of exception to the 'new spirit of capitalism'. Indeed, it seems to us that Schmitt, not Spinoza or Deleuze, is the grammatician of the project regime. And this is the case precisely insofar as the project regime can turn nomadism into a reactionary state of (normalized and justified) exception that aims at preserving rather than changing business as usual. If anything, the project regime is the Spinozism or Deleuzianism *of capital*:

> If we can say that Fordism incorporated, and rewrote in its own way, some aspects of the socialist experience, then post-Fordism has dismissed both Keynesianism *and* socialism. Post-Fordism, hinging as it does upon the general intellect and the multitude, puts forth, *in its own way*, typical demands of communism (abolition of work, dissolution of the State, etc.). Post-Fordism is the communism of capital.
>
> (Virno 2004: 111)

Capital reads Spinoza and Deleuze 'in its own way', creating its own Spinozism/ Deleuzianism and by turning immanence into a transcendent rule. Our point is that this logic of indistinction (immanence/transcendence, capitalism/ communism, and so on) itself is Schmittian. The paradoxical logic of the project regime consists in its including and excluding immanence in the same movement, for inclusion here amounts to transforming immanence into transcendent rule (Albertsen 2001). 'Communism of capital', however, is not communism. If the logic of normalized exception serves capital in the form of post-Fordism, the political task, to paraphrase Benjamin, is 'to bring about a real state of emergency' that can improve the critical position in the struggle against post-Fordist capital.

Which brings us to the second problem. In any critique of capital it is fatal to recall the immanence of capital. Capital has no ethical code defined once and for all and therefore, as already Marx saw it, it functions like a specter, a vampire (see 1973: 646). Having no ethical autonomy, it forever needs justification from elsewhere, from other orders than itself, that is, the regimes of justification (Boltanski and Chiapello 1999: 58–9; Guilhot 2000: 357). It can even appropriate the criticism of itself, turning anti-consumerism into a commodity. Or, as is the case with contemporary marketing, advertising and other branches of communication, capital can seize hold of even the notion of creativity, the 'concept itself', reducing critique to sales promotion (see Deleuze and Guattari 1994: 10–11).

The constitutive role of critique for capital explains why the multitude is the fundamental creative force that keeps power and capital afloat, not the other way around; the 'final word on power is that resistance comes first' (Deleuze 1988: 89). Criticism precedes, not follows, justification, that is, in principle, capital can capture every kind of critique. Nothing is critical once and for all. And in this respect the transformation of contemporary 'society' into an unstable bio-political field is co-terminus with the logic of capital. Indeed, capital seems to be the only link between diverse, multiple camps, especially those which take privatized consumption as their primary reason to exist. Further, the ever-growing diversification of contemporary camps is possible only to the extent that they can be held together by capital. For the same reason, the reference of each camp to a particular 'territory' is what hides its universal, anonymous, and 'ex-territorial' logic, a logic, which, being indifferent to the particular, operates *per causas* and administers the particular contexts directly, with the cruelty of the sovereign exception.

To the extent the camp signals the disappearance of 'society', its explosion in the global and implosion in the individual, it also brings with it a mobile form of sociality to be performed and re-performed constantly. What remains unchanging in temporary 'settlements' is the recognition that there is no 'society' out there. Against 'society', the logic of the camp promotes unbonding as a form of relation and as a 'good' which is not common. And not surprisingly, in a 'society under siege' (Bauman 2002), that is, when 'society' can no longer repress or promise salvation, the idea of 'society' can only be staged as a spectacle, as a simulacrum of a 'society' that can only pretend to exist. Hence the popularity of the reality TV show *Big Brother* as the tragicomic reversal of Foucault's panopticon. Reality TV is a testimony to the disappearance of society, its 'unreality', and to the *Unsicherheit* which follows. Thus everything is staged for the gaze of a spectral, unreal 'society', in the camp called *Big Brother* reality TV show. In this, reality and representation enter into a zone of indistinction and it becomes impossible whether the 'actors' are objects of desire or abjects. The logic of the camp, one must add, is not only what remains operative when 'society' disintegrates but also what causes this disintegration.

Distant critique?

In a sense, there is no 'question' of the camp. Answers to the question of the camp are already given: opinion, business, efficiency, creativity, community, civic life, and project. And 'to the answer already contained in a question . . . one should respond with questions from another answer' (Deleuze and Guattari 1987: 110). Regarding the critique of the camp, our question from another answer was nomadism. It is obvious that the camp must be criticized and resisted in a creative way because it is creative. Regarding the camp, the problem of critique is to acquire a consistency, without which there will be only two options: an anti-nomadic critique of the camp, on the one hand, or a pseudo-nomadic critique with no consistency, on the other. A nomadic critique demands the creation of 'a plane of absolute immobility or absolute movement', a 'movement that can be carried to infinity' (ibid.: 255; 1994: 39). 'Infinite movement' here does not refer to spatiotemporal coordinates but to nomadism as deviation, as 'spiritual exercise'.

From Castoriadis to Bauman, we are reminded that ours is a society which no longer questions itself and feels released from the necessity of justifying itself. Which does not mean that the critique of reality as such has ceased to exist; there is much critique in our society, but critique does not reach far: 'the unprecedented freedom which our society offers its members has arrived . . . together with unprecedented impotence' (Bauman 2000: 23). Interestingly in this context, Boltanski's *Distant Suffering* investigates the contemporary possibilities of translating knowledge/critique into action. His question revolves around the possibilities of moral action at a distance *vis-à-vis* a mobile power that can act at a distance. What realistic chance do we have to act, for instance, when we, the spectators, witness in the media the distant suffering of those in, say, (refugee, rape, detention, sex, . . .) camps scattered in different parts of the world? What form of commitment follows the knowledge of the camp? The crucial moment in this respect is the moment of transformation from the state of being a spectator, a receiver of information, into the position of an actor, a transformation, which is 'the political moment par excellence' (Boltanski 1999: 31).

We can recall Bourdieu for a last time at this point. He states, in the interview mentioned above, that he is sure that Chirac has read *The Weight of the World*. But Bourdieu is equally sure that Chirac has not done anything about the misery depicted in the book (Pécseli 1995: 14). This cynicism, that knowing but continuing to do otherwise, lies at the heart of the moral/political problem of the camp. Post-politics means the disappearance of the link between knowledge and action.

The relationship between critique and the camp, in other words, is not only an epistemological but also a political problem, a problem of action. Watching those held in the camps on television people can be shocked but this in no way guarantees commitment. Considering that people can only digest a certain amount of horror at a time and that indifference to distant others is an easy option, commitment has a weak chance to materialize (Boltanski 1999: 10; Bauman 2002: 211). If it does materialize, however, there are two common forms of commitment: denunciation (e.g. finding indignation by denouncing the perpetrators of the horror) or sentimentalism. Both options take one away from action: 'resentment = denunciation + sentiment' (Boltanski 1999: 132). But there is a third kind of commitment, 'aesthetic commitment', by which one dares to cast eyes on the evil without the imaginary benefits of denunciation and sentimentalism. This form of commitment, related to trust in the power of speech, is the only realistic basis for political action informed by morality, a 'politics of pity'. That is, pity can be a political issue only through dialogue and engagement, only in the public sphere (ibid.: 186).

Hence 'the crisis of pity' that characterizes the time of the camps. If speech and recognition are necessary for a politics of pity, for a morality that can have consequences, the camp signals the demise of confidence in speech. As Bauman argues, we are losing faith in the effectiveness of speech, because we are losing faith in the effectiveness of political action. Which is why today's 'agora' seems to be emptied out by the processes of privatization (Bauman 1999: 2). To be sure, today, with increasing networking and mobility, all kinds of interdependencies between different, locally disconnected but globally connected, camps proliferate and intensify. But technologies of camping do not really eradicate the distance between knowledge and action, between moral awareness and political consequence. Rather, the opposite is the case. The gap is becoming deeper and wider, taking the form of a fundamental contradiction, that of between freedom *de jure* and freedom *de facto* (see ibid.: 83–4; 2000: 38, 43).

All *dispositifs* of power, as Deleuze and Guattari (1987: 217) insist, are primarily defined by their impotence or what escpaes them. There is always a line of flight. This is, as we argued before, extremely relevant to recall in today's post-political society, which makes escape infinitely easy, and infinitely dangerous. Hence individual flight must connect, connect also to collective politics. And *this* is the task of sociology which has lost its 'society'.

What follows is that *sociology is needed today more than ever before*. The job in which sociologists are experts, the job of restoring to view the lost link between objective affliction and subjective experience, has become more vital than ever.

(Bauman 2000: 211)

The task of sociology is to formulate the experience of the space opened up in between flight and the political, or, to re-use a concept dear to both Bourdieu and Bauman, to add 'understanding' (consciousness) to the life of the planetary middle 'class' subjected to the powers of camping.

8

ETHICS AFTER THE CAMP

> Then one day, for no apparent reason, a dog wandered into camp. The prisoners, dreaming of America and Americans, called the dog Bobby, and Bobby got into the habit of greeting them with a happy bark when they lined up in the morning and when they returned from work at night. For him – without question – we were men.
>
> (Levi, quoted in Finkielkraut 2000: 4)

Can there be an ethics of the camp that can regulate the conduct of 'insiders' and 'outsiders', or, is the precondition of an ethical stance a commonality that has vanished with the generalization of the camp? How are we to relate to *homo sacer* with whom we can share nothing except his fundamental nakedness? Can one imagine an ethics that can make naked life (of the self and the other) its point of departure? And above all, can the world of camps be made hospitable? As we have shown throughout this book, the particularistic ethics promoted by the camp do not provide consistent answers to such questions. Ethics, in other words, remains one of the most problematical aspects regarding the generalization of the camp. Hence in this final chapter we deal with the camp in terms of ethics. We start with one of the most outrageous attempts to articulate an ethics of the camp in the history, Adolf Eichmann's distorted Kantianism. Then we contrast it with Agamben's ethics of testimony. Following this juxtaposition, we ask how the ethics of testimony can achieve a politically explicit form. Finally, to be able to move beyond the logic of the camp, we focus on the concepts of right and hospitality and investigate their potentiality regarding the camp.

Eichmann's Kant

What was most disturbing in Eichmann's trial in Jerusalem was his claim that in practice he had followed Kant's categorical imperative. Had Arendt, on the other hand, not stated that Eichmann was incapable of moral reflection, that his obedience was 'blind'? Arendt believed that Eichmann's being expressed a 'banality' of the evil, that is, an evil emanating not from a will (to do evil) but from a lack of thinking, of moral reflection. Eichmann was not a pathological criminal; 'banality' was a quality of his being rather than of his evil, which was 'monstrous' (Arendt 1978: 4). Eichmann followed the law, but did so 'blindly', without ethical reflection. He *chose* not to measure his acts up against moral standards. It is not obvious, therefore, how Eichmann could conceive of himself as a Kantian who strived to live according to the moral law.

The reason for Eichmann's distortion of Kantian ethics is already obvious in the first formulation of the categorical imperative (to make one's maxim universal law). The moral law is not obeyed for specific causes but solely because it is a law. The moral act is to be understood not as an expression of the good but as pure duty: your duty is . . . to do your duty (Žižek 1996: 79). This, for Eichmann, became the duty to follow the Führer's will. Precisely because this duty was imperative (categorical), he could avoid thinking. For him there existed no difference between the Führer's will and the moral law, or in more general terms, between legality and morality. He could thus recognize his subjection to Hitler's will as an unproblematic act. He had personally sworn him the oath of allegiance and this included an obligation towards his word of command (Arendt 1992: 149). The Führer's word was given immediately and imperatively. It had the power of the law and hence was not to be doubted (ibid.: 148). Arendt writes on Eichmann's use of the categorical imperative that:

> [Eichmann had] distorted it to read: Act as if the principle of your actions were the same as that of the legislator or of the law of the land – or, in Hans Frank's formulation of the 'categorical imperative in the Third Reich,' which Eichmann might have known: Act in such a way that the Führer, if he knew your action, would approve it.
>
> (ibid.: 136)

Eichmann's distortion of the categorical imperative was consistent with what Arendt and Eichmann himself called a version of Kant 'for the household use of the little man' (ibid.: 136). In this respect, Arendt is aware that Eichmann describes himself as an 'idealist': as a man who lived for his idea and was ready to sacrifice everything for it, including his family and himself (ibid.: 242). He had feelings and needs but they should retreat if they came into conflict with his 'idea' (ibid.: 42). The Nazis saw their killings as moral acts. It was an act where one bracketed one's subjective preferences and considerations, an act that could thus be understood as ethical. Crime was thus given a moral status.

The feeling of duty towards the Führer, the readiness to kill, and Eichmann's Kantianism are in reality of a piece. Just as Kantianism demands the complete disregard of all selfish considerations and motives, the Führer demanded that everybody unselfishly worked for the *Fatherland*. Thus, what was disquieting regarding Eichmann's evil was, according to Arendt, the fact that it was without personal motives. Eichmann distorted the categorical imperative by understanding it as a rule to be followed blindly. Such 'principled' evil had not been seen before. It is striking in this respect that the Nazis increased the speed of the extermination of Jews when they started to lose the war and thereby wasted decisive resources that could have been employed in the war. It was as if their 'idealism' mattered most, even more than their own lives and the fate of Germany.

For Kant, moral law appears only negatively as the experience of guilt. That one can never live up to the ethical demand, this *a priori* guilt, is what Kant understands as radical evil (Žižek 1997: 28). It is a guilt that originates in the fact that the human being can freely choose evil. Without this radical evil the moral law would have to phenomenologize itself in positive precepts and would thus become a codex which one then could follow blindly (ibid.: 228–9). Eichmann does not accept this radical evil. In other words, he does not accept that he has his own will, which is why he does not feel a need for moral reflection. His conscience is pure.

> [W]hat made it possible for the Nazis to torture and kill millions of Jews was not simply that they thought they were gods, and could therefore decide who would live and who would die, but the fact that they saw themselves as *instruments* of God (or some other Idea), who had already decided who could live and who must die. Indeed, what is most dangerous is not an insignificant bureaucrat who thinks he is God but, rather, the God who pretends to be an insignificant bureaucrat. One could even say that, for the subject, the most difficult thing is to accept that, in a certain sense, she is 'God', that she has a choice.
>
> (Zupančič 2000: 97)

We can now specify exactly the meaning of Kant's 'Du kannst, denn du sollst!' – you can because you must. No reference to a duty can be accepted as an excuse. If one refers to duty in doing one's duty, one oversees that one precisely should act out of duty (*aus Pflicht* and not *pflichtmässig*) (Zupančič 2000: 13–16). The ethical practice is always linked to a subjective element, a will, which must be acknowledged. The difference between acting *dutifully* and acting *out of duty* can be used to clarify in which way Eichmann is mistaken in his use of Kant's categorical imperative. The strength of Kantian ethics lies precisely in its undecideability: the moral law does not tell me *what* my duty is; it only tells me *that* I must do my duty: 'the ethical subject bears full responsibility for the concrete universal norms he follows – that is to say, the only guarantor of the universality of positive moral norms is the subject's own contingent act of performatively assuming these norms' (Žižek 1997: 221).

Eichmann was, in Arendt's view, frighteningly normal. The problem was that he did not 'think', that is, he was not able to reflect morally. He did not have the capacity to put himself in others' place and thus he did not doubt the words of Führer. He was 'banal' in the sense of thinking in rigid terms and his dependency on others.

> Except for an extraordinary diligence in looking out for his personal advancement, he had no motives at all. And this diligence in itself was in no way criminal; he certainly would never have murdered his superior in order to inherit his post. He *merely*, to put the matter colloquially, never realized what he was doing. . . . He was not stupid. It was sheer thoughtlessness – something by no means identical with stupidity – that predisposed him to become one of the greatest criminals of that period.
>
> (Arendt 1992: 287–8)

Lack of thinking, however, need not, automatically, lead to the inhumane treatment of the other. That is, Eichmann's rigidity may explain his adherence to the *Fatherland* but not the denigration of the Jews. The missing link here is the dehumanization of the other. Arendt repeatedly stresses that Eichmann was not an anti-Semite, but in doing so she misses an important point: Eichmann's world did not stop at the gate to the camp. He transposed the distinction between the human and the nonhuman onto another distinction, that of between the private and the public. In private, he could behave morally; in the public sphere, he behaved instrumentally. The concept of cynicism may illuminate this split.

As a cynic, Eichmann knew very well that the Nazi ideology is a construction, that the Führer was not God, and that the Jew was not a devil. But nevertheless he carried on, in practice, as if these were uncontestable truths. On several occasions he even distanced himself from anti-Semitism. For instance, he claimed several times that he personally had nothing against Jews (ibid.: 26). He even helped some Jews privately. However, helping an individual (private) Jew does not immunize one against the (public) ideology. Eichmann's 'distance' did not undermine but merely sustained his anti-Semitism. It is precisely through the (mis)conception of a 'I' outside the reach of ideology that the ideology is sustained. The exceptions to the public rule (e.g. helping individual Jews) sustain the rule (extermination of the Jews). Eichmann's cynicism finds perhaps its best expression when he mentions one of his Jewish 'friends', Storfer, who by a mistake ended up in a concentration camp. Here is what Arendt writes about Eichmann's last meeting with Storfer. As it is central to our analysis, we quote at length:

> Eichmann had received a telegram from Rudolf Höss, Commandant of Auschwitz, telling him that Storfer had arrived and had urgently requested to see Eichmann. 'I said to myself: O.K., this man has always behaved well, that is worth my while . . . I'll go there myself and see

what is the matter with him. And I go to Ebner [chief of the Gestapo in Vienna], and Ebner says – I remember it only vaguely – 'If only he had not been so clumsy; he went into hiding and tried to escape,' something of the sort. And the police arrested him and sent him to the concentration camp, and according to the orders of the Reichsführer [Himmler], no one could get out once he was in. Nothing could be done, neither Dr. Ebner nor I nor anybody else could do anything about it. I went to Auschwitz and asked Höss to see Storfer. 'Yes, yes [Höss said], he is in one of the labor gangs.' With Storfer afterward, well, it was normal and human, we had a normal human encounter. He told me all his grief and sorrow: I said: 'Well, my dear old friend [*Ja, mein lieber guter Storfer*], we certainly got it! What rotten luck!' And I also said: 'Look, I really cannot help you, because according to orders from the Reichsführer nobody can get out. I can't get you out. Dr. Ebner can't get you out. I hear you made a mistake, that you went into hiding or wanted to bolt, which, after all, *you* did not need to do.' [Eichmann meant that Storfer, as a Jewish functionary, had immunity from deportation.] I forget what his reply to this was. And then I asked him how he was. And he said, yes, he wondered if he couldn't be let off work, it was heavy work, And then I said to Höss: 'Work – Storfer won't have to work!' but Höss said: 'Everyone works here.' So I said: 'O.K.,' I said ' I'll make out a chit to the effect that Storfer has to keep the gravel paths in order with a broom,' there were little gravel paths there, 'and that he has the right to sit down with his broom on one of the benches.' [To Storfer] I said: 'Will that be all right, Mr. Storfer? Will that suit you?' Whereupon he was very pleased, and we shook hands, and then he was given the broom and sat down on his bench. It was a great inner joy to me that I could at least see the man with whom I had worked for so many long years, and that we could speak with each other.' Six weeks after this normal human encounter, Storfer was dead – not gassed, apparently, but shot.

(ibid.: 50–1)

Do we encounter here a lack of thinking or cynicism? Surely both. It is obvious that Eichmann cannot reflect on his practice. At the same time, however, the quote expresses his cynicism. Eichmann sees the ideology (Nazism) as an external framework he can distance himself from. However, despite his 'distance' to the ideology (e.g. being Storfer's sympathetic friend), he insists on the ideology in practice. Does the quote express anti-Semitism? Yes, in the sense that Eichmann accepts Storfer's fate as a natural consequence of his 'misbehaving'. The meeting with Storfer indicates that the Jews became human first when they (deserve to) become Eichmann's friends. As Göbbels claimed, everybody had their favourite Jews. This, however, did not stop the murder of six million Jews.

What becomes problematical in Eichmann's practice is the fate of the universal. And here we face the problem of the camp: a categorical and 'unselfish' ethics is no longer sufficient. The crucial question is no longer the content of an ethical stance. Rather, the question is to decide who counts as subjects worthy of ethical concern in the first place. Regarding the question of rights, for instance, the character and content of particular rights increasingly seem less significant compared with the right to have rights, that is, the right to belong to a common humanity. Then the question becomes, what would an ethics, which takes this right-less, naked and inhuman being as its point of departure, be like? As a first attempt to articulate such an ethics, let us now discuss Agamben's reflections on testimony. A truly universal ethics is one which testifies to the nakedness of *homo sacer*, a nakedness that is, we conclude, shared by all.

Testimony

Only if the experience of abandonment can escape every kind of law, it becomes possible to imagine the 'outside' of the paradox of sovereignty. This, however, involves 'nothing less than an attempt to think the politico-social *factum* no longer in the form of a relation' (Agamben 1998: 60). In this context Agamben sets the concept of 'testimony' against the sovereign exception. Testimony, in the case of the Holocaust for instance, materializes a crucial ambivalence in that verification and understanding can never coincide (Agamben 1999a: 12). Inasmuch as this ambivalence is the home ground for ethics and politics, the task consists of bearing testimony to something, which is impossible to bear testimony to. Testimony urges one to communicate what is incommunicable: the 'remnant' or the remainder (e.g. of Auschwitz), which designates not a relation but the *relating* of the relation.

> Here, it is not a matter of relating to something, but of *being* in relation, of entering the relation and touching its factuality, its *that*-it-relates. Only from such a perspective can a remainder reveal itself to be a 'being together' which no longer appears to have a 'relational form.' In order not to relate, and to break with the 'logic of sovereignty' . . . one must maintain oneself in the relating of the relation.
>
> (Düttmann 2001: 5)

To speak of a singular event (e.g. the Holocaust) as a remnant is not a matter of disclosing its positional network (e.g. through a testimony) or sublimating it as a unique isolated event. Rather, what is at stake here is 'to become testimony and to stop testifying to something – to Auschwitz' (ibid.). What the indifference to the network of the singularity illuminates is that any insight must initiate 'an abstraction and an idealization which is incompatible with the idea of a constitutive link, or relation, between a cognitive act and a proper name' (ibid.). Whenever 'testimony' becomes a testimony *to* something, we can be sure that this something reintroduces relation (and thus the logic of sovereignty).

> This is why those who assert the unsayability of Auschwitz today should be more cautious in their statements. If they mean to say that Auschwitz was a unique event in the face of which the witness must in some way submit his every word to the test of an impossibility of speaking, they are right. But if, joining uniqueness to unsayability, they transform Auschwitz into a reality absolutely separated from language, if they break the tie between an impossibility and a possibility of speaking that, in the Muselmann constitutes testimony, then they unconsciously repeat the Nazis' gesture; they are in secret solidarity with the Arcanum imperii.
>
> (Agamben 1999a: 157)

To understand what is meant by testimony, it is worth unpacking the concept of 'the unspeakable'. Trezise counts three meanings of 'the unspeakable', which also sums up the debate on the uniqueness of the Holocaust. First, the unspeakable is what cannot be uttered, what cannot be understood and therefore cannot be represented. The Holocaust transgresses our categories and therefore no description can do justice to it. The second meaning of the unspeakable emerges as to the dimensions and character of an evil act, e.g. the 'unspeakable evil' of Nazism. Finally, there is a third meaning which takes the form of a prohibition against utterance or narration. In this sense the unspeakable refers to something sacred or a taboo (Trezise 2001: 39).

Adorno's famous dictum 'To write poetry after Auschwitz is barbaric' and 'after Auschwitz one cannot write poetry' and even that 'all post-Auschwitz culture, including its urgent critique, is garbage' (Adorno 1973: 367), is often utilized as an axis around which the discussion of the representation of the Holocaust revolves (Trezise 2001: 43). In an essay titled 'Commitment' Adorno emphasizes that he wants to stick to his original wording and explains that it has two central meanings: first, every artistic representation of naked violence contains in itself the possibility of being in receipt of a desire to confront it. Following this, and second, any representation will invest meaning in what has no meaning. There is thus established an emancipating distance through which horror is relieved (ibid.: 44).

For Agamben, the Holocaust is unique in its dimensions and character (the second meaning of the unspeakable). Similarly, the Holocaust is the limit of the language and the speakable (the first meaning of the unspeakable). Agamben claims, for instance, the unfortunate term Holocaust is an attempt at giving meaning to something that has no meaning (1999a: 31). He does not, however, accept that the Holocaust is a mystical event that contains a sacred aura (the third meaning of the unspeakable) (ibid.: 31–3). To say this would be playing the Nazis' own game. How can one avoid the apparently logical step from the first two understandings of the unspeakable to the third? The solution is to emphasize the aporetic character of testimony. We are urged to communicate what is incommunicable.

Levi repeatedly emphasized that those who survived were not the real witnesses. The *Muselmann* would have been a real witness. The survivor is the exception, the drowned the rule (ibid.: 33). Therefore meaningful remembrance must relate itself to the fundamental nakedness of the subject, and thus always take place by delegation:

> At first it appears that it is the human, the survivor, who bears witness to the inhuman, the Muselmann. But if the survivor bears witness for the Muselmann – in the technical sense of 'on behalf of' or 'by proxy' ('we speak in their stead, by proxy') – then according to the legal principle by which the acts of the delegated are imputed to the delegant, it is in some way the Muselmann who bears witness.
>
> (ibid.: 120)

Testimony does not guarantee the factual truthfulness of a given utterance and thus does not enable a definitive historical archivation. The Holocaust is that which resists archivation because as unspeakable it escapes both the appropriating memory and the willed forgetting. But then, how can we keep alive the aporia, the tension between speech and naked life, between the traumatized testimony and the repressed memory, and thus 'mediate' between the past and the present? How can one represent the impossibility of depicting horror? 'Remnant' expresses that which cannot be destroyed, a residue of the past that refuses to disappear: 'the remnants of Auschwitz – the witnesses – are neither the dead nor the survivors, neither the drowned nor the saved. They are what remains between them' (ibid.: 164).

Further, Agamben uses the concept of shame to describe the relationship between the *Muselmann* and those who bear witness. What is central here is not the subject of shame, but its object. We are ashamed of the acts where we are not able to establish a distance to our acts, that is, our nakedness. What creates the feeling of shame is that which cannot be appropriated: the nakedness of the subject (ibid.: 105). Shame does not originate from a consciousness of a lack, which one attempts to distance oneself from; rather, one is ashamed of not being able to escape oneself. More technically, shame is produced when the subject acts as a subject for his own de-subjectivation (ibid.: 106):

> To be ashamed means to be consigned to something that cannot be assumed. But what cannot be assumed is not something external. Rather, it originates in our own intimacy; it is what is most intimate in us (for example, our own physiological life). Here the 'I' is thus

overcome by its own passivity, its own sensibility; yet this expropriation and desubjectification is also an extreme and irreducible
presence of the 'I' to itself. It is as if our consciousness collapsed and,
seeking to flee in all directions, were simultaneously summoned
by an irrefutable order to be present at its own defacement, at the
expropriation of what is most its own. In shame, the subject thus has
no other content than its own desubjectification; it becomes witness
to its own disorder, its own oblivion as a subject. This double
movement, which is both subjectification and desubjectification, is
shame.

(ibid.: 105–6)

One can live in shame, and certainly everybody in the camps did. Those who
did not hit the bottom avoided this fate by stealing from other inmates or by
working in *Sonderkommando* or by overtaking policing functions in the camps
(ibid.: 24). That is, it was impossible to preserve one's dignity; the inmates
occupied what Levi characterized as a grey zone, in which the distinctions
between executioner and victim, good and evil, worthy and unworthy lose their
meaning (ibid.: 21). In this respect, the condition of the *Muselmann* is not the
lowest form of being in an ethical hierarchy of forms of being but that which
makes the whole hierarchy meaningless (ibid.: 63). If ethical categories no
longer make sense in this grey zone, it is because they are not genuinely ethical
categories (ibid.: 63). Auschwitz is, in this sense, the test of ethics, a test a
genuine ethics must pass through (ibid.: 13). An ethics after the Holocaust
must start at the point at which worth disappears and the naked life reveals
itself (ibid.: 69).

Shame has an active and a purely receptive pole. The *Muselmann* incarnates
the first and the person who bears testimony the other. What is significant is
the relationship between these two poles; testimony is, as the appropriation of
something that cannot be appropriated, precisely such a relation. Agamben
seeks to identify this relationship through a series of concepts such as auto-
affection, immanence and the existence of the grammatical 'I'. This 'I' has
no substance in itself. It is merely the link between a series of utterances. As
such, the grammatical 'I' refers to the same nakedness, which the *Muselmann*
incarnates (ibid.: 116). The 'grammatical I' marks a non-being, which is the
condition of all being. Testimony emerges at the point at which the mute gives
the speaking subject a voice, and the speaking subject bears testimony to
the impossibility of speaking with one's own voice (bears testimony to
that which cannot be communicated and represented) (ibid.: 120). It is only
because we all share in common the fundamental nakedness of the *Muselmann*,
because human life is precarious and vulnerable, we can bear testimony to
the *Muselmann*. 'The witness' survival of the inhuman is a function of the
Muselmann's survival of the human. What can be infinitely destroyed is what
can infinitely survive' (ibid.: 151).

Shame is essentially the guilt of having survived, of knowing that others died in one's place. One mourns the other in having outlived him or her, for having abandoned the other. And what must be forgiven is thus simply this living on. And this *a priori* guilt turns the death of the other into something different, into an equivalent of murder to which one must confess and be forgiven (Derrida 2002b: 381–4):

> There would be, there sometimes is, a feeling of guilt, muted or acute, for living, for surviving, and therefore an injunction to ask for forgiveness, to ask the dead or one knows not who, for the simple fact of being there, alive, that is to say, for surviving, for being here, still here, always here, here where the other is no longer – and therefore to ask for forgiveness for one's being-there, a being there originarily guilty.
>
> (ibid.: 382–3)

And then again, there emerges the question of who has the right to forgive and who to receive this forgiveness. As a proper name Auschwitz here works as a metaphor for all those who died and to whom we have to speak. Perhaps there is even a duty to speak for and in behalf of those who are living but in their lack of a voice is already counted as dead. It might be that the authenticity of humanity is that of a speechless and precarious being: an anonymous corporeality of pure helplessness; man as a poor forked animal (Caldwell 2004: 43). Considered in this way, the discourse of human rights is a discourse in permanent crisis, a crisis, which stems from the fact that the abstract nakedness of simply being a human being no longer provides it with a sacred core (Arendt 1973: 299).

The right to have rights

> We became aware of the existence of a right to have right (and that means to live in a framework where one is judged by one's actions and opinions) and a right to belong to some kind of organized community, only when millions of people emerged who had lost and could not regain these rights because of the new global political situation. The trouble is that this calamity arose not from any lack of civilization, backwardness, or mere tyranny, but, on the contrary, that it could not be repaired, because there was no longer any 'uncivilized' spot on the earth, because whether we like it or not we have really started to live in One World. Only with a completely organized humanity could the loss of home and political status become identical with expulsion from humanity altogether.
>
> (Arendt 1973: 296–7)

When human rights were most downtrodden, another right announced itself, the right to have rights (ibid.: 298). This newly discovered right was not a

181

civil right and barely a juridically defined right. It did not and still does not belong to the family of rights (the celebrated political, social and economical rights) for it is what conditions them, and as such this 'right' necessarily resists the very language of rights (Hamacher 2004: 353). In fact, it is not a right at all because it is given exclusively to the citizens of states. Hence innumerable times throughout history this 'right' to belong to a common humanity has proven unenforceable for those unprotected by a state, e.g. refugees.

The double title of the *Déclaration des droits de l'homme et du citoyen* is thus a pleonastic one. The first term, *l'homme* is defined and contained in the other, *citoyen*. Man is defined in terms of his citizenship and is entitled to human rights only in this capacity. Instead of the universalistic concept of *Man* we are left with a political concept of *men* as citizens who stand against other citizens (Hamacher 2004: 347). Thus, the first article of the *Déclaration*, which states that 'all men are born and remain free and equal in rights', must be taken literally. What matters is the fact of birth through which bare life is included in the nation and in the apparatus of the state (Agamben 1995: 128). Since birth comes into being as nation, the difference between the two moments potentially disappears (Agamben 2000: 21). Thus, it is always governments that define the standards of human rights within their borders and act as representatives of humanity within the international realm. In other words, human rights depend on an alien power to implement them, which makes them vulnerable to the will and interests of this power.

Hence the 'rights of man' is always a confusing, perplex concept. The crisis of the concept is perhaps best illuminated by the figure of the refugee (see Chapter 4). Breaking the continuity between man and citizen, nativity and nationality, the refugee illustrates that human rights are neither sacred nor inalienable: 'Bringing to light the difference between birth and nation, the refugee causes the secret presupposition of the political domain – bare life – to appear for an instant within that domain' (Agamben 1998: 131). The paradox here is this: the difference between birth and nation is marked by a passport, the lack of which becomes the reason for denying rights:

> One assumes that what one calls, in a word, a 'sans-papiers,' is lacking something. He is 'without.' She is 'without.' What is he or she lacking, exactly? Lacking would be what the alleged 'paper' represents. The right, the right to a right. One assumes that the 'sans-papiers' is in the end 'sans droit,' 'without right' and virtually outside the law . . . What he is lacking, in truth, the lack he is being imputed and that one wants to sanction, that one wants to punish – let us not deceive ourselves, and I would like to show this, intentionally using this very precise word – is a *dignity*. The 'sans-papiers' would be lacking dignity . . . One refuses this dignity to those one is accusing . . . of being 'unworthy of living on our soil'.
>
> (Derrida 2002a: 135–6)

It is precisely in being abandoned from the domain of rights that the refugee turns out to be the core figure around which an ethics of the camps can be articulated. The refugee reveals the limits of a system based on the jurisdiction of nation-states and points, as does the *Muselmann*, towards a coming community in which the naked being is raised to the dignity dreamt of in the *Declaration*. Thus, the fact of birth not only signals the inscription into the nation but can also refer to the equality of all human beings. That is, it can underline the fact that all are born as subjects of right. This implies that 'the right to have rights' can correspond to the naked body of *human sacer*, man in his nakedness. The Man mentioned in the *Declaration* is not a particular being but one liberated from the particularities of given communities by the fact of being just human (Deranty 2004: 19–21). The task, then, is to reconstruct political thought with reference to the figure of the refugee, 'the only imaginable figure of the people in our day' (Agamben 1995: 114).

The abstract right to have rights might be understood as the right to a future community, which contains the possibility of having rights, of using, changing and expanding rights, a possibility offered to 'each and everyone, whoever or whatever he, she or it may be' (ibid.: 353–4). It is the right of the human in its abstract nakedness, that is, before its profession, citizenship, deeds and identifications (ibid.: 354). It is, however, crucial to remember that rights are not static and immutable entities. Rather, they are historical, shifting conditions of human freedom and emancipation. In other words, the realm of rights is a political battlefield. Thus rights, especially the attribution of them to some and not others, can become a means of repression, but they are also weapons in the struggle of the oppressed against oppression.

Balibar's concept 'equaliberty' is here useful. There can be no liberty without equality and no equality with liberty; the two terms stand in a relation of mutual implication (Balibar 2004: 313). The subject of equaliberty positions itself as a bearer of universal demands. It is sufficient 'simply to be a human *being, ohne Eigenschaften*' (a man without properties). The 'without' here might refer to a virtually infinite category, including the 'san-papiers', 'sans-abri', the 'sans-emploi,' the 'sans-logis,' or 'sans-diplôme' – the people without papers, homes, jobs or skills (Derrida 2002a: 139). The subjects without properties stand, in their without-ness, as the vanguards of an 'intensive' universality which forbids exclusion from citizenship in the name of determinations of condition, status, or nation. Emphasis, in this context, is on the negative. Universality is strived for in fighting particular wrongs, in negating the negative (Balibar 2004: 312). Through this fight the concept of universality is widened and intensified. As such, equaliberty is the demand for popular sovereignty, a principle of universal reciprocity (ibid.: 318–19).

Balibar's being *ohne Eigenschaften* is indebted to Marx's concept of the 'universal class', which is simultaneously a class and a non-class, or, more precisely, a class whose entire being resides in alienation. For Marx, the proletariat is the vanguard of universality not because it is the most exploited class but because it is a 'living contradiction' giving body to the inconsistency of the capitalist whole (Žižek 1999a: 225). The universal class is the reverse of reciprocity and as such what commands its unconditional realization (Balibar 2002: 6). It is a part of no part, the part, which does not belong to the whole, a party without a parliament. The universal class is the part, the party of the universal, whose emancipation serves as the criterion of a general emancipation. That is, politics of the universal class is a matter of elevating the specific into a stand-in for the universal (Žižek 1999a: 208).

If equaliberty is understood in Balibar's general sense, then the history of emancipation is not primarily one of demanding still unknown rights, but a struggle to enjoy rights that has already been declared (Balibar 2002: 6). To say that the 'men without' form a universal class means, in this context, that we are all refugees (Agamben 1995: 119). Or, we are all 'sans-papiers' (Derrida 2002a: 139). The problem is not only the fragile status of the excluded but rather that 'we are all "excluded" in the sense that our most elementary, "zero", position is that of an object of biopolitics and that eventual political and citizenship rights are given to us as a secondary status?' (Žižek 2002: 95). Then, if we all are naked, how can a solidarity between camps emerge?

Hospitality

Ethics is the question of care for the other, a question of welcoming the other, of hosting him or her. But hospitality is not an ethics among others. One is mistaken if one sets out to cultivate *an* ethics of hospitality. Ethics *is* hospitality and at the same time one of the most precious human rights (Derrida 2000b: 4):

> Insofar as it has to do with the *ethos*, that is, the residence, one's home, the familiar place of dwelling, inasmuch as it is a manner of being there, the manner in which we relate to ourselves and to others, to others as our own or as foreigners, ethics is hospitality; ethics is so thoroughly coextensive with the experience of hospitality.
>
> (Derrida 2001: 16–17)

This ethics is a matter of enabling openings and recognition (Dikeç 2002: 229). Opening towards and recognition of the other. Ethics is thus a question of relationships, of relating differently, without following the path of sovereignty and abandonment. The subject is, to paraphrase Levinas, simultaneously host and hostage. Subject *for* the other, the one who welcomes him, the one who resides over the home, but also subject *of*, the one who is exposed to the other and put into question by the other's very being. And here we have the recurring theme of the face in Levinas. Although the other is an abandoned subject stripped down to a fundamental nakedness, there is still the anguish of the face, which, in a silent but imperative voice, commands: 'Do not kill'.

This silent voice is the beginning of ethics and, by the same token, of the weakening or becoming minor of the sovereign power.

The other (the refugee, the stranger or just simply the neighbour) is the one who begs for hospitality in a language which is not his own. And herein consists a first and unavoidable act of violence. In determining the other as stranger, the conditionality of family, nation, state and citizenship is already presupposed (Derrida 2000b: 8). Thus, the other is subjected to the laws of the visiting country, the rules of hospitality. The foreigner must accept that his host is the master (Derrida 2000a: 15). Hence the tension, the double bind, inscribed at the heart of hospitality: hospitality is a right, a duty and an obligation but at the same time is conditioned by the host, who opens his home. The law of hospitality is the law of the household, the law of place: house, hotel, hospital, hospice, family, city, nation, language. It is a law of space, which delimits the place and time of hospitality, which thus turns to be a conditioned gift (Derrida 2000b: 4). The first condition is that the guest accepts that it is not his or her home, that he or she is welcomed but is not at home. The host must remain the master, regardless of the extent of his or her generosity. That is, the ultimate act of border crossing becomes conditional with respect to another threshold that is not to be passed (ibid.: 14).

The border crossed is one between 'the familial and the non-familial, between the foreign and the non-foreign, the citizen and the non-citizen, but first of all between the private and the public, private and public law, etc.' (Derrida 2000a: 49). What marks this border between inside and outside, familiar and foreign is the door, an opening towards the other and towards infinity (Derrida 1999: 26). There can be no habitable home without openings, without doors and windows that allow passage to the outside. On the other hand, if there is a door, there will no longer be unconditional hospitality. Sovereignty is exactly the ability to close the door, to abandon a subject. If there is a door there will also be a key and someone holding this key. Hence the distinction between visitation (with key) and invitation (without key), between entering (lacking a key) and coming (having one's own key), and between conditional and unconditional hospitality, a distinction between hospitality as it exposes itself to the visit, to the visitation, and the hospitality that adorns and prepares itself in invitation (Derrida 2000a: 61; 2000b: 14; 2002b: 362).

To interrogate this fragile balance between the border as a place of filtering and of welcoming let us, for a moment, turn to Kant's 'Third Definitive Article of a Perpetual Peace', where he introduces the right to hospitality, the right of the stranger not to be treated with hostility and the right to asylum. It is as if Kant's idea is an elaborated notion of the classic idea of sanctuary provided by churches. There is, Kant claims, a right to communal possession of the earth's surface. The earth is a globe, that is a finite area, and one is thus to tolerate the company of others. No one has the right to any particular portion of the earth (Kant 1970: 106). Crucially, however, this genuinely ethical right is put under erasure as soon as it is uttered, which is also expressed in the subtitle: 'Cosmopolitan (Cosmopolitical) Right shall be Limited to Condition of Universal Hospitality' (ibid.: 105). As Derrida remarks, the text establishes, on the one hand, a regulative Ideal, but it sets, on the other, certain delimitations, which implies that this ideal must necessarily have a history, that it is in the making (2000b: 10). The natural right to hospitality does not extend beyond the conditions making it possible to enter into relations with natives.

But there are less obvious conditions. The right to unconditional hospitality is a cosmo*political* right, protecting citizens against hostile treatment when entering another state. In other words, the right to unconditional hospitality is a right and not a matter of philanthropy (Kant 1970: 105). Strangers might in fact be turned away if this is done without causing harm. As Kant laconically stresses, this is a right which implies that savage nations are no longer allowed to make a meal out of the stranger (ibid.: 103, 105–6). The restriction on cannibalism can also be given a more metaphoric and updated interpretation in the sense of a right to keep one's foreignness, the right not to be assimilated. As Bauman (1995: 18) argues using Lévi-Strauss's concepts, there are two predominant strategies of dealing with the stranger. One is anthropophagic and aims at assimilating the stranger's strangerhood; the other is anthropoemic and aims at banishing, excluding the stranger. Eating up versus vomiting. The question never raised by either strategy is being *for*, what we can do for the stranger. Rather, today the figure of the stranger arouses fear, hospitality has become subject to the possession of passports, bank statements and invitation letters. Further, the pretext of combating 'bogus refugees' or economic immigrants constantly denigrates the status of the strangers as something unwanted. Indeed, hospitality has become a crime, as is the case when people hide foreigners whose applications of asylum have been rejected:

> What becomes of a country, one must wonder, what becomes of a culture, what becomes of a language when it admits of a 'crime of hospitality,' when hospitality can become, in the eyes of the law and its representatives, a criminal offense?
>
> (Derrida 2002a: 133)

Hospitality is a self-contradictory concept, which can only destruct itself (Derrida 2000b: 5), a concept defined by its very impossibility, by a non-dialectizable antinomy. It deconstructs the very idea of being at home and as such of the self and its other (ibid.: 364). On the one hand, the unconditional imperative principle of radical hospitality, a hyperbolic principle, which defies all laws and identities, and on the other all the innumerable conditions (see Derrida 2000a: 77). There is a plight to question the authority of the logos and ethnos. But the tension is not only one between the host and the other exposed to the welcoming gesture. The host has to keep within the laws of hospitality and transgress them, and so does the guest. Hospitality must never simply be a duty, a law. One must welcome without the 'must' (Derrida 2002b: 361):

> For to be what it 'must' be, hospitality must not pay a debt, or be gov-
> erned by a duty: it is gracious, and 'must' not open itself to the guest
> [invited or visitor], either 'conforming to duty' or even, to use the
> Kantian distinction again, 'out of duty.' This unconditional law of
> hospitality, if such a thing is thinkable, would then be a law without
> imperative, without order and without duty. A law without law,
> in short. For if I practice hospitality 'out of duty', this hospitality
> of paying up is no longer an absolute hospitality, it is no longer
> graciously offered beyond debt and economy, offered to the other, a
> hospitality invented for the singularity of the new arrival, of the
> unexpected visitor.
>
> (Derrida 2000a: 83)

The unexpected visitor! Hospitality is a risk, too. Hospitality in Latin has a rather troubling origin, carrying with it its own opposite, hostility. The visitor may take the host as his hostage (Derrida 2000b: 3). Without running this risk, there can be no hospitality, no unconditional letting the other come, no pre-ontological and affirmative yes to the other (Derrida 1999: 35). One must run the risk of being overtaken, surprised and even raped and stolen from (Derrida 2002: 360–1). Or, even further, hospitality requires that one continu-ously struggles to transgress the conditions restricting hospitality. It is the urge to do the impossible, to transgress the aporetic paralysis.

But what is significant in terms of ethics is the demand for developing hospitality into a culture of hospitality, to 'multiply the signs of anticipation, construct and institute what one calls the structure of welcoming, a welcoming apparatus' (Derrida 2002b: 360–1). Even in keeping within the law of uncon-ditional hospitality one needs laws to make it effective and to avoid the risk of becoming an abstract, utopian and illusory idea (Derrida 2000a: 79). Ethics, and thus hospitality, are not just a matter of the two, of the self and the other. There is, as Levinas stressed, always 'a third'. One cannot give all to the other, for there will always come another. A sort of mediation is thus necessary and in this respect the third is the beginning of justice as law. The exterior of the third will, however, always disturb the relation of the two. No ethics without perjury (Derrida 1999: 29–33). The other is the birth of the question, not just of ethics, but also of the subject itself. The other brings the subject into question. Ethics is thus not just a question of the other but also a self-questioning.

Ethics, in short, urges a reversal: the one who invites becomes the invited; the one who gives receives. Ethics demands a constant process of engagement and role exchange. It is the other, who, in accepting the hospitality of the host, makes his home a hospitable one, a true home (Derrida 2000b: 9; 1999: 41–2).

Crossing the threshold is entering and not only approaching or coming. Strange logic, but so enlightening for us, that of an impatient master awaiting his guest as a liberator, his emancipator. It is *as if* the stranger or foreigner held the keys. This is always the situation of the foreigner, in politics too, that of coming as a legislator to lay down the law and liberate the people or the nation by coming from outside, by entering into the nation or the house, into the home that lets him enter after having appealed to him. . . . [It is as if] the stranger could save the master and liberate the power of his host; it's as if the master, qua master, were prisoner of his place and his power, of his ipseity, of his subjectivity (his subjectivity is hostage).

(Derrida 2000a: 123)

Crossing a threshold, becoming other, a stranger to oneself, but still unavoidably trapped in the logic of the house, the subject easily becomes a hostage caught in a home of closed doors and windows. Ethics is situated on a threshold; it *is* a threshold and this more than ever in the era of generalized camping. Ethics insists on the threshold without which there would be no home, no place of asylum and no welcoming of the other. But it also demands that this threshold is crossed. Hospitality must never be reduced to a duty: the law of hospitality has to be reinvented every time an other is encountered. Ethics is, in short, a double bind. It is never pure, always a becoming. But how can one become other? And is there a nakedness which is not already trapped in the order of law and identity?

Naked at last sight

This is the anti-pampering experience. Feel like a mud bath? That's fine, but you'll find it in the gutter. Need to lose some pounds? A health farm can do that for you. But having no money to buy food is more efficient. The Peacemaker Centre . . . has been organising the retreats on the streets of New York for a decade and has already had more than 300 takers. Usually, they arranged in small groups of say about 10 people, each paying $150 in advance. And their ho-bo holidays last from three to five days.

(Usborne 2004)

Its rules are clear and simple: do not bring money; do not clean yourself; do not wear any new clothes, any jewellery, including watches and earrings; and do not forget to take a few plastic bags with you. This is what you need to improve your begging skills and to survive the latest de-stressing technique called 'street retreat' (Rees-Tonge 2004). It involves living the life of the homeless for a few days at a time. As Bernie Glassman, one of its spiritual leaders, puts it: 'Each retreat gives the retreatant a glimpse into what it is like to be ignored by society and what it feels like to be treated like an object by other people' (ibid.). Promising a 'plunge into the unknown', the idea that emerged among New York missionaries in the 1960s is now spreading in the USA and making its way to European cities.

It is significant that street retreat emerges in the contemporary 'reflexive' society whose ultimate suspicion is its own inauthenticity, that it is a fake paradise, a spectacle, deprived of a material solidity. Characteristic for such a society is that the social itself 'acquires the features of a staged fake' (Žižek 2002: 13–14). And when social reality appears as its opposite, as a spectacle, 'experience' increasingly refers to reaching out to the extreme, touching the void. The 'crash'. In a society in which everything is perceived to be a simulacrum, the 'hysteria' is the production of the real (Baudrillard 1994: 23). The suffering in a mean street can in this sense serve as a reminder of the real and is a testimony to a civilization for which everyday life is banal and the repetitive is death, a civilization, whose main feature is the 'passion of the real' (Badiou, quoted in Žižek 2002: 5–6).

The nature of the staged reality is, however, paradoxical. In other words, the idea that street retreat is that of the real, that it signifies the discovery of a real world behind the simulacra, is problematical. Being staged, experience itself acquires the characteristics of a dramatic, fantastic production. The 'real' itself becomes the simulacrum of a fantasy. In this sense, street retreat is more than anything else a journey to Benjamin's 'phantasmagoria', the fantasy-street.

If this is naïve, and sad, it is not only because the retreatants have a return ticket to civilization nor because they are transforming the street, the 'agora', into a 'phantasmagoria' in their paradoxical search for the real. But because the retreatants can be likened to Hegel's 'beautiful soul' who engages with the social world without recognizing his or her own active role in its production. There is, however, no neutral and un-deterritorialized ground upon which an innocent experience of the homelessness is possible. The homeless are a product of the American class structure. They are the homeless because the middle class, to which the retreatants belong, are the middle class. It is this knowledge of the real that is disavowed in the phantasmagoria.

Traditionally, spiritual retreats occur in peaceful, restful locations. But this one runs on the rough American streets instead. The retreatants belong to the higher segments of the middle class; among them are popular writers such as Tom Wolfe. The challenge is to find a place to sit down, not to mention a meal, or a bathroom. For some, it is the first and only time that they will struggle to find something to eat. Some, however, can endure more. But for all of them, freedom is becoming socially naked. Strip your 'identity' and leave it behind, at home. Becoming naked is a precondition for safety in the fantasy-street. Which is why the retreatants can claim that they are safe, much safer than in their clothes, during their retreat. 'Most people walk around in huge bubbles of security, but on the street retreat you learn that you can survive without the apartment, the job, the lifestyle' (a retreatant, quoted in Rees-Tonge 2004).

Bracketing their class, lifestyles, jobs, families, friends for a short while, that is, stripping their life from its 'form', street retreatants try to reach a kernel: bare life, the common denominator of humanity. As one of the retreatants says, 'spiritual awakening happens through the recognition that we are all human beings. We can get on with people regardless of their economic scale and find common ground' (CBS Radio Network 2002). Indeed, it is as if the disappearance of the self follows the disappearance of the experience. And precisely at this point the 'experiment' of street retreat meets its opposite:

> Two decades ago, the German left-wing weekly journal *Stern* con- ducted a rather cruel experiment: it paid a group of destitute homeless men and women to be thoroughly washed, shaved, and then delivered to the top fashion designers and hair dressers; in one issue, the journal then published two large parallel photos of each person: as a destitute homeless man or woman, dirty and unshaven; and dressed by a top designer. The result was somehow uncanny: although it was clear that we were looking at the same person, the effect of the different dress, and so on, was that our belief that, beneath different appearances, there is one and the same person was shaken. Not only their appear- ances were different: the deeply disturbing effect of these changes of appearance was that we, the spectators, somehow perceived a different personality beneath the appearances.
>
> (Žižek 2003b: 151–2)

Appearances, or forms, matter. Stripping the 'form' off a form of life, one reaches not an essential kernel but merely a void, a void in which the 'bare life' of the homeless dressed up as as a member of the middle class and of the retreatant dressed up as a homeless person become formally indistinguish- able. The self consists of the 'form' of life. And in both experiments we are confronted with the *mise en scène* of the contemporary fantasy world, a consumer culture focused on things about to disappear. The expectation is of course that these objects will spread light, illuminate, a last time before they disappear completely. The surrealist belief in the revolutionary potential of the things about to disappear, to be forgotten. Disappearance is to be alive.

One is tempted to ask: how is the retreatant, then, confronted with the 'real' homeless, with human waste, in the phantasmagoria? Does he feel what Baudelaire felt when an unknown woman 'passing by' in the crowd enters into Baudelaire's vision/world in the deafening crowd of the street: 'A flash . . . then night! – O lovely fugitive/ . . . /Shall I never see you till eternity?' (quoted in Benjamin 1983: 45). This momentary encounter, this shock, experienced just before one's object of desire disappears into the crowd, just before one is helplessly blown into the future while desperately trying to look back (*Angelus Novus*), is perhaps what comes closest to the experience of the real. 'The delight of the city-dweller is not so much love at first sight as love at last sight'

(Benjamin 1983: 45). In the world of disappearances it is not only unbonding but also bonding that fascinates – bonding, 'not at first sight but at last sight'.

What makes street retreat disturbing is that it is not an original experience at all. In fact, as we discussed, the concentration camp was the place in which naked body was introduced to the West in the figure of *homo sacer*, the human being excluded from the *polis* while being totally exposed to its *police*. Who is *homo sacer* in today's New York, if not the homeless whose life is abandoned by what we call civilization but remains at its mercy, a life that comes closest to a life in the 'state of nature'? And is it not precisely the opposite movement, that of, becoming *homo sacer*, the street retreatants subject themselves to, when they engage in their 'plunge into the unknown'? Or, are we not confronted here with the identity of the opposites?

Which brings to mind *Dawn of the Dead*, George Romero's 1978 film about zombies, in which the menaced consumers fortify themselves in a shopping mall, their 'temple, a cathedral of commodities'. The satire of the movie builds upon the indifference between the consumers of the phantasmagoria and the living-dead that attack them. 'The customers gobble up clothes, gadgets and snacks; the zombies gorge on human flesh' (Conrad 2004). Romero's 'silent majority', the animated corpses as exemplary citizens, is the point at which the consumption of objects about to disappear overlaps with the wasted or disappearing subjects.

The new street, or rather, the camp, is the place in which the body (of the homeless) becomes a spectacle, the spectacle (the identity of the middle class), a body. The body without an image, the homeless, meets the image without a body, the paranoiac consumer who suspects that his life is not real. And it is this paranoia that addresses the street as a forest that enslaves and promises freedom only to bare life. To those 'bodies' that have to hide their identity to survive.

To end with, in her essay on judgment, Arendt shows that rule following cannot be reconciled with the criteria of judgment. In this context she stresses the difference between *Kritik der Reinen Vernunft* and *Kritik der Urteilskraft*. Whereas the first understands morality as rule following (qua deduction), the latter constitutes an actively judging subject, a subject whose judgments invent the rule rather than following a given rule. The concept of taste is here of crucial importance for it is what mediates between the universal and the particular. As taste tells us what is 'tasty' or 'not tasty', political judgments tells us what is 'good' or 'bad'. The predicative activity of judgment presupposes thinking, that is, questioning everything including established truths (Arendt 1978: 174).

The choice between an ethics of norm and an ethics of exception is an open one. It is, namely, a choice, a judgment. Both ethics may inform genuine ethical judgments but they can, both, be perverted form. That is, the moral situation is an ambivalent one; the only yardstick is hospitality, the responsibility for the other, knowing, at the same time, that too much of it would cause domination, whereas a lack of it would amount to indifference. The moral self is born in this condition of uncertainty; the moral actor can never feel certain with respect to being moral: one would never have a definitive description of how one can respond to the other, or 'touch', without 'grasping' at one extreme and without, at the other extreme, becoming 'indifferent' to the other (see Bauman 1993: 92–4). And crucially in this respect, norm and exception are entwined. Thus the rule must be reinvented every time it is followed. Along the same lines, hospitality is both an opening and a closure: something unconditional, which, however, has to find a legal or semi-legal form. The third always stands in between the self and the other.

There can be no ethics without risk, the leitmotif and the driving force of the camp. The camp is the materialization of the avoidance of the unprepared encounter, an attempt to avoid (the confrontation with) the other. Its instruments, neutrality and segregation, make it impossible, by defining others *before* they are met, to confront others and to take choices. The logic of the camp is, from the point of ethics, to kill the beneficial anarchy of communication between the one and the other. Ethics, on the other hand, urges risk taking. It is in this effort that we discover that the camp is not just a matter of walls and fences but also of doors and windows. And it is only in this risk taking, that is, in becoming minor, one can defeat the logic of sovereignty:

> Why are there so many becomings of man, but no becoming-man? First because man is a majoritarian par excellence, whereas becomings are minoriarian; all becoming is a becoming-minoritarian. When we say majority, we are referring not to a greater relative quantity but to the determination of a state or standard in relation to which larger quantities, as well as the smallest, can be said to be minoritarian: white-man, adult-male, etc. Majority implies a state of domination, not the reverse . . . It is important not to confuse 'minoritarian', as a becoming or process, with a 'minority' as an aggregate or a state. Jews, Gypsies, etc., may constitute minorities under certain conditions, but that in itself does not make them becomings. One reterritorializes, or allows oneself to be reterritorialized, on a minority as a state; but in a becoming, one is deterritorialized. Even blacks, as the Black Panthers said, must become-black. Even women must become-women. Even Jews must become-Jewish . . . As Faulkner said, to avoid ending up a fascist there was no other choice than to become-black.
>
> (Deleuze and Guattari 1988: 291–2)

BIBLIOGRAPHY

Adorno, T.W. (1973) *Negative Dialectics*. New York: Continuum.

Agamben, G. (1993) *The Coming Community*. Minneapolis and London: University of Minnesota Press.

Agamben, G. (1995) 'We Refugees', *Symposium* 49(2): 114–20.

Agamben, G. (1997) 'Beyond Human Rights', in P. Virno and M. Hardt (eds) *Radical Thought in Italy*. Minneapolis: University of Minnesota Press, pp. 158–64.

Agamben, G. (1998) *Homo Sacer: Sovereign Power and Bare Life*. Stanford, CA: Stanford University Press.

Agamben, G. (1999a) *Remnants of Auschwitz: The Witness and the Archive*. New York: Zone Books.

Agamben, G. (1999b) *The Man Without Content*. Stanford, CA: Stanford University Press.

Agamben, G. (2000) *Means Without End: Notes on Politics*. Minneapolis: University of Minnesota Press.

Agamben, G. (2001) 'Heimliche Komplizen: Über Sicherheit und Terror', *Frankfurter Allgemeine Zeitung*, No. 219, September 20, p. 45.

Agamben, G. (2003a) 'The State of Emergency', available on www.generation-online. org/p/fpagambenschmitt.htm

Agamben, G. (2003b) 'The State of Exception', *Lettre Internationale* 1: 31–3.

Agamben, G. (2004a) '"I Am Sure that You Are More Pessimistic Than I Am": An Interview with Giorgio Agamben', *Rethinking Marxism* 16(2): 115–24.

Agamben, G. (2004b) 'Non au tatouage biopolitique', *Le Monde*, January 10.

Agamben, G. (2004c) *The Open: Man and Animal*. Stanford, CA: Stanford University Press.

Albertsen, N. (1995) 'Kunstværket, en sansningsblok under evighedens synsvinkel. Spinoza, Wittgenstein, Deleuze', in N. Lehmann and C. Madsen (eds) *Deleuze og det æstetiske. Æstetikstudier II*. Århus: Aarhus Universitetsforlag, pp. 135–62.

Albertsen, N. (2001) 'Spinoza, imperiet og kapitalismens nye ånd. Til fornyelsen af den sociale og æstetiske kritik af kapitalismen', paper given at the seminar, 'Globalisering, Kunst, fællesskabsfølelser og offentlighedsformer', Fællesæstetisk forskergruppe, *Center for Tværæstetiske Studier*, Aarhus Universitet, 3 December.

Albertsen, N. (2003) 'Conatus og intellektuel kærlighed. Spinozismen i Bourdieu', paper presented at the conference 'Kritiske Perspektiver på Bourdieus forfatterskab', Kritisk Profil og Sociologisk Forum, University of Aarhus.

Albertsen, N. and Diken, B. (2001) 'Mobility, Justification, and the City', *Nordic Journal of Architectural Research* 14(1): 13–24.

Al-Qattan, O. (2001) 'Disneyland Islam', *Open Democracy*, available on www. opendemocracy.net

Amin, S. and Thrift, N. (2002) *Cities: Reimagining the Urban*. London: Polity Press.

Andersen, H.C. (1965) *Eventyr og Historier*. vol. II. Copenhagen: Gyldendal.

Arendt, H. (1973) *The Origins of Totalitarianism*. New York: Harcourt Brace and Company.

Arendt, H. (1978) *The Life of Mind*. San Diego: Harcourt Brace and Company.

Arendt, H. (1992) *Eichmann in Jerusalem: A Report on the Banality of Evil*. London: Penguin.

Arendt, H. (1994) *Essays in Understanding 1930–1954*. New York: Harcourt Brace and Company.

Askin, K.D. (1997) *War Crimes Against Women: Prosecution in International War Crimes Tribunals*. The Hague: Martinus Nijhoff Publishers.

Augé, M. (1995) *Non-places: Introduction to an Anthropology of Supermodernity*. London: Verso.

Aure, M. (2004) 'Actors and Agency in Russian-Norwegian Rural, Regulated, Short-term Labour Migration', paper presented at the seminar 'Embeddedness and Migration – Local Dynamics in a Mobile World', Klasvik, 24–28 March.

Balakrishnan, G. (2000) *The Enemy: An Intellectual Portrait of Carl Schmitt*. London: Verso.

Balibar, É. (2002) *Politics and the Other Scene*. London: Verso.

Balibar, É. (2004) 'Is a Philosophy of Human Civic Rights Possible? New Reflections on Equaliberty', *The South Atlantic Quarterly* 103(2–3): 311–22.

Barber, B.R. (1996) *Jihad vs. McWorld: How Globalism and Tribalism are Reshaping the World*. New York: Ballantine Books.

Barrett, F. (1998) 'How Did the British Turn Ibiza into the Gomorrah of the Med?' *The Mail*, August 30.

Barthes, R. (1981) *Camera Lucida*. New York: Hill and Wang.

Bataille, G. (1993) *The Accursed Share*. vols II and III. New York: Zone Books.

Bataille, G. (1997) 'Architecture', in N. Leach (ed.) *Rethinking Architecture: A Reader in Cultural Theory*. London: Routledge, pp. 21–2.

Bataille, G. (2001) *Eroticism*. London: Penguin.

Batty, D. (2001) 'Doctor Plans Euthanasia Boat in UK Waters', *The Guardian*, June 19.

Baudrillard, J. (1988a) *Selected Writings*. London: Polity Press.

Baudrillard, J. (1988b) *Ecstasy of Communication*. Paris: Semiotext(e)/Pluto.

Baudrillard, J. (1990) *Fatal Strategies*. Paris: Semiotext(e)/Pluto.

Baudrillard, J. (1993) *The Transparency of Evil*. London: Verso.

Baudrillard, J. (1994) *Simulacra and Simulation*. Ann Arbor, MI: The University of Michigan Press.

Baudrillard, J. (2002) *The Spirit of Terrorism*. London: Verso.

Baudrillard, J. (2003) *The Spirit of Terrorism*. 2nd edn. London: Verso.

Bauman, Z. (1989) *Modernity and the Holocaust*. Cambridge: Polity Press.

Bauman, Z. (1991) *Modernity and Ambivalence*. Cambridge: Polity Press.

Bauman, Z. (1992) *Intimations of Postmodernity*. London: Routledge.

Bauman, Z. (1993) *Postmodern Ethics*. Oxford: Blackwell.

Bauman, Z. (1995) *Life in Fragments*. Oxford: Blackwell.

Bauman, Z. (1998a) 'What Prospects of Morality in Times of Uncertainty?', *Culture and Society* 15(1): 11–22.

Bauman, Z. (1998b) *Globalization: The Human Consequences*. New York: Columbia University Press.

Bauman, Z. (1999) *In Search of Politics*. Cambridge: Polity Press.

Bauman, Z. (2000) *Liquid Modernity*. London: Polity Press.

Bauman, Z. (2002) *Society Under Siege*. Cambridge: Polity Press.

Bauman, Z. (2003) *Liquid Love*. Cambridge: Polity Press.

Bech, H. (1999) *Leisure Pursuit: Studies in Modernity, Masculinity, Homosexuality and Late Modernity. A Survey of Some Results*. Copenhagen: Sociologisk Institut.

Beck, U. (2002) 'The Terrorist Threat: World Risk Society Revisited', *Theory, Culture and Society* 19(4): 39–55.

Beck, U. and Beck-Gernsheim, (1999) *The Normal Chaos of Love*. Cambridge: Polity Press.

Belge, M. (2001) 'Inside the Fundamentalist Mind', available on www. opendemocracy.net

Benjamin, W. (1983) *Charles Baudelaire: A Lyric Poet in the Era of High Capitalism*. London: Verso.

Benjamin, W. (1992) *Illuminations*. Fulham: Fontana Press.

Bentham, J. (1988) *An Introduction to the Principles of Morals and Legislation*. Buffalo, NY: Prometheus Books.

Bentham, J. (1995) *The Panopticon Writings*. London: Verso.

Berger, J. and Mohr, J. (1975) *A Seventh Man: The Story of a Migrant Worker in Europe*. Harmondsworth: Penguin.

Bickermann, E. (1929) 'Die Römische Kaiserapotheose', *Archiv für Religionswissenschaft* 27: 1–34.

Bigo, D. (2002) 'Security and Immigration: Toward a Critique of the Governmentabilility of Unease', *Alternatives* 27: 63–92.

Bin Laden, O. (2001a) 'Text of Osama Bin Laden Statement', October 7. http://users.skynet.be/terrorism/html/laden_statement.htm

Bin Laden, O. (2001b) 'Text of Osama Bin Laden Statement', November 3. http://users.skynet.be/terrorism/html/laden_statement_3.htm

Bin Laden, O. (2001c) 'Muslims Have the Right to Attack America', *The Observer*, November 11. www.observer.co.uk

Bin Laden, O. (2002a) 'Bin Laden's New Audiotape', November 12. http://users.skynet.be/terrorism/html/laden_statement_6.htm

Bin Laden, O. (2002b) 'Full Text: Bin Laden's "Letter to America"', *The Observer*, November 24. www.observer.co.uk

Bin Laden, O. and Miller, J. (2001) 'To Terror's Source', interview with Bin Laden, May 1998. http://abcnews.go.com/sections/world(DailyNews/miller_binladen_980609.html

Bolt, M. (2003) 'At vidne om det personlige', in S. Iversen, and H.S. Nielsen and D. Ringgard (eds) *Ophold: Giorgio Agamben's Litteraturfilosofi*. Copenhagen: Gyldendal, pp. 10–41.

Boltanski, L. (1999) *Distant Suffering: Morality, Media and Politics*. Cambridge: Cambridge University Press.

Boltanski, L. and Chiapello, È. (1999) *Le Nouvel esprit du capitalisme*. Paris: Gallimard.

Boltanski, L. and Thévenot, L. (1991) *De la Justification: Les économies de la grandeur*. Paris: Gallimard.

Boltanski, L. and Thévenot, L. (2000) 'The Sociology of Critical Capacity', *European Journal of Social Theory* 2(3): 359–77.

Borowski, T. (1976) *This Way for the Gas, Ladies and Gentlemen*. London: Penguin.

Bourdieu, P. (1989) *Distinction*. London: Routledge.

Bourdieu, P. (1999) 'Understanding', in P. Bourdieu *et al. The Weight of the World*, London: Polity Press, pp. 607–626.

Bourdieu, P. and Wacquant, L.J.D. (1992) 'The Purpose of Reflexive Sociology', in P. Bourdieu and L.J.D. Wacquant, *An Invitation to Reflexive Sociology*. Cambridge: Polity Press, pp. 61–216.

Bourdieu, P. *et al.* (1999) *The Weight of the World*. London: Polity Press.

Bowcott, O. (2003) 'Massive Flop. Ali G Fails to Win Respect in the US', *The Guardian*, 24 February.

Bozovic, M. (1995) 'Introduction: "An Utterly Dark Spot"', in J. Bentham *The Panopticon Writings*. London: Verso, pp. 1–27.

Bracewell, W. (2000) 'Rape in Kosovo: Masculinity and Serbian Nationalism', *Nations and Nationalism* 6(4): 563–90.

Braidotti, R. (1997) 'In the Sign of the Feminine: Reading Diana', http://muse.jhu. edu/journals/theory_and_event/v001/1.4symp_int.html

Braidotti, R. (2004) 'From "Biopower" to the politics of "Life Itself"', paper presented at the conference 'What's Life Got to Do with It?', Lancaster University, June 11.

Bright, M. (2001) 'Fury over 'Slave Pay' to Refugees', *The Observer*, September 2.

Bush, G.W. (2001a) 'Statement by the President in his Address to the Nation', September 11. www.yale.edu/lawweb/avalon/sept_11/pres_state001.htm

Bush, G.W. (2001b) 'Remarks by the President', September 12. www.yale.edu/ lawweb/avalon/sept_11/president_005.htm

Bush, G.W. (2001c) 'Proclamation 7462 of September 13', September 13. www.yale. edu/lawweb/avalon/sept_11/proc002_091301.htm

Bush, G.W. (2001d) 'Washington D.C., 'The National Cathedral', September 14. www.yale.edu/lawweb/avalon/sept_11/

Bush, G.W. (2001e) 'Remarks by the President upon Arrival at The South Lawn', September 16. www.yale.edu/lawweb/avalon/sept_11/president_015.htm

Bush, G.W. (2001f) 'Presidential Address to the Nation', October 7. www.yale.edu/ lawweb/avalon/sept_11/president_035.htm

Bush, G.W. (2001g) 'Remarks by the President at the Department of Defense Service of Remembrance', October 11. www.yale.edu/lawweb/avalon/sept_11/president_ 050.htm

Bush, G.W. (2001h) 'Radio Address by the President to the Nation', November 24. www.yale.edu/lawweb/avalon/sept_11/president_107.htm

Bush, G.W. (2002a) 'Bush's National Security Strategy', *The New York Times*, September 20.

Bush, G.W. (2002b) 'President Bush Delivers Graduation Speech at West Point', June 1. http://www.whitehouse.gov/news/releases/2002/06/20020601-3.html

Butler, J. (2000) *Antigone's Claim: Kinship Between Life and Death*. New York: Columbia University Press.

Butler, J. (2004) *Precarious Life: The Powers of Mourning and Violence*. London: Verso.

Butts, C. (1997) *Is Harry on the Boat?* London: Orion.

Caldwell, A. (2004) 'Bio-Sovereignty and the Emergence of Humanity', *Theory and Event*, http://muse.jhu.edu/journals/theory_and_eventv007/7.2caldwell.html

Callinicos, A. (1982) *Is There a Future for Marxism?* London: Macmillan Press.

Calvino, I. (1997) *Invisible Cities*. London: Vintage.

Cambridgeshire Against Refugee Detention (2002) 'Asylum Accommodation Center Sites Named', http://www.scrf.ucam.org/card

Campbell, D. (2002) 'In Woomera', *The Guardian Weekly*, May 25, pp. 25–31.

Caputi, J. (1999) 'The Second Coming of Diana', *NWSA Journal* 11(2): 103–23, http://muse.jhu.edu/journals/nwsa_journal/v011/11.2caputi.html

Carroll, R. (1998) 'Not Raving but Clowning', *The Guardian*, September 1.

Castells, M. (1977) *The Urban Question*. London: Edward Arnold.

Castells, M. (1996) *The Information Age*. vol. I: *The Rise of the Network Society*. Oxford: Blackwell.

CBS Radio Network (2002) 'Street Retreat', http://www.acfnewsource.org/religion/street_retreat.html

Chancey, J.R. (1999) 'Diana Doubled: The Fairytale Princess and the Photographer', *NWSA Journal* 11(2): 163–75, http://muse.jhu.edu/journals/nwsa_journal/v011/11.2caputi.html

Colebrook, C. (2002) *Understanding Deleuze*. Sydney: Allen & Unwin.

Conrad, P. (2004) 'The Art of Pain', *The Observer*, April 4.

Cowan, R. (2001) 'Stormy Forecast for the Abortion Ship', *The Guardian*, June 16.

Daly, F. (2004) 'The Non-Citizen and the Concept of "Human Rights"', *Borderlands*, 1.

Danner, M. (2004a) 'Torture and Truth', *New York Review of Books* 51(10), June 10.

Danner, M. (2004b) 'The Logic of Torture', *New York Review of Books* 51(11), http://necessaryprose.com/torture.htm

Davis, M. (1990) *City of Quartz*. London: Vintage.

Davis, M. (1999) *Ecology of Fear*. Basingstoke: Picador.

Deleuze, G (1983) *Nietzsche and Philosophy*. New York: Columbia University Press.

Deleuze, G. (1988) *Foucault*. Minneapolis and London: University of Minnesota Press.

Deleuze, G. (1990) *Expressionism in Philosophy: Spinoza*. New York: Zone Books.

Deleuze, G. (1994) *Difference and Repetition*. London: The Athlone Press.

Deleuze, G. (1995) *Negotiations*. New York: Columbia University Press.

Deleuze, G. (2004) *Desert Islands and Other Texts 1953–1974*. Los Angeles: Semiotext(e).

Deleuze, G. and Guattari, F. (1983) *Anti-Oedipus: Capitalism and Schizophrenia*. Minneapolis: University of Minnesota Press.

Deleuze, G. and Guattari, F. (1987) *A Thousand Plateaus: Capitalism and Schizophrenia II*. Minneapolis and London: University of Minnesota Press.

Deleuze, G. and F. Guattari (1994) *What is Philosophy?* London: Verso.

Deleuze, G. and Parnet, C. (1987) *Dialogues*. New York: Columbia University Press.

Denike, M. (2003) 'The Devil's Insatiable Sex: A Genealogy of Evil Incarnate', *Hypatia* 18(1): 10–43.

Deranty, J.-P. (2004) 'Agamben's Challenge to Normative Theories of Modern Rights', *Borderlands*, www.borderlandsejournal.adelaide.edu.au/vol3no1_2004

Derrida, J. (1999) *Adieu to Emmanuel Levinas*. Stanford, CA: Stanford University Press.

Derrida, J. (2000a) *Of Hospitality: Anne Dufourmantelle invites Jacques Derrida to Respond*. Stanford, CA: Stanford University Press

Derrida, J. (2000b) 'Hospitality', *Angelaki* 5(3): 3–18.

Derrida, J. (2001) *Cosmopolitanism and Forgiveness*. London: Routledge.

Derrida, J. (2002a) *Negotiations*. Stanford, CA: Stanford University Press.

Derrida, J. (2002b) *Acts of Religion*. London: Routledge

Desert Storm (2002) 'An Engagement with the Real', http://antimedia.net/desertstorm/dialogue.shtml

Dikeç, M. (2002) 'Pera Peras Poros: Longings for Spaces of Hospitality', *Theory, Culture and Society* 19(1–2): 227–47.

Dillon, D. (1994) 'Fortress America', *Planning*, June, pp. 8–12.

Dillon, M. (1996) *Politics of Security*. London: Routledge.

Dillon, M. (1999) 'The Scandal of the Refugee: Some Reflections on the "Inter" of International Relations and Continental Thought', in D. Campbell and M.J. Shapiro (eds) *Moral Spaces*. Minneapolis: University of Minnesota Press, pp. 92–124.

Dillon, M. and Reid, J. (2001) 'Global Liberal Governance: Biopolitics, Security and War', *Millennium* 30(1): 1–26.

Douglas, M. (1966) *Purity and Danger*. London: Routledge.

Drobisch, K. and Wieland, G. (1993) *System der NS-Konzentrationslager 1933–39*. Berlin: Akademie Verlag.

Düttmann, A.G. (2001) 'Never Before, Always Already: Agamben and the Category of Unrelation', *Angelaki: Journal of the Theoretical Humanities*, www.tandf.co.uk/journals/titles/rangintheory.html

ECRE (2002) *Setting Limits: Research Paper on the Effects of Limits on the Freedom of Movement of Asylum Seekers within the Borders of European Union Member States*. London: European Council on Refugees and Exiles.

Eriksen, T. (1998) 'Historiens undtagelsestilstand. En bemærkning til Walter Benjamins reception af Carl Schmitts suverænitetsteori', in T. Eriksen and H.J. Thomsen (eds) *When I'm Sixty-Four*. Viborg: Modtryk, pp. 242–72.

Euben, R.L. (2002) 'Killing (For) Politics. Jihad, Martyrdom, and Political Action', *Political Theory* 30(1): 4–35.

Evren, S. (2004) *Torture and its Show*. Unpublished manuscript.

Falk, R. (2002) 'The New Bush Doctrine', *The Nation*, www.thenation.com/docprint. mhtml?I=20020715ands=falk

Finkielkraut, A. (2001) *In the Name of Humanity: Reflections on the Twentieth Century*. London: Pimlico.

Firestone, R. (1999) *Jihad: The Origin of Holy War in Islam*. Oxford: Oxford University Press.

Fisher, S.K. (1996) 'Occupation of the Womb: Forced Impregnation as Genocide', *Duke Law Journal* 46(1): 91–134.

Fiskesjö, M. (2003) *The Thanksgiving Turkey Pardon, the Death of Teddy's Bear, and the Sovereign Exception of Guantánamo*. Chicago: Prickley Paradigm Press.

Foucault, M. (1977) *Discipline and Punish*. London: Penguin.

Foucault, M. (1978) *The History of Sexuality: An Introduction*. vol. 1. New York: Vintage Books.

Foucault, M. (1980) *Power/ Knowledge. Selected Interviews and Other Writings 1972–1977 by Michael Foucault*. New York: Harvester Wheatsheaf.

Foucault, M. (1991) *Discipline and Punish: The Birth of the Prison*, London: Penguin.

Foucault, M. (1997) 'Of Other Spaces: Utopias and Heterotopias', in N. Leach (ed.) *Rethinking Architecture*. London: Routledge, pp. 350–6.

Foucault, M. (2001) 'Friendship as a Way of Life', in C. Kraus and S. Lotringer (eds) *Hatred of Capitalism*. New York: Semiotext(e), pp. 297–302.

Foucault, M. (2002) *Power: Essential Works of Foucault 1954–1984*. London: Penguin.

Foucault, M. (2003a) *Society Must Be Defended*. London: Penguin.

Foucault, M. (2003b) *Abnormal: Lectures at the Collège de France 1974–1975*. London: Verso.

George, L.N. (2002) 'The Pharmacotic War on Terrorism: Cure or Poison for the US Body Politic?', *Theory, Culture and Society* 9(4): 161–86.

Gerecht, R.M. (2002) 'The Gospel According to Osama Bin Laden', http://www.afgha.com/article.php?sid=11840andmode=threadandorder=0

Ghaith, A.S. (2001) 'Text of Al-Qaida's Statement' (October 9), http://users.skynet.be/terrorism/html/laden_statement_2.htm

Giddens, A. (1992) *The Transformation of Intimacy: Sexuality, Love and Eroticism in Modern Societies*. London: Polity Press.

Giddens, A. (1994) *Beyond Left and Right: The Future of Radical Politics*. Oxford: Polity Press.

Gill, A.A. (2004) 'The Hitchcock of Painting', *Sunday Times Magazine*, April 25, pp. 38–48.

Gillan, A. (2002) 'Erotic Emma: Drunk and at Risk', *The Guardian*, June 22.

Gilroy, P. (1999) 'Between Camps: Race and Culture in Postmodernity: An Inaugural Lecture', *Economy and Society* 28(2): 183–97.

Girard, R. (1977) *Violence and the Sacred*. Baltimore, MD: Johns Hopkins University Press.

Goldstein, J.S. (2001) *War and Gender: How Gender Shapes the War System and Vice Versa*. Cambridge: Cambridge University Press.

Graham, S. and Marvin, S. (2001) *Splintering Urbanism: Networked Infrastructures, Technological Mobilities, and the Urban Condition*. London: Routledge.

Grosrichard, A. (1998) *The Sultan's Court*. London: Verso.

Guilhot, N. (2000) 'Review of Luc Boltanski and Eve Chiapello's *Le Nouvel Esprit du Capitalisme*', *European Journal of Social Theory* 3(3): 355–64.

Gülçür, L. and Ilkkaracan, P. (2002) 'The "Natasha" Experience: Migrant Sex Workers from the Former Soviet Union and Eastern Europe in Turkey', *Women Studies International Forum* 25(4): 411–21.

Gutman, R. (1993) *A Witness to Genocide*. New York: Macmillan.

Haarder, B. (2002) 'Besvarelse af spørgsmål nr 40 stillet af Integrationsudvalg til ministeren for Flytgninge, Indvandrere og Integration den 7. juni 2002' (Almen. del – bilag 124). J-nr: 2002/4011–43. www.folketinget.dk/Samling/20012/udvbilag/UUI/Almdel_bilag167.htm – 15k

Hallward, P. (2003) *Badiou: A Subject to Truth*. Minneapolis: The University of Minnesota Press.

Hamacher, W. (2004) 'The Right to Have Rights (Four-and-a-Half Remarks)', *The South Atlantic Quarterly* 103(2–3): 343–356.

Hardt, M. (2002) 'Folly of our Masters of the Universe', *The Guardian*, December 18.

Hardt, M. and Negri, A. (2000) *Empire*. Cambridge, MA: Harvard University Press.

Harris, L. (2002) 'Al Qaeda's Fantasy Ideology', *Policy Review* 114, http://www.policyreview.org/AUG02

Harvey, D. (1973) *Social Justice and the City*. London: Edward Arnold.

Hefner, R.W. (2001) 'September 11 and the Struggle for Islam', www.ssrc.org/sept11/essays/hefner_text_only.htm

Hobbes, T. (1990) *Behemoth or The Long Parliament*. Chicago: The University of Chicago Press.

Hobbes, T. (1991) *Man and Citizen (De Hominie and De Cive)*. Indianapolis: Hackett Publishing Company.

Hobbes, T. (1999) *Leviathan*. Cambridge: Cambridge University Press.

Home Office (2002) 'Still No Decision on Accommodation Centre for Asylum Seekers', press release, May 14, www.west-lindsey.gov.uk/Asylum_Seekers/default.htm

Homer-Dixon, T. (2002) 'The Rise of Complex Terrorism', http://globalpolicy.org/wtc/terrorism/2002/0115complex.htm

Hopkins, N. (1999) 'High Anxiety'. *The Guardian*, August 19.

Houellebecq, M. (2002) *Platform*. London: William Heinemann.

Hubert, S.F. (1999) 'Two Women, Two Songs: The Subversive Iconography of "Candle in the Wind"', *NWSA Journal* 11(2): 124–37, http://muse.jbu.edu/journals/nwsa_journal

Human Rights and Equal Opportunity Commission (2002) *Human Rights*, http://www.humanrights.gov.au/human_rights/asylum_seekers/index.html

Human Rights Watch (1993) *War Crimes in Bosnia-Hercegovina. Vol. II.* New York: Human Rights Publications.

Huntington, S.P. (1997) *The Clash of Civilizations and the Remaking of World Order*. London: Simon and Schuster.

Illuminati, A. (2003) 'Postfordisten Spinoza', *Agora* 2(3): 317–29.

Januszczak, W. (2004) 'Truly, Deeply, Sadly'. *Sunday Times Magazine*, May 30, pp. 6–7.

Johnson, J.T. (1997) *The Holy War Idea in Western and Islamic Traditions*. Philadelphia, PA: The Pennsylvania State University Press.

Johnson, R. (2002) 'Defending Ways of Life: The (Anti-) Terrorist Rhetorics of Bush and Blair', *Theory, Culture and Society* 19(4): 211–31.

Jones, A. (1994) 'Gender and Ethnic Conflict in Ex-Yugoslavia', *Ethnic and Racial Studies* 17(1): 115–34.

Jones, J. (2004) 'All the Lonely People', *The Guardian*, May 19.

Joxe, A. (2002) *Empire of Disorder*. New York: Semiotext(e).

Juergensmeyer, M. (2000) *Terror in the Mind of God: The Global Rise of Religious Violence*. Berkeley, CA: University of California Press.

Kafka, F. (1976) *The Castle*. Harmondsworth: Penguin.

Kagan, R. (2002) 'Power and Weakness', *Policy Review* 113: 3–28.

Kant, I. (1970) 'Perpetual Peace: A Philosophical Sketch', in H. Reiss (ed.) *Kant's Political Writings*. Cambridge: Cambridge University Press, pp. 93–130.

Kantorowicz, E.H. (1957) *The King's Two Bodies: A Study in Mediaeval Political Theology*. Princeton, NJ: Princeton University Press.

Kaplan, C. (1995) '"A World Without Boundaries": The Body Shop's Trans/national Geographics', *Social Text* 13(2): 45–66.

Kaplan, C. (1996) *Questions of Travel: Postmodern Discourses of Displacement*. London and Durham, NC: Duke University Press.

Katz, N. (2000) '"Women's Issues" Women on Waves", http://womensissues.about.com/library/weekly/aa042701a.htm

Kellner, D. (2002) 'September 11, Social Theory and Democratic Politics', *Theory, Culture and Society* 19(4): 147–59.

Kermani, H. (2002) 'Roots of Terror: Suicide, Martyrdom, Self-Redemption and Islam', www.opendemocracy.net

Kesic, V. (2002) 'Muslim Women, Croatian Women, Serbian Women, Albanian Women . . .', in D.I. Bjelic and O. Savic (eds) *Balkan as Metaphor: Between Globalization and Fragmentation*. Cambridge, MA: The MIT Press, pp. 311–22.

Kierkegaard, S. (1962a) 'Afsluttende uvidenskabelig Efterskrift', in *Samlede værker*. vol. IX. Copenhagen: Gyldendal.

Kierkegaard, S. (1962b) 'Enten – Eller', in *Samlede værker*. vols II, III. Copenhagen: Gyldendal.

Kierkegaard, S. (1962c) 'Frygt og bæven', in *Samlede værker*. vol. V. Copehagen: Gyldendal.

Koolhaas, R. *et al.* (1995) *S, M, L, XL*. New York: The Monacelli Press.

Kranzfelder, I. (2002) *Hopper*. Cologne: Taschen.

Kristeva, J. (1982) *Powers of Horror: An Essay on Abjection*. New York: Columbia University Press.

Lacan, J. (1977) *Écrits: A Selection*. London: Routledge.

Larsen, J.V. (2003) 'Holland bygger fæstninger', *Politiken*, January 18.

Lash, J. (1993) *Twins and the Double*. London: Thames and Hudson.

Latour, B. (1996) 'On Actor-Network Theory: A Few Clarifications', *Soziale Welt* 47: 369–81.

Laustsen, C.B. and Wæver, W. (2000) 'In Defence of Religion: Sacred Referent Objects for Securitization', *Millennium: Journal of International Studies* 29(3): 705–39.

Levinas, E. (1985) *Ethics and Infinity: Conversations with Philippe Nemo*. Pittsburgh, PA: Duquesne University Press.

Littlewood, I. (2001) *Sultry Climates: Travel and Sex Since the Great Tour*. London: John Murray.

Lotringer, S. and Virilio, P. (1997) *Pure War*. New York: Columbia University Press.

Luhmann, N. (1989) *Ecological Communication*. Cambridge: Polity Press.

Luhmann, N. (1992) 'Kontingenz als Eigenwert der Modernen Gesellschaft', in *Beobachtungen der Moderne*. Braunschweig: Der Westdeutsche Verlag.

Luhmann, N. (1994) 'The Idea of Unity in a Differentiated Society', paper presented at the XIIIth Sociological World Congress, 'Contested Boundaries and Shifting Solidarities', Bielefeld, Germany.

Luhmann, N. (1995) *Social Systems*. Stanford, CA: Stanford University Press.

Lyon, D. (2001) *Surveillance Society: Monitoring Everyday Life*. Buckingham: Open University Press.

Lyon, D. (2003) *Surveillance after September 11*. Cambridge: Polity Press.

MacCannell, D. (1999) 'New Urbanism and Its Discontents', in J. Copjec and M. Sorkin (eds) *Giving Ground: The Politics of Propinquity*. London: Verso, pp. 106–30.

MacCannell, J.F. (2000) 'Urban Perversions', *Third Text* 54: 65–74.

Macnamara, D. (2002) 'History of Sexual Violence', http://www.interactivetheatre.org/resc/history.html

Marx, K. (1973) *Grundrisse*. Harmondsworth: Penguin.

Metz, C. (1990) 'Photography and Fetish', in C. Squires (ed.) *The Critical Image: Essays on Contemporary Photography*. Seattle: Bay Press, pp. 155–64.

Miller, J.A. (1987) 'Jeremy Bentham's Panopticon Device', *October* 41: 3–29.

Miller, J.A. (1989) 'Extimité', *Prose Studies* 11(3): 121–31.

Miller, W.I. (1997) *The Anatomy of Disgust*. Cambridge, MA: Harvard University Press.

Morrow, L. (1993) 'Unspeakable', *Time*, February 22, p. 50.

Moussalli, A.S. (1999) *Moderate and Radical Islamic Fundamentalism: The Quest for Modernity, Legitimacy, and the Islamic State*. Gainesville, FL: University of Florida Press.

Münkler, H. (2002) 'The Brutal Logic of Terror: The Privatization of War in Modernity', *Constellation* 9(1): 66–73.

Musil, R. (1996) *The Man Without Qualities*. London: Vintage.

Nbembe, A. (2003) 'Necropolitics', *Public Culture* 15(1): 11–40.

Negri, T. (2003a) 'The Ripe Fruit of Redemption', http://www.generation-online.org/t/negriagamben.htm

Negri, T. (2003b) 'Public Sphere, Labour, Multitude. Strategies of Resistance in Empire', http://www.generation-online.org/t/common.htm

Nielsen, T. (2000) *Formløs*. Aarhus: The Aarhus School of Architecture.

Nikolic-Rastanovic, V. (1996) 'War and Violence against Women', in J. Turpin and L.A. Lorentzen (eds) *The Gendered New World Order: Militarism, Development, and the Environment*. London: Routledge, pp. 195–210.

Noor, F.A. (2001) 'The Evolution of "Jihad" in Islamist Political Discourse: How a Plastic Concept Became Harder', http://www.ssrc.org/sept11/essays/noor_text_only.htm

Osborn, A. (2001) 'Danish Voters Swing to the Right', *The Guardian*, November 21.

Osborn, A. (2003) 'Sailing Close to the Wind', *The Guardian*, June 20.

Palaver, W. (1992) 'A Girardian Reading of Schmitts' Political Theology', *Telos* 94: 43–68.

Pan, D. (1992) 'Enemies, Scapegoats and Sacrifice: A Note on Palaver and Ulmen', *Telos* 93: 81–8.

Pécseli, B. (1995) 'La misère du monde – og sociologiens kald', ant interview withmed Pierre Bourdieu, *Social Kritik* 37: 5–15.

Pettman, J.J. (1996) 'Boundary Politics: Women, Nationalism and Danger', in M. Maynard and J. Purvis (eds) *New Frontiers in Women's Studies: Knowledge, Identity and Nationalism*. London: Taylor and Francis.

Pilger, J. (2001) 'A War in the American Tradition', *The New Stateman*, October 15.

Plet, R.J.V. (1994) 'Auschwitz: From Architect's Promise to Inmate's Perdition', *Modernism/Modernity* 1(1): 80–120.

Poster, M. (1996) 'Database as Discourse, or Electronic Interpellations', in P. Heelas *et al*. (eds) *Detraditionalization*. Oxford: Blackwell.

Rasch, W. (2003) 'Human Rights as Geopolitics: Carl Schmitt and the Legal Form of American Supremacy', *Cultural Critique* 54(1): 120–47.

Rasmussen, M.B. (2003) 'Forkansning, geografi, globalisering', *Mutant* 3: 1–9.

Razac, O. (2002) *Barbed Wire: A History*. London: Profile Books.

Rees-Tonge, J. (2004) 'For $150 You, Too, Can be a Spiritual Down and Out', *The Sunday Times*, April 25.

Reid, J. (2002) 'The Contemporary Strategisation of City Spaces: Thoughts on the Relations between War, Power and Transurbanism', paper presented at the conference, 'Cities as Strategic Sites', Manchester.

Rifkin, J. (2000) *The Age of Access: How the Shift from Ownership to Access is Transforming Capitalism*. London: Penguin.

Ritzer, G. and Liska, A. (1997) '"McDisneyization" and "Post-tourism": Complementary Perspectives on Contemporary Tourism', in C. Rojek and J. Urry (eds) *Touring Cultures*. London: Routledge, pp. 96–109.

Roberts, C. and Throsby, K. (2003) 'Discarded, Wasted or Spare? Human Embryos in the New Biotech Economies', paper presented at Department of Sociology, Lancaster University, November 15.

Rogozinski, J. (1993) 'Hell on Earth: Hannah Arendt in the Face of Hitler', *Philosophy Today* 3: 257–74.

Rose, N. (1999) *Powers of Freedom: Reframing Political Thought*. Cambridge: Cambridge University Press.

Roy, A. (2001) 'Den uendelige retfærdigheds logic', in C. Clausen and R.Ø. Madsen (eds) *Tirsdag 11. september 2001. Eftertanker*. Copenhagen: Tiderne Skifter, pp. 79–91.

Roy, O. (2001) 'Neo-Fundamentalism', http://www.ssrc.org/sept11/essays/roy_text_only.htm

Rushdie, S. (2001) 'Den skjulte krig kan ikke vindes', *Information*, October 4.

Ruthven, M. (2001) 'Cultural Schizophrenia', *Open Democracy*, available on www.opendemocracy.net

Salzman, T.A. (1998) 'Rape Camps as a Means of Ethnic Cleansing: Religious, Cultural, and Ethical Responses to Rape Victims in the Former Yugoslavia', *Human Rights Quarterly* 20(2): 348–78.

Sante, L. (2004) 'Tourists and Tortures', *The New York Times*, May 11.

Sassen, S. (2001) 'Entrapments Rich Countries Cannot Escape: Governance Hotspots', http://www.txt.de/b_books/texte/ny911/english/SassenSaskia.html

Saunders, M. and Glenn, G. (1996) *Dicing with Di: The Amazing Adventures of Britain's Royal Chasers*. London: Blake.

Schmitt, C. (1985a) *Political Theology: Four Chapters on the Concept of Sovereignty*. Cambridge, MA: The MIT Press.

Schmitt, C. (1985b) *The Crisis of Parliamentary Democracy*. Cambridge, MA: The MIT Press.

Schmitt, C. (1996) *The Leviathan in the State Theory of Thomas Hobbes: Meaning and Failure of a Political Symbol*. London: Greenwood Press.

Schmitt, C. (2003) *Nomos of the Earth in the International Law of Jus Publicum Europaeum*. New York: Telos Press.

Seifert, R. (1994) 'War and Rape: A Preliminary Analysis', in A. Stigelmayer (ed.) *Mass Rape: The War against Women in Bosnia-Herzegovina*. Lincoln, NE: University of Nebraska Press, pp. 54–72.

Sennett, R. (1986) *The Fall of Public Man*. London: Faber and Faber.

Sennett, R. (1990) *The Conscience of the Eye*. London: Faber and Faber.

Sennett, R. (1994) *Flesh and Stone*. London: Faber and Faber.

Sennett, R. (1996) 'The Foreigner', in P. Heelas, S. Lash and P. Morris (eds) *Detraditionalization*. Oxford: Blackwell, pp. 173–99.

Sennett, R. (1999) 'The Spaces of Democracy', in R. Beauregard and S. Body-Gendrot (eds) *The Urban Moment: Cosmopolitan Essays on the Late 20th Century City*. London: Sage, pp. 273–85.

Sennett, R. (2000) 'Cities Without Care or Connection', *New Statesman*, June 5, pp. 25–7.

Simmel, G. (1971) 'The Stranger', in D.N. Levine (ed.) *On Individuality and Social Forms*. Chicago and London: The University of Chicago Press, pp. 143–9.

Simmel, G. (1997) 'The Bridge and the Door', in N. Leach (ed.) *Rethinking Architecture: A Reader in Cultural Theory*, London: Routledge, pp. 64–8.

Skejlsbæk, I. (2001) 'Sexual Violence and War: Mapping Out a Complex Relationship', *European Journal of International Relations* 7(2): 211–37.

Sofos, S.A. (1996) 'Inter-ethnic Violence and Gendered Constructions of Ethnicity in Former Yugoslavia', *Social Identities* 2(1): 73–91.

Sofsky, W. (1997) *The Order of Terror: The Concentration Camp*. Princeton, NJ: Princeton University Press.

Sontag, S. (1977) *On Photography*. London: Penguin.

Sontag, S. (2004) 'What Have We Done?', *The Guardian*, May 24.

Sørensen, M. (2002) 'Indeni er jeg allerede død', *Berlingske Tidende*, June 19.

Sorkin, M. (1999) 'Traffic in Democracy', in J. Copjec and M. Sorkin (eds) *Giving Ground: The Politics of Propinquity*. London: Verso, pp. 1–18.

Stark, J. (2001) 'Suicide After Auschwitz', *The Yale Journal of Criticism* 14(1): 93–114.

Stigelmayer, A. (1994) 'The Rapes in Bosnia Herzegovina', in A. Stigelmayer (ed.) *Mass Rape. The War against Women in Bosnia-Herzegovina*. Lincoln, NE: University of Nebraska Press, pp. 82–169.

Sullivan, S. (2002) 'POW's or Unlawful Combatants?', http://www.crimesofwar. org/print/expert/pow-intro-print.html

Thrift, N. (1997) 'The Rise of Soft Capitalism', *Cultual Values* 1(1): 29–57.

Trezise, T. (2001) 'Unspeakable', *The Yale Journal of Criticism* 14(1): 39–66.

UN (1994) *Final Report of the Commission of Experts Established Pursuant of Security Council Resolution 780*, 49th Sess., Annex, U.N. Doc. S/1994/674, at 55–69.

Usborne, D. (2004) 'Bums's Rush', *Nine to Five and Midweek*, May 17.

Velidakis, L. and Harris, P. (2002) 'Rape Claims Can't Stop the Party in Top Greek Resort', *The Observer*, June 30.

Veloso, M.F.M.D. (2004) Performing Art: Reinventing Avant-garde Practice and the Role of the Artist. PhD thesis submitted at Department of Media and Communication, Goldsmiths College, University of London.

Verstrate, G. (2001) 'Technological Frontiers and the Politics of Mobility in the European Union', *New Formations* 43: 121–49.

Virilio, P. (1997) 'The Overexposed City', in N. Leach (ed.) *Rethinking Architecture*. London: Routledge, pp. 381–90.

Virilio, P. (2002) *Ground Zero*. London: Verso.

Virno, P. (2004) *A Grammar of the Multitude*. Los Angeles: Semiotext(e).

Wæver, O. (1997) *Concepts of Security*. Copenhagen: University of Copenhagen, Department of Political Sciences.

Walters, W. (2002) 'Deportation, Expulsion and the International Police of Aliens', *The Journal of Citizenship Studies* 6(3): 265–92.

Webster's New Encyclopedic Dictionary (1993) Cologne: Könemann.

Wheatley, J. (2001) 'Going Up', *Swissair Gazette* (2): 50–7.

White, M. and Travis, A. (2002) 'Blunkett Defends "Swamping" Remark', *The Guardian*, April 25.

Williams, R. (1989) *Resources of Hope*. London: Verso.

Wilson, S. (1997) 'The Indestructable Beauty of Suffering: Diana and the Metaphor of Global Consumption', http://muse.jhu.edu/journals/theory_and_event/v001/ 1.4symp_int.html

Women on Waves (2003) 'Report Poland', http://www.womenonwaves.nl/

Wong, Y.-S. (2004) 'En Passant', http://www.arts.ualberta.ca/vcr/operators.htm

Woolf, M. (2004) 'Scanner Will Lay Bare the Secrets of all Air Travellers', *The Independent*, May 10.

Žižek, S. (1991) *For They Know Not What They Do*. London: Verso.

Žižek, S. (1993) *Tarrying with the Negative. Kant, Hegel, and the Critique of Ideology*. Durham, NC: Duke University Press.

Žižek, S. (1994) 'Introduction. The Spectre of Ideology', in S. Žižek (ed.) *Mapping Ideology*. London: Verso, pp. 1–33.

Žižek, S. (1996) *The Indivisible Remainder: Essays on Schelling and Related Matters*. London: Verso.

Žižek, S. (1997) *The Plague of Fantasies*, London. Verso.

Žižek, S. (1999a) *The Ticklish Subject: The Absent Center of Political Ontology*. London: Verso.

Žižek, S. (1999b) 'Carl Schmitt in the Age of Post-Politics', in C. Mouffe (ed.) *The Challenge of Carl Schmitt*. London: Verso, pp. 18–37.

Žižek, S. (2000) *The Fragile Absolute*. London: Verso.

Žižek, S. (2001a) *Did Somebody Say Totalitarianism? Five Interventions in the (Mis)use of a Notion*. London: Verso.

Žižek, S. (2001b) *On Belief*. London: Routledge.

Žižek, S. (2002) *Welcome to the Desert of the Real*, London: Verso.

Žižek, S. (2003) *Organs Without Bodies*. London: Routledge.

Žižek, S. (2003b) *The Puppet and the Dwarf: The Perverse Core of Christianity*. Cambridge, MA: The MIT Press.

Žižek, S. (2004) 'What Rumsfeld Doesn't Know That He Knows About Abu Ghraib', in *In These Times*, http://www.inthesetimes.com/site/main/article/what_rumsfeld_doesnt_know_that_he_knows_about_abu_ghraib/

Žižek, S. and Daly, G. (2004) *Conversations with Žižek*. Cambridge: Polity Press.

Žižek, S. and Hanlon, C. (2001) 'Psychoanalysis and the Post-Political: An Interview with Slavoj Žižek', *New Literary History* 32(1): 1–21.

Zolberg, A. (2001) 'Guarding the Gates in a World on the Move', http://www.ssrc.org/sept11/essays/zolberg_text_only.htm

Zulaika, J. (2002) 'The Self-Fulfilling Prophecies of Counterterrorism', *Radical History Review* 85: 191–9.

Zupančič, A (2000) *Ethics of the Real: Kant, Lacan*. London. Verso.

INDEX

LIBRARY, UNIVERSITY OF CHESTER

An environmentally friendly book printed and bound in England by www.printondemand-worldwide.com

PEFC Certified

This product is
from sustainably
managed forests
and controlled
sources

www.pefc.org

PEFC/16-33-415

This book is made entirely of chain-of-custody materials; FSC materials for the cover and PEFC materials for the text pages.

#0206 - 140313 - C0 - 234/156/12 - PB